William Marshal's Wife

William Marshal's Wife

Isabel de Clare, Woman of Influence

Julia A. Hickey

PEN & SWORD
HISTORY

First published in Great Britain in 2023 by
Pen & Sword Military
An imprint of Pen & Sword Books Limited
Yorkshire – Philadelphia

ISBN 978 1 39904 327 4

A CIP catalogue record for this book is
available from the British Library

Typeset by Mac Style
Printed in the UK by CPI Group (UK) Ltd, Croydon, CR0 4YY.

Pen & Sword Books Limited incorporates the imprints of After
the Battle, Atlas, Archaeology, Aviation, Discovery, Family History,
Fiction, History, Maritime, Military, Military Classics, Politics,
Select, Transport, True Crime, Air World, Frontline Publishing, Leo
Cooper, Remember When, Seaforth Publishing, The Praetorian Press,
Wharncliffe Local History, Wharncliffe Transport, Wharncliffe True
Crime and White Owl.

For a complete list of Pen & Sword titles please contact

PEN & SWORD BOOKS LIMITED
47 Church Street, Barnsley, South Yorkshire, S70 2AS, England
E-mail: enquiries@pen-and-sword.co.uk
Website: www.pen-and-sword.co.uk
or
PEN AND SWORD BOOKS
1950 Lawrence Rd, Havertown, PA 19083, USA
E-mail: Uspen-and-sword@casematepublishers.com
Website: www.penandswordbooks.com

Contents

Illustrations

Principalities of Wales map
Ireland in the Middle Ages map, 1915
De Clare coat of arms The Priory Church of St Mary, Usk
Arms of William Marshal, 1st Earl of Pembroke
Effigy of Richard 'Strongbow' de Clare, Christchurch Cathedral Dublin
Tintern Abbey
Chepstow, Striguil, Castle
Chepstow Castle doors
Chepstow Castle keep
Goodrich Castle
Pembroke Castle
Usk Castle
Effigy of William Marshal, 1st Earl of Pembroke, Temple Church, London
Effigy of Gilbert Marshal, 4th Earl of Pembroke, Temple Church, London
Gilbert de Clare, 4th Earl of Hertford, 5th Earl of Gloucester, Tewkesbury Abbey
De Clare Earls of Gloucester, Tewkesbury Abbey
Llywelyn ap Iorwerth, St Mary's Church, Trefriw, Denbighshire
Henry III's coronation, Gloucester Cathedral

Simplified table of the de Clare family showing Isabel de Clare's ancestry

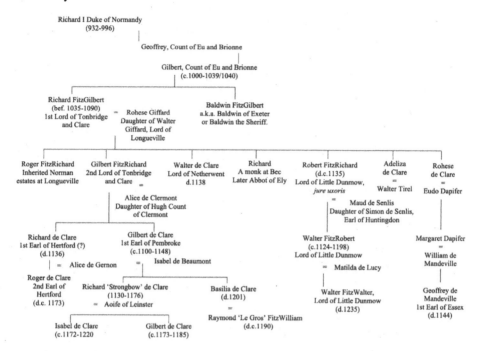

Simplified table showing the Earls of Hertford and Gloucester

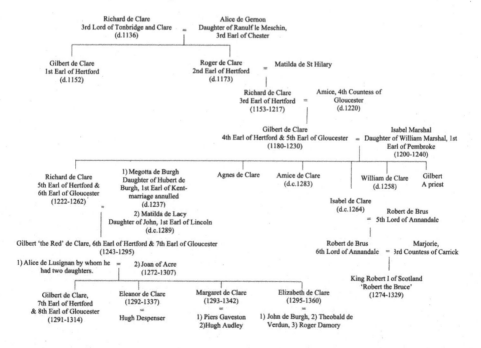

Simplified Table of the Marshal family: the male line

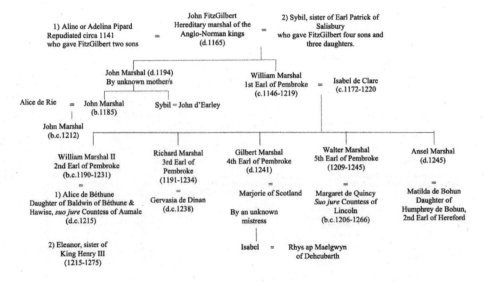

1) Aline or Adelina Pipard
Repudiated circa 1141
who gave FitzGilbert two sons
=
John FitzGilbert
Hereditary marshal of the
Anglo-Norman kings
(d.1165)
=
2) Sybil, sister of Earl Patrick of
Salisbury
who gave FitzGilbert four sons and
three daughters.

John Marshal (d.1194)
By unknown mother/s

William Marshal
1st Earl of Pembroke
(c.1146-1219)
=
Isabel de Clare
(c.1172-1220)

Alice de Rie = John Marshal
(b.1185)

Sybil = John d'Earley

John Marshal
(b.c.1212)

William Marshal II
2nd Earl of Pembroke
(b.c.1190-1231)
=

Richard Marshal
3rd Earl of
Pembroke
(1191-1234)
=

Gilbert Marshal
4th Earl of Pembroke
(d.1241)
=

Walter Marshal
5th Earl of Pembroke
(1209-1245)
=

Ansel Marshal
(d.1245)

1) Alice de Béthune
Daughter of Baldwin of Béthune &
Hawise, *suo jure* Countess of Aumale
(d.c.1215)

Gervasia de Dinan
(d.c.1238)

Marjorie of Scotland

By an unknown
mistress

Margaret de Quincy
Suo jure Countess of
Lincoln
(b.c.1206-1266)

Matilda de Bohun
Daughter of
Humphrey de Bohun,
2nd Earl of Hereford

2) Eleanor, sister of
King Henry III
(1215-1275)

Isabel = Rhys ap Maelgwyn
of Deheubarth

Simplified tables of Marshal family: Isabel de Clare and William Marshal -female lines of descent

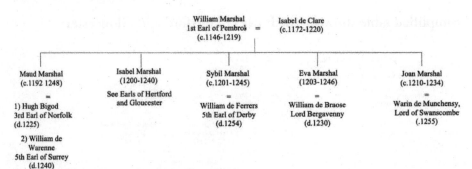

William Marshal
1st Earl of Pembroke
(c.1146-1219)
=
Isabel de Clare
(c.1172-1220)

Maud Marshal
(c.1192 1248)
=

Isabel Marshal
(1200-1240)

See Earls of Hertford
and Gloucester

Sybil Marshal
(c.1201-1245)
=

Eva Marshal
(1203-1246)
=

Joan Marshal
(c.1210-1234)
=

1) Hugh Bigod
3rd Earl of Norfolk
(d.1225)

William de Ferrers
5th Earl of Derby
(d.1254)

William de Braose
Lord Bergavenny
(d.1230)

Warin de Munchensy,
Lord of Swanscombe
(.1255)

2) William de
Warenne
5th Earl of Surrey
(d.1240)

Maud Marshal descendants

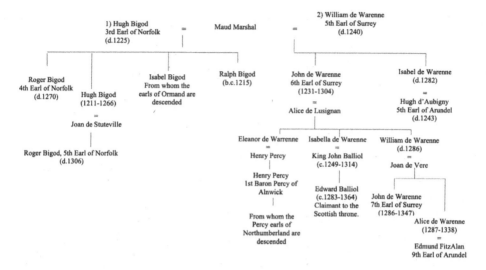

Sybil Marshal descendants

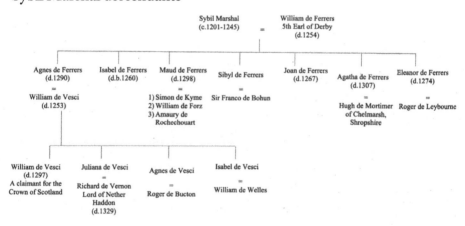

Eva Marshal descendants

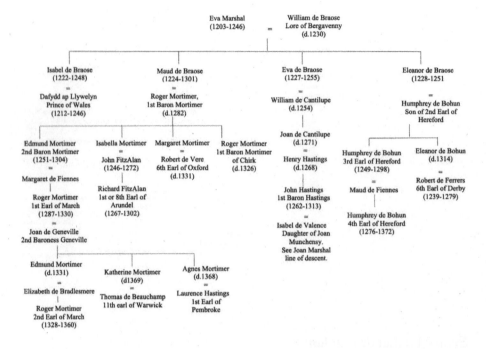

Eva Marshal (1203-1246) = William de Braose Lore of Bergavenny (d.1230)

Isabel de Braose (1222-1248) = Dafydd ap Llywelyn Prince of Wales (1212-1246)

Maud de Braose (1224-1301) = Roger Mortimer, 1st Baron Mortimer (d.1282)

Eva de Braose (1227-1255) = William de Cantilupe (d.1254)

Eleanor de Braose (1228-1251 = Humphrey de Bohun Son of 2nd Earl of Hereford

Edmund Mortimer 2nd Baron Mortimer (1251-1304) = Margaret de Fiennes — Roger Mortimer 1st Earl of March (1287-1330) = Joan de Geneville 2nd Baroness Geneville

Isabella Mortimer = John FitzAlan (1246-1272) — Richard FitzAlan 1st or 8th Earl of Arundel (1267-1302)

Margaret Mortimer = Robert de Vere 6th Earl of Oxford (d.1331)

Roger Mortimer 1st Baron Mortimer of Chirk (d.1326)

Joan de Cantilupe (d.1271) = Henry Hastings (d.1268) — John Hastings 1st Baron Hastings (1262-1313) = Isabel de Valence Daughter of Joan Munchensy. See Joan Marshal line of descent.

Humphrey de Bohun 3rd Earl of Hereford (1249-1298) = Maud de Fiennes — Humphrey de Bohun 4th Earl of Hereford (1276-1372)

Eleanor de Bohun (d.1314) = Robert de Ferrers 6th Earl of Derby (1239-1279)

Edmund Mortimer (d.1331) = Elizabeth de Bradlesmere — Roger Mortimer 2nd Earl of March (1328-1360)

Katherine Mortimer (d1369) = Thomas de Beauchamp 11th earl of Warwick

Agnes Mortimer (d.1368) = Laurence Hastings 1st Earl of Pembroke

Joan Marshal descendants

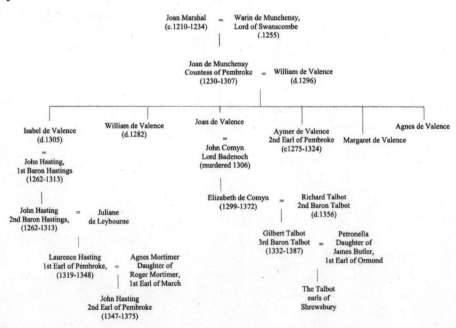

Joan Marshal (c.1210-1234) = Warin de Munchensy, Lord of Swanscombe (.1255)

Joan de Munchensy Countess of Pembroke (1230-1307) = William de Valence (d.1296)

Isabel de Valence (d.1305) = John Hasting, 1st Baron Hastings (1262-1313)

William de Valence (d.1282)

Joan de Valence = John Comyn Lord Badenoch (murdered 1306)

Aymer de Valence 2nd Earl of Pembroke (c1275-1324)

Margaret de Valence

Agnes de Valence

John Hasting 2nd Baron Hastings, (1262-1313) = Juliane de Leybourne

Laurence Hasting 1st Earl of Pembroke, (1319-1348) = Agnes Mortimer Daughter of Roger Mortimer, 1st Earl of March — John Hasting 2nd Earl of Pembroke (1347-1375)

Elizabeth de Comyn (1299-1372) = Richard Talbot 2nd Baron Talbot (d.1356)

Gilbert Talbot 3rd Baron Talbot (1332-1387) = Petronella Daughter of James Butler, 1st Earl of Ormond — The Talbot earls of Shrewsbury

Introduction

Isabel de Clare, Countess of Pembroke, daughter of Richard 'Strongbow' of Striguil and Aoife of Leinster fulfilled the role that every comital wife of the period was expected to play, exerting power within her marriage, family networks and management of her domains. Her husband, William Marshal, was a man who would advise four kings and become regent to another. His political activism took Isabel to the heart of the realm's turbulent politics and put her under a spotlight during the years when King John alienated his magnates, the First Barons War and into the regency of King Henry III.

It is impossible to know exactly what Isabel or her mother Aoife of Leinster looked like. There are no portraits of them and no surviving tomb effigies thanks to Henry VIII's destruction of the monasteries during the 1530s. History does not record exactly when Isabel was born or what her education was like. Nor is it possible to know when, of even if, Isabel fell in love with William Marshal, the Angevin tournament hero epitomising chivalry both on and off the battlefield. Instead, as well as drawing on any information specific to Isabel, it becomes important to capture something of the essence of a medieval aristocratic childhood, marriage and maternity. Isabel, one of the feudal elite, can be glimpsed in the surviving records of the period; in the great medieval stronghold at Chepstow and in the sources which paint a more general picture of medieval life. As Hilary Mantel said in her first BBC Reith Lecture of 2017, 'Evidence is always partial. Facts are not truth, though they are part of it'.[1] But as this is history rather than fiction, there must be corroboration.

The political choices and marriages made by Isabel de Clare's ancestors, not to mention the twists and turns of fortune's wheel, resulted in her becoming one of the wealthiest heiresses of the period. At a time when land equated to wealth and power Isabel, her daughters and granddaughters were the personification of both. Before their weddings, women were legally the property of their fathers or guardians. After they took their marriage vows all they owned belonged to their husbands. Coverture meant that a woman's official identity merged with that of her husband. She remained in the shadows of her spouse, legally and administratively, until she became a widow. Isabel's own life story becomes a matter of reading between the lines and interpreting the evidence, which is partial at best.

Isabel de Clare, Countess of Netherwent and Pembroke and Lady of Leinster was much more than a vessel by which her patrimony was passed into the hands of William Marshal and to his heirs. The *Histoire* depicts a woman who spent her life at her husband's side: advising and supporting him; administering and holding the estates and castles that were rightfully hers through force of arms; smoothing a way through the social and political world of the thirteenth century; giving him the love and support that he needed to fulfil his role as Henry III's regent; and imbuing the same dedication to land and family in her own daughters.

Isabel de Clare's marriage to William Marshal and subsequent birth of her children effectively reassigned the estates and power, which she personified, into the hands of a new Marshal dynasty. William Marshal, loyal servant of the Plantagenet monarchy, became Earl of Pembroke *jure uxoris*[2] and took control of his wife's lands. What is helpful to our understanding of Isabel's relationships both with her birthright and her husband, is that Marshal acknowledged his indebtedness to his wife and, on occasion, spoke plainly that without her, he would have nothing. Thanks to Marshal's recognition that as a fourth son he had married well above his social status, Isabel signed writs and took an active role in the administration and protection of her patrimony. Even so, the number of charters associated with her can be counted on both hands.

The countess first appears in the historical record as a ward of the Crown, a marginalised heiress waiting in the wings for a husband to be chosen for her. Henry II selected a man he could trust to control her patrimony on the Welsh Marches and in Ireland. His successor, King Richard I, recognised the soundness of the decision. He also wanted to bind Isabel's prospective husband to his own cause. William Marshal rose through his service to the Angevin monarchy of Henry II and his sons who took their identity from the County of Anjou ruled by the king's father Geoffrey. The count used to wear a sprig of yellow broom in his hat, in Latin called *Planta Genista*, from where the Plantagenet name by which Henry II's line of medieval kings is also known.

By the time of Marshal's marriage to Isabel, who was approximately 18-years of age, he was in his early forties. His bride had never set eyes on him before the morning she became his wife. A political marriage turned them into a power couple but personal love and devotion, if Marshal's biography paints a truthful picture, followed. Popular culture, subsequent to the rediscovery of the *Histoire de Guillaume le Marechal*, known as the *Histoire*, at an auction in 1861, created an enduring image of chivalry and romance around William's relationship with Isabel. The countess, it appears, was beautiful and intelligent, emerging as a 'significant actor'[3] working in partnership with her husband to preserve and care for her estates and family. Isabel travelled throughout England,

Normandy, Wales and Ireland, gave birth to ten children who survived to adulthood, withstood siege at Kilkenny Castle, advised her husband on family matters and was a patron of the Church. She knew kings and princes but was equally comfortable in the company of freebooters and barons.

The *Histoire* creates a tableau of Marshal's death which places Isabel at the heart of the dying earl's counsels for the future wellbeing not only of his family but also for the government of England. The countess's guiding hand can be seen in the manner by which the Marshal estates in Normandy, England, Wales and Ireland flourished and the speed by which Henry III's regents allied the king to William the Younger through marriage soon after his parents' deaths.

After Marshal's death, like other widows of the medieval period including her own mother, Isabel took effective control of her dower lands demonstrating an agency at odds with medieval views of feminine frailty. It was only during widowhood that most women were able to act in the legal capacity of *femme sole*, making their own decisions and acting of their own accord regarding their estates and property. However, unlike her daughters, Maud, Countess of Norfolk and Surrey and Eva, Lady of Bergavenny, Isabel did not live long enough to come under public scrutiny and into administrative records beyond the early days of her widowhood. Sources, still scant, paint a fuller picture of Maud and Eva's activities after the death of their husbands. Neither Isabel, her daughters nor the aristocratic women like them were the cyphers that the Church and law might have wished to depict. But, like all powerful women of the era, they walked a fine line between the domestic and public spheres.

Female power came from an aristocratic woman's role as a wife, a mother and then as a widow. Quite simply, they were women with the resources, prestige and relationships to exert influence on familial networks and beyond. Foucault explains that power is not always grounded in domination but reflects an ability to persuade; to sway decisions in one direction or another.[3] Isabel's power was more nuanced than the exploration of charters and rolls allows. However, 'the complexities and contradictions'[4] of medieval society, or of any society, are not always easy to either catalogue or evidence.

There are examples of powerful women wielding public authority, in a range of contexts throughout the period, who might be described as exceptional. Isabel was born in about 1172. A year later, Henry II's queen, Eleanor of Aquitaine, was imprisoned for rebelling against her husband. Marshal and Isabel's wedding celebrations in 1189 commenced with the death of the king and the freeing of his widow from captivity at Sarum Castle. Eleanor would live until she was 82-years of age, become the virtual ruler of her son Richard I's kingdom in his absence on the Third Crusade and emerge from semi-retirement at Fontevraud Abbey to help secure John's, her last remaining son, succession a decade later. As the Duchess of Aquitaine, she was one of the wealthiest and best educated women in Europe and, when Isabel knew her, she played an active role in the government of her sons. Despite the scandals that attached themselves to Eleanor's name throughout her life and the power that she wielded, there were occasions when the chroniclers had very little to say about her.

If Eleanor is the most famous woman of the twelfth century, she had contemporaries like Isabel who had their own place in history because of their birth rights and their own roles in the turbulent events of the period. In Ireland, Rohesia de Verdun, born in about 1204, commissioned the building of Castleroche Castle and is said to have had its architect thrown from one of the tower windows to ensure that he never shared its secrets. As a *femme sole*, owning property and making her own decisions, she gained a reputation more akin to the fantasy world of *Game of Thrones* than the subservient role provided by the limitations of medieval Church and State. In Wales, Isabel's neighbour, Matilda de Braose, born sometime in the early 1150s, was said to have built the castle at Hay in one night, such was her formidable reputation. Matilda remains famous because of her family's disastrous clash with King John and her own tragic death. Less well remembered is that she was a worthy castellan, defending Painscastle in Elfael against the Welsh for three weeks before the siege was raised. Nichola de la Haye, the daughter of a minor Lincolnshire lord, inherited the Constableship of Lincoln Castle. She was in her mid-sixties when she played a vital role in its defence against rebel English barons and the forces of the dauphin, Louis of France in 1217. She had already defended the castle against William Longchamp in the reign of King Richard I. She was described as a woman 'whose strength and tenacity saved England'[5] even though the monastic chronicler Richard of Devizes did not think it a 'womanly' pastime.[6] Nor was she particularly well rewarded, although both John and his son Henry III acknowledged her role. Four days after the Battle of Lincoln, her grandson-in-law, William II Longspée was granted the shrievalty of Lincolnshire which Nichola had held since the previous year. He contended that the Constableship was his as well. It was an argument that continued until his death in 1226.

Isabel was not an exceptional woman – she, her mother, her daughters, and aristocrats like them were women of their times who worked for the betterment of their families and preservation of what was rightfully theirs. Marshal's countess emerges from the shadows as a woman who was a worthy successor of her forefathers. When Isabel died in 1220, she left a cohesive network of family alliances that established the Marshal dynasty. No one could have predicted that fortune's wheel would turn against the male line within a generation leaving only females to inherit all that Isabel and Marshal achieved through their lives together.

The familial and political alliances that Isabel provided for her daughters was replicated in her granddaughters' unions. The countess's bloodline was embedded in the Marches of Wales and in the struggles not only for the Scottish Crown but the English one as well. Her descendants have included kings of Scotland since King Robert I, all the monarchs of England since the reign of King Henry IV, the Despenser, Beauchamp and Neville Earls of Warwick, the Stafford dukes of Buckingham, and all six of King Henry VIII's wives.

Chapter 1

The de Clare Family Establishes Itself

Isabel de Clare's mother, Aoife, was an Irish princess and her father, Richard 'Strongbow' de Clare, was descended from the dukes of Normandy through Godfrey, the eldest of Duke Richard I's illegitimate children by an unknown mistress. It is perhaps not surprising given her ancestry that she has been described as 'a great lady in a long tradition of powerful Norman aristocratic women'.[1] She was not someone to be side-lined even if the Church and State preferred to view all women as morally, physically and intellectually inferior to their male counterparts.

The men in Isabel's family were battle hardened warriors who acquired land on both sides of the Channel, in Wales and in Ireland by dint of conquest and royal patronage. Godfrey received Brionne and Eu from his father but Eu, a buffer zone which lay on the northern edge of the duchy, reverted to William, another of Duke Richard I's illegitimate sons, soon after Godfrey's death.[2] Gilbert FitzGodfrey, the son of Godfrey, continued to lay claim to his father's domain at Eu even though, as Count of Brionne, he remained one of the most important landholders in Normandy. His tenacity and ambition were perhaps not surprising. Duke Richard I's grandson was something of a chip off the old block. The monk Gilbert Crispin, a friend of Lanfranc at Bec[3] and later Abbot of Westminster, described Gilbert as 'a man ferocious of mind and immensely powerful, and greedy for matchless reputation'.[4]

In January 1035, Gilbert, who was first cousin to Duke Robert I of Normandy, was appointed as one of the guardians to the duke's 7-year-old son, William, while the duke went on pilgrimage to the Holy Land. There were some who whispered that Gilbert enjoyed the favours of William's mother, Herleva, before she became Duke Robert's mistress and that Gilbert's own illegitimate son, Richard FitzGilbert, was in fact William's half-brother. The origin of the gossip is likely to have been founded on supposition based on the favour shown by both the Conqueror and his youngest son, King Henry I, to Isabel's family.

Duke Robert died unexpectedly on his way home from Jerusalem at the beginning of July. His son William, became Duke of Normandy. Naming him heir to the duchy was a risk, not because he was illegitimate; Christian marriage was still being standardised in Normandy at that time. The real problem lay in the new duke's youth. Other claimants to the duchy were grown men with supporters of their own. Life became more perilous for everyone as various branches of the ducal family vied for their own advancement and the ruling elite took the opportunity to settle old grudges amongst themselves. William of Jumièges writing the *Deeds of the Dukes of Normandy*, shortly after the conquest of England explained that men who could afford it built earth works and castles to protect themselves but 'having dared to establish themselves securely in their fortifications, they immediately hatched plots and rebellions and fierce fires were lit all over the country'.[5]

Even so, Archbishop Robert of Rouen, the most dominant of William's guardians as well as the boy's great-uncle was able to maintain control over the various counter-claimants for the duchy until his own death in 1037. Soon afterwards, civil order faltered and almost failed. Alan of Brittany who replaced the archbishop as William's senior guardian and tutor was killed either late in 1039 or early in 1040. All the men appointed by Duke Robert before his departure to rule during the boy's minority, were picked off one by one. Osbern, Duke Robert's trusted steward, was slain in the room where William slept and in 1040, Turold who was described as one of the boy's tutors was also assassinated.

Gilbert FitzGodfrey was murdered at about the same time as Turold.[6] He was killed by his cousin Ralph de Gacé, one of the sons of Archbishop Robert of Rouen. The political crisis in Normandy deepened. Gilbert's sons, Richard and Baldwin, born between 1030 and 1035, under the care of their own guardians escaped to safety in Flanders at the court of Count Baldwin V. Brionne, an arrondissement of Bernay, was given into the custody of another of their cousins, Guy of Burgundy, who was one of Duke William's household companions. But Guy, a younger son of the Count of Burgundy, was not satisfied with the grant made at the expense of Isabel's ancestors. He became increasingly discontented and, in 1047, was drawn into a revolt against William. He was a legitimate grandson of Duke Richard II so had his own claim to the duchy which he sought to win on the battlefield. William and his feudal overlord, King Henri I of France, defeated Guy's army at the Battle of Val-ès-Dunes near Caen that summer. Guy retreated to the castle at Brionne. After a protracted siege the castle surrendered and was absorbed into the ducal estates.[7]

In 1050, Duke William, having survived his childhood and secured Normandy, married Matilda, the daughter of Baldwin V of Flanders. Richard and Baldwin, grown to adulthood, returned to the duchy to serve the duke as their father did before them. There is evidence of them witnessing William's charters from the 1050s onwards. Orderic Vitalis, a contemporary monastic chronicler, stated that William 'had a special regard for Richard and Baldwin, the sons of Count Gilbert, and advanced them in the world, both on account of their nearness of blood and their own valour'.[8] They were granted Obrec, Bienfaite, Meulles and Le Sap but the County of Brionne remained alienated. Robert of Toriginy recorded that Gilbert's grandson Roger unsuccessfully tried to pay for the return of Brionne into the family's hands in 1087.[9]

More immediately, William arranged that his cousins should marry. Baldwin was wedded to Emma who was William's own niece, or cousin, depending on the source. Richard, from whom Isabel was descended, was united with Rohese Giffard, sister of Walter Giffard, Lord of Longueville who was one of the duke's most trusted companions. Longueville was one of the select group of men who attended Duke William's council at Lillebonne to plan the invasion of England in January 1066.

Wace's *Chronicle of the Norman Conquest*, commissioned by King Henry II, places Richard and Baldwin at Senlac at the battle which saw King Harold and his house carls slaughtered and opened the way for William to become king.[10] The Conqueror rewarded Richard and Baldwin generously in the aftermath of his victory. Baldwin was granted lands in the West Country becoming the Sheriff of Devon in 1068. Richard was settled with estates, including the honours of Clare in Suffolk and Tonbridge in Kent where he built a motte and bailey castle to guard the crossing of the Medway. William of Jumièges told the tale of a rope being used to measure a league, or two miles, round the castle at Brionne which remained in the Conqueror's hands. The rope was fetched across the Channel to Kent so that it could gauge the same area around Richard's new motte and bailey castle at Tonbridge. The domain was a liberty which held legal privileges exempting it from the rule of Kent's sheriff. It was permitted the right to hold its own court. The area became known as known as the Lowy, or League, of Tonbridge. Some of the land claimed by Richard was appropriated from the Archbishop of Canterbury's estates and subject to dispute even after Lanfranc of Bec, appointed by King William as Archbishop in 1070, established his rightful overlordship. Richard built another castle at Clare and a third overlooking the Weald at Bletchingley in Surrey. FitzGilbert's castles were an instrument of feudal domination but they also expressed his military and political power.

Isabel's forefather continued to extend his landholdings throughout the Conqueror's lifetime and continued to be a trusted servant of the Crown. In 1073 during the duke's absence from England, Richard acted as justiciar alongside William de Warren dispensing justice and maintaining order on the king's behalf. Two years later he helped to suppress a revolt against William. By 1087 the Domesday book valued Richard's estates at £873.[11] He was amongst the wealthiest men in the country with property in nine counties. He can be found in the records across the period as Richard FitzGilbert, Richard of Bienfaite,[12] Richard of Tonbridge and latterly as Richard of Clare. In time de Clare would become the name by which the family was known although they were never earls of Clare.

After the Conqueror's death in 1087 the king's eldest son, Robert Curthose, inherited Normandy while his second son, William Rufus, became king of England. The following year Richard of Tonbridge's sons, and maybe even Richard himself, joined the Conqueror's half-brothers Bishop Odo and Robert of Mortain in rebellion against the king to put Curthose on the English throne. The *Anglo-Saxon Chronicle* described the realm as 'greatly stirred up, and filled with much treachery'.[13] It recorded that Gilbert and his elder brother, Roger de Clare, were besieged for only two days in Tonbridge Castle before 'the English went and broke into the castle'.[14] Gilbert, wounded in the encounter, was pardoned but only after the king ordered that the castle should be razed to the ground. Richard, if he had not already done so after William the Conqueror's death in 1087, withdrew to the priory he founded at St Neots, in Huntingdonshire, and remained there until his own death in 1090.

Following the pattern established by William the Conqueror, Richard's elder son, Roger FitzRichard de Clare, inherited the family's Norman estates while Gilbert, from whom Isabel was descended, received his father's extensive English lands.

In 1095, despite the failures of 1088 and the risk associated with unsuccessful rebellion, Gilbert was drawn into a second plot led by Robert de Mowbray, Earl of Northumbria and William of Eu, Lord of Hastings against King William II. On this occasion Gilbert experienced second thoughts and revealed what he knew of the scheme to the king before the plot came to fruition. William Rufus was swift to exact his vengeance. The Earl of Northumbria surrendered his estates and was imprisoned at Windsor before eventually being permitted to become a monk at St Albans Abbey. William of Eu was blinded and castrated although his son was permitted to inherit the barony of Hastings as well as the countship of Eu. The *Anglo-Saxon Chronicle* added that, 'many others [were deprived of] their lands; some men were taken to London and there mutilated'.[15] Gilbert retained his lands but he never recovered the king's full favour. It is unclear why, in 1095, he changed his mind about supporting Robert Curthose's claim to the throne. The decision was clearly justified as Earl Robert of Northumbria and William of Eu were not the only barons to be destroyed by their involvement in a series of planned uprisings that dogged William Rufus's reign.[16] Perhaps Gilbert recognised that fortune's wheel was often propelled on a downward trajectory by the king's wrath and, as a consequence, was careful in his decision making.

Five years later the *Anglo-Saxon Chronicle* documented that on 2 August 1100 'King William was shot with an arrow by his own men as he was hunting'.[17] Later chroniclers embellished the manner of the king's death but everyone agreed that it was Gilbert's brother-in-law, Walter Tirel, who shot the arrow; intentionally or not. William of Malmesbury described the king's younger brother, Henry, deserting Rufus's body so that he could secure the royal treasury at Winchester before hastening to London. He was crowned three days after William's death on Sunday 5 August. It was left to Gilbert de Clare and his younger brother, Robert, to cover the king's body and to arrange for a bier to transport it back to Winchester before joining Henry on the dash to obtain his crown. Other men who were with William's hunting party that day chose to rush in the direction of their own estates with the intention of securing their possessions. They knew that Henry's bid for the throne would not go uncontested. The Treaty of Caen signed in 1091 recognised Robert Curthose, on his way back to Normandy from the First Crusade, as the rightful king. Either King Henry I, who was the Conqueror's youngest son, took advantage of an unexpected opportunity arising from an unfortunate hunting accident or there was a plot to assassinate his predecessor.

Without more substantial evidence the assertion that Rufus's death was murder is nothing more than a conspiracy theory. It was suspected that the de Clares protected their kinsman by marriage, Tirel, who escaped to Normandy immediately after the killing. William of Malmesbury did not name Gilbert as one of Tirel's protectors nor did he describe the king's death as murder. He recorded that it was Tirel who fired the deadly arrow but that 'there were none to pursue him: some helped his flight; others felt sorry for him'.[18] It was certainly to the financial and political advantage of the de Clares to support Henry's claims to the throne. While the kingdom was in a state of turmoil and with the threat of invasion over his head the monarch needed to conciliate his barons.

The new king was swift to make a proclamation condemning his brother's reign and to issue a coronation charter that swore to 'abolish all the evil customs by which the kingdom of England has been unjustly oppressed'.[19] Among the charter's witnesses were members of the powerful Beaumont family from whom Isabel was descended: Gilbert's cousin Walter Giffard, 1st Duke of Buckingham whose loyalty to the new king would fail in 1101; and Eudo Dapifer, William Rufus's steward who had been present in the New Forest on the fateful day that William died. Eudo was a powerful man who acquired vast estates through his service to the Norman kings. Since about 1088 he was also

Gilbert's brother-in-law, through his marriage to Rohese de Clare. Gilbert and the barons to whom he was related continued to back Henry in the hope of reaping dividends from his elevation to the throne. Gilbert's uncle, Walter Giffard, was made Bishop of Winchester the day after Henry became king. It was part of a bid to ensure that the clergy backed Henry's claim rather than Robert Curthose's but it was also a tantalising promise of the rewards to come for men like Gilbert FitzRichard de Clare.

The de Clares enjoyed significant favour in the form of estates and offices throughout King Henry I's lifetime. Gilbert's youngest surviving brother, Robert, received lands including Little Dunmow in Essex as well as becoming Constable of Baynard's Castle in London. Richard de Clare, a monk, became the Abbot of Ely[20] increasing the family's sphere of influence in East Anglia. In 1119, Walter de Clare was given the lordship of Netherwent on the Welsh Marches with its principal castle at Chepstow or Striguil as it was then known. The castle, set high on a cliff above the Rive Wye, was thought to have originally been built by William FitzOsbern shortly after the conquest of England. More recent research suggests that it was William I who gave the orders that it should be built in stone.[21]

Marcher lordships were on the margins of Crown control; a buffer zone between England and Wales. They were not assimilated into the English county administrative structure which included a sheriff appointed by the monarch to oversee law and order. Royal writ did not extend into the Marches unless there was treason involved. Later Norman kings including William Rufus, Henry I and Stephen licensed individual Norman barons to seize control of specified areas inside Wales and hold them against the Welsh if they were able. Barons and their families living on the frontier fought private military campaigns, were a law unto themselves, and so far as the Welsh were concerned little better than bandits. Walter de Clare was expected to hold the border for the king but as with other Marcher lords his authority within his own domain was far-reaching.

Walter's new life as a frontier baron was not an isolated one. His elder brother Gilbert had been a formidable presence in the Marches for almost a decade. In 1110, Gilbert was granted the lordship of Ceredigion following the kidnap of King Henry I's one-time mistress, Nest of Wales, by Owain ap Cadwgan and the failure of Owain's father, the Prince of Powys, to control his son. The *Brut* provides a detailed account of the king offering Gilbert the lordship, providing he could take and hold on to it. Henry, a pragmatist, saw the benefit of extending Anglo-Norman control into Wales as well as the chance to install barons in the borders who owed their position to him. Too many of his existing Marcher barons defied the Crown and feuded amongst themselves. The de Clares, who were always swift to recognise opportunities for personal gain, had, according to the *Brut*, pestered the king for years for the right to move across the English border into Wales.

Gilbert established castles at Ceredigion overlooking the River Teifi and at Aberystwyth as well as a series of smaller forts which made control of the region possible. Gilbert's privileges included complete jurisdiction over his border domain as well as his territories within Wales. He was permitted to hold his own courts, appoint his own sheriffs and establish his own markets without the need for the king's charter. Even so, the lordship of Ceredigion was not without its difficulties. Griffith ap Rhys put the earth and timber fortification at Aberystwyth under siege in 1116. Although ap Rhys was not successful on that occasion, it was captured by the Welsh twenty years later. The de Clare family understood that their hold on the Marches and Wales meant that residence in disputed lands equated to a life often lived in a state of actual or threatened war. It was something that they were well used to across the generations. The kingdoms of Wales were difficult to conquer and the castles that Gilbert and other Anglo-Norman lords built in the region were never wholly effective.

By the time Gilbert died in 1117, he had augmented his already substantial fortunes and made politically strategic marriages for his children. The prescriptions of primogeniture observed by the Normans throughout the medieval period preserved family estates in tact from one generation to the next. Richard FitzGilbert, Gilbert's eldest son, inherited the honours of Clare and Tonbridge as well as the lordship of Ceredigion. Richard's marriage to the sister of Ranulf de Gernon, 4th Earl of Chester gained him political affiliations in the Marches as well as his wife Adeliza's dowry lands in Lincolnshire and Northampton.

Gilbert FitzGilbert, Isabel de Clare's grandfather, inherited nothing from his father. He was a man without wealth or land of his own. The *Gesta Stephani* described him as a poor knight.[22] The best that younger sons like him could hope for was making a good marriage or a position as a household knight. Fortunately for Gilbert his uncles – Walter, Lord of Netherwent and Roger of Clare who held the family's Norman fief – left no direct heirs when they died in 1137 and 1131 respectively. Gilbert inherited their lands and titles. His good fortune was augmented by the fact that, sometime before 1130, King Henry I arranged for him to marry Isabel de Beaumont, a daughter of Isabel de Vermandois and her first husband Robert Beaumont, 1st Earl of Leicester and Count of Meulan.

Isabel de Beaumont was one of the king's many mistresses and had given Henry a daughter before he settled the manor of Barrow in Suffolk upon her and married her to Gilbert.[23] The intention was to draw the de Clare family into his own extended kinship network in an attempt to ensure their continuing loyalty to him and his only surviving heir, the Empress Matilda. It has been suggested that Gilbert's acquisition of his uncles' estates during the reign of King Stephen derived from the support of his wife's powerful family who regarded his advancement as of benefit to themselves.[24] Power was based in both land ownership and influential kinship networks. Wives and daughters were the glue that cemented alliances.

King Henry I was overtaken by disaster on 25 November 1120 when his only legitimate male heir, William Adlin, drowned. His vessel, *The White Ship*, sank as it left the harbour at Barfleur. The king was left with only one lawful daughter, Matilda, married to the Holy Roman Emperor since 1114. Henry wedded for a second time to Adeliza of Louvain in an attempt to secure the succession. Although he fathered children with his mistresses, including his daughter by Isabel de Beaumont, Adeliza gave him no more heirs. In 1125 Matilda's husband Henry V, the Holy Roman Emperor, died. The following Christmas, King Henry I required all his barons to swear an oath recognising Matilda as his successor even though a woman had never before ruled England in her own right. Gilbert de Clare's elder brother Richard was among their number. In the spring of 1131 England's barons repeated the oath that they would accept Matilda as their queen. Many barons were hostile not only to the idea of a woman ruling them but to the empress's new husband, Geoffrey of Anjou.

Chapter 2

The Anarchy

When King Henry I died on 1 December 1135 the bonds of political stability that the king imposed upon his magnates cracked. Matilda, who was pregnant, was in Anjou but her cousin Stephen of Blois, a grandson of William the Conqueror, was closer in Boulogne. Aside from the advantage of being male, he had sons, was well liked, and hastened to England as soon as he heard news of Henry's death. He was crowned on 22 December 1135 having secured the royal treasury at Winchester in a move which mirrored the actions of his uncle thirty-five years earlier.

In Wales, the death of King Henry I was followed by an upsurge of violence against the Anglo-Norman interlopers. A Welsh raid on the Gower led by the lord of Brycheiniog inflicted a reverse on Anglo-Norman pretensions in the region.[1] Richard, Gilbert's elder brother, and founder of the senior branch of the de Clare family in England, was ambushed on his way to Ceredigion and killed on 15 April 1136 at the hands of Iorwerth ab Owain, Lord of Caerleon. Owain ap Gruffud and his brother invaded Richard's Welsh lordship and seized the lands he held in Wales apart from Ceredigion Castle. Richard's widow, Adeliza, had to be rescued from the besiegers by an expedition sent from Gloucester. The *Gesta Stephani* blamed the disaster on the death of the king but other writers including Gerald of Wales suggest that trouble was brewing before Henry's death.

War blossomed between Stephen and Empress Matilda in England. Concentration on events in the east left Marcher lords exposed to the attacks of the renascent Welsh. By 1138, all of the de Clare fortifications in Ceredigion, excluding Ceredigion Castle which could be resupplied from the sea, and everything west of the River Usk were lost. Other Marcher lords struggled to cling to the gains they had made in Wales. Without a strong king they became resentful of the situation in which they found themselves. Robert, Earl of Gloucester, Matilda's illegitimate half-brother, proved a staunch supporter of his sister from the spring of 1138 onwards when he renounced his fealty to Stephen. The majority of Marcher lords, if they had not done so before, also joined with the Angevin cause because it suited their personal loyalties and ambitions.

The chaos of conflict provided openings for self-reliant and resourceful men who won the king's confidence. Gilbert FitzGilbert, Isabel de Clare's grandfather, served King Stephen with loyalty throughout much of the nineteen years' war which followed Henry I's death. He turned from a landless younger son into a powerful political player. In about 1137 or 1138, in addition to the lordship of Netherwent, Gilbert was also granted the lordship of Pembroke and elevated to an earldom. The information was recorded by Orderic Vitalis and in the *Register of Tintern Abbey*.[2] Gilbert, whose family was a cadet branch of the de Clares, also received the important rape of Pevensey and its castle on the south coast. The new Earl of Pembroke, it seemed, was a man who could be trusted and the king, who was known for his excessive generosity, heaped rewards upon him.

Gilbert had the wealth but not yet the opportunity to reconquer the lands in Ceredigion and Dyfed that had been lost in 1136 when his brother was killed and which his nephew, Richard, elevated to the earldom of Hertford by Stephen, did not attempt to reclaim. The *Anglo-Saxon Chronicle* described the years when Stephen and Matilda fought for the throne as 'an evil time'.[3] It recorded casual savagery, torture, famine and starvation as armies that crossed the realm like locusts destroyed everything that they came across. In the Marches, border barons who were well practised in violence capitalised on the civil war as a license to behave in England as they behaved in the Marches and in Wales; as 'warlords and chancers'.[4]

They aligned themselves according to kinship connections and where they saw most advantage for themselves, including with the Welsh. Owain ap Gruffudd's brother, Cadwalladr, strengthened his hold on Ceredigion by a treaty made, after 1140, with Ranulf de Gernon, 4th Earl of Chester. The confederacy was cemented with a marriage between Cadwalladr and Alice de Clare, the daughter of the murdered Richard. Cadwalladr became Chester's nephew and Gilbert FitzGilbert's cousin by marriage. Kinship and intermarriage helped to build some stability although it was not always to the monarch's advantage.

Ranulf exemplified the ruthless opportunism that prevailed among the barons. His only loyalty was to himself. Many of his decisions were driven by a belief that the honour of Carlisle was justly his own inheritance by right of his mother Lucy de Taillebois. Ranulf's father resigned the claim to the lordship in 1120 in return for licence to enter his cousin's earldom of Chester when Richard d'Avranches drowned during the sinking of the White Ship. King Henry I wanted no overmighty subjects but the family never gave up hope of regaining their northern estates. In 1136, King Stephen ceded the Cumbrian honour to Henry of Scotland as part of a treaty with Henry's father,

King David I. The earl disguised his outrage at the loss until, two years later, Stephen arranged a wedding between Henry and Adeline de Warenne whose half-brothers Waleran and Robert de Beaumont were Ranulf's main rivals for power in the Midlands. Festering resentment escalated into a personal war waged in the Midlands and the Marches against Robert Beaumont, 2nd Earl of Leicester who commanded an army on Stephen's behalf. The conflict reverberated through the region for more than a decade.

In January 1141, Ranulf was able to seize Lincoln Castle which his half-brother, William de Roumare, claimed as part of his own rightful inheritance from their mother. When Stephen laid siege to the castle with Ranulf, his half-brother and their wives inside it, the earl escaped to raise more troops. Among them were a Welsh contingent who joined his army as part of Cadwalladr's alliance with him. He also sought the help of his father-in-law, Robert of Gloucester, who offered aid only when Ranulf agreed to switch sides. Stephen was heavily outnumbered and was captured by the Empress's army on 2 February during the First Battle of Lincoln.

In 1145, or early in 1146, Ranulf switched sides once more, not only to retain Lincoln Castle but because he was still agitating for the return of the honour of Carlisle. His chance of achieving his goal with the support of the Empress was thwarted when Matilda allied herself with David of Scotland. Furthermore, the earl wanted the king, who was released six months after his capture at Lincoln during a prisoner exchange, to take part in a campaign against the Welsh fearing, as he did, that the disorder in England would lead to an attack on his own territory in the Marches.

Despite coming to terms with Stephen in 1145, the rapprochement between Ranulf and the king was an uneasy one especially when it was discovered that the earl wanted Stephen to take part in a campaign against the Welsh. The suggestion provoked an argument from men who remembered that there was a contingent of Welshmen present at the Battle of Lincoln in 1141. They persuaded the king to have Ranulf arrested in direct contravention to Stephen's earlier promises to the earl. The immediate result was an attack by the Welsh on the palatinate of Chester which was halted on 3 September 1146 by the earl's seneschal at Nantwich. In England, Ranulf was forced to surrender various castles, including Lincoln, as well as providing hostages as guarantors of his continued loyalty to the Crown before he was freed. Gilbert FitzRichard, 1st Earl of Hertford, was among the men forced to become a hostage as surety for his uncle, Ranulf of Chester's, future conduct. As soon as he was released, Ranulf declared the oath that was exacted from him was invalid, declared himself for Matilda once more and set about recovering the castles at Lincoln and Coventry which had been seized on Stephen's orders.

The earl's rebellion would continue until at least 1149 but the chronicles are silent on the manner of its conclusion.

Gilbert FitzRichard, 1st Earl of Hertford was imprisoned when Ranulf broke the terms of his agreement with the king. Stephen refused to release FitzRichard until he placed all his own castles into royal custody. It was either that or exile. Slow to learn from the example set by Ranulf, the king extracted oaths of loyalty from FitzRichard and freed him. Unsurprisingly, the 1st Earl of Hertford joined with Ranulf in rebellion once he regained his liberty. The king promptly confiscated all his estates.

Gilbert, Earl of Pembroke and his son, Richard, despite a brief waiver of loyalty in 1141 after Stephen's capture at Lincoln, were unusual in their sustained support for the king rather than shifting allegiance to the Angevins to suit their own ends. In 1147, Gilbert briefly deserted the king. The goodwill that existed between the two men was tainted because of the circumstances in which Gilbert's nephew, Gilbert de Clare, 1st Earl of Hertford, either acting as the senior representative for de Clare family interests or ambitious for the acquisition of territory for himself, asked the king for his nephew's sequestered estates by right of birth even though FitzRichard's younger brother had a better claim than his own. Stephen refused Gilbert's request. He had his own doubts about the cadet branch of the de Clare family. The king's concerns were justified when Gilbert, following the rejection of his demands, joined in the rebellion against Stephen not because of a newfound devotion to Matilda but because he had been thwarted.

The *Gesta Stephani* recorded the king's anger at Gilbert's treachery. Stephen believed that the earl owed all his advances to his own generosity. He moved quickly to secure Kent believing that the earl would attempt to defend Tonbridge and then marched on Pevensey where he found his recalcitrant subject. The garrison was blockaded and starved into submission.[5] Eventually both the earls of Pembroke and Hertford were re-established on Stephen's side and even regained their confiscated lands as, eventually, did their kinsman Ranalf of Chester. The loss of his estates and newfound honours was something that Gilbert preferred not to countenance and the king was not in a position where he could afford to alienate the de Clare family, or even the treacherous Ranulf.

Gilbert died in 1148 and was succeeded by his son Richard, Isabel's father, better known to history as Strongbow. Unfortunately for Richard, his father's bid to acquire land and power based upon Stephen's claim to the crown was about to unravel. The year before Gilbert's death, Matilda's son, Henry FitzEmpress, launched a small invasion of England but lacked both men and money. His mercenaries were paid off by King Stephen and the boy returned to Normandy. For the time being England continued to be relatively peaceful.

Undeterred, Henry returned in 1149 and formed an alliance with the Earl of Chester who was able to resolve his property disputes with King David of Scotland as part of an Angevin coalition. The earl set aside his claim to Carlisle in return for the honour of Lancaster and a marriage between one of his sons and a daughter of Henry of Scotland's. It was an outcome that seemed certain to guarantee Ranulf's loyalty to the Angevins. However, the coalition collapsed when Stephen upped the stakes by recognising the earl's dominance in the Midlands.

In 1153, Henry arrived in England with another army; the circumstances were considerably changed from his earlier attempts to claim his mother's kingdom. He was the duke of both Normandy and Anjou and was married to Eleanor of Aquitaine giving him control of her duchy as well as his own domains. Stephen was forced to declare a winter truce after he failed to force Henry into a decisive battle. While the king returned to London, Henry used the opportunity to win Strongbow's Beaumont kinsmen over to his own side and to secure the Midlands. He also re-purchased Ranulf's support with the grant of estates in Staffordshire. The terms of Henry's agreement ended hostilities between the earls of Chester and Leicester. FitzEmpress now controlled the north, the Midlands and the south-west of England.

Although sporadic fighting continued, Theobald of Bec, the Archbishop of Canterbury, was able to broker a peace deal in the summer of 1153. The Treaty of Wallingford allowed Stephen to remain king until his death on the proviso that Matilda's son would be his successor. It was a temporary truce but when Stephen's eldest son and heir, Eustace IV Count of Boulogne, died of a seizure in August 1153 it became permanent. Even King Stephen's younger son, William, Earl of Surrey by right of his wife Isabel de Warenne was prepared to recognise Henry as king in return for assurances regarding his rights to his wife's estates and title. The Anarchy was over. Strongbow de Clare was one of the signatories of the Treaty of Wallingford that cemented the end of the war, as was his cousin, Roger de Clare, 2nd Earl of Hertford, younger brother to the luckless Gilbert FitzRichard, 1st Earl of Hertford.

Less than a year after the treaty was agreed Stephen died and Henry FitzEmpress ascended to the throne as King Henry II. The future suddenly looked much less secure for men like Strongbow whose families fought against the Empress Matilda and her son and who had failed to turn their coats in sufficient time to win favour with them. Orderic Vitalis recognised that the de Clares 'were driven by the changeable gales of unstable fortune'.[6]

The 1st Earl of Hertford's support for Matilda prior to his death in 1152 was, however, sufficient to exonerate the senior line of the de Clare family. Roger de Clare, 2nd Earl of Hertford was welcome at Henry II's court. By

1157 he had royal permission to take and hold whatever lands in Wales he could. Strongbow's maternal uncle, Robert Beaumont 2nd Earl of Leicester, whose principal actions between 1141 and 1149 could be seen in the light of a private war with his rival Ranulf of Chester defected to Henry FitzEmpress in 1153. His timely decision ensured that he remained in the office of Chief Steward of England and Normandy and was further rewarded with the role of chief justiciar as soon as Henry became king.

Strongbow, by contrast, was not welcome at court and, even worse, he was not licensed to enter his estate as the 2nd Earl of Pembroke when King Henry II was crowned on 19 December 1154. Nor did Henry, in his capacity as Duke of Normandy, choose to recognise Strongbow's claim to Orbec and Bienfaite inherited by Gilbert from Roger de Clare. Henry elected to demonstrate his authority among the Marcher lords by diminishing Strongbow. He and his father played too notable a part in Stephen's reign for the son of the Empress Matilda to let bygones be bygones.

Chapter 3

The Earl and the King of Leinster

Gerald of Wales, the Cambro-Norman chronicler who nursed a FitzGerald family grudge against Strongbow, would write of Isabel's father 'his name was greater than his means, his descent than his talents'[1] suggesting that Henry's decision to withhold the earldom of Pembroke had less to do with the king than Strongbow's own failure to play the political game as effectively as his ancestors had done. His family's past seemed destined to be greater than their future at the start of King Henry II's reign.

In 1148, after his father's death, Strongbow inherited the lordship of Netherwent and the earldom of Pembroke even though he was not yet 21-years old. The name Strongbow either arose from a misinterpretation of Striguil as Chepstow Castle was then known, his use of Welsh archers among his levies, or his own prowess with a longbow. In addition to Chepstow and its associated lands in the Marches of Wales, Netherwent was composed of sixty-five knights' fees[2] (approximately 97,500 acres). De Clare witnessed the Treaty of Windsor of 1153 as an earl.[3] However, at Henry II's coronation the following year and, later, when the royal court gathered in the spring of 1155, Strongbow was only recognised as the Lord of Netherwent holding the lands between the rivers Wye and Usk. He was denied the earldom of Pembroke, its strategically important castle and its estates. He continued to be denied license to enter his father's estates at Orbec and Bienfaite. The reason for depriving Strongbow of his inheritance is not documented. It can only be surmised that the king did not trust his loyalty to the new regime and that de Clare's ties to his mother's Beaumont kinsmen were insufficient, or his establishment as a significant Marcher lord not to their benefit, for them to try and sway the king's mind in his favour.

By the end of 1158 Henry II had established his authority in his realm, come to terms with the Scots and forced Owain ap Gruffud to surrender both territory in Wales and hostages. Having achieved his purpose, the king turned his attention back to the other side of the Narrow Seas as the English Channel was then called.

Royal approval continued to elude Isabel's father throughout the next decade. In 1164, Henry dispersed the estates of Walter Giffard, 2nd Earl of Buckingham who had no direct heirs of his own. The king had no intention of passing the earl's estates to his collateral heirs of whom Strongbow was one through his descent from Rohese Giffard. Instead, the king alienated most of the honour of Giffard for himself and used some of the land to reward men whose loyalty he could trust. One such was his Constable in Normandy, Richard du Hommet who received land in Buckinghamshire and Norfolk as well as several estates in Normandy.[4]

It was a blow to Strongbow who owed money to Aaron of Lincoln, King Henry II's wealthy Jewish financier. He mortgaged some of his property to make ends meet. As well as potential payment for the earlier building works undertaken at Pembroke before Henry became king there were the expenses of maintaining his fortifications in the Marches. In addition, de Clare, like all of Henry's other barons, was required to pay feudal dues including *servitium debitum*, or knight service, and scutage. The king was intent on re-establishing the dominance of the monarchy over England's barony. He also needed the revenue to fund his military campaigns to subdue rebellions in Brittany and Aquitaine as well as to wage war against the French. Scutage, the so-called shield money, paid by a feudal tenant in lieu of military service was levied five times between Henry's coronation and 1165 at the rate of one or two marks per knight's fee.[5] Magnates including Strongbow were required to dig deep into their coffers. In 1166, Henry required that every baron complete a census return detailing each knight they held enfeoffed to ensure that the exchequer maximised the returns gained from scutage.

One solution to Strongbow's problems would have been for him to marry an heiress. It would ensure the continuation of his line; ease his financial burden and build a political alliance with another family. As lord of Netherwent, de Clare held lands directly from the king, so he would have expected a marriage with a woman whose lands and wealth were proportionate to his own. But, for a wedding to take place royal permission was required. Henry was well aware of the potential influence that an unbridled Marcher lord could bring to bear upon English politics. The king had no intention of loosening his grip on Strongbow either by returning his patrimony or permitting him to make a good marriage. Unwed, deprived of his rightful inheritance, in debt and with little likelihood that Henry would return Strongbow to favour it seemed that the cadet branch of the de Clare family was destined to wither within a generation.

Fortune's wheel began to turn in de Clare's favour with the arrival of a boat from Ireland which docked at Bristol in the summer of 1166. The vessel was not in itself unusual. There were strong trading links between the port, which was the third most important city in the kingdom, and the south west of Ireland. This particular boat carried Diarmait Mac Murchada who was

King of Leinster, his wife Mór, their daughter Aoife and a small band of loyal supporters. The king's enemies had overrun his land, left his stone hall at Ferns in ruins and burned its longphort, or shore fort, to the ground. When Aoife looked back in the direction of the Irish coast, she may have spared a thought for the predicament of her half-brother, Énna, who had fallen into the hands of the King of Osraige, a former adherent of their father.

The weary refugees made their way to the home of Bristol's town reeve whose duties were similar to those of a magistrate. Robert FitzHarding was a wealthy and well-connected merchant who traded with Ireland. Diarmait already knew him and was aware of his influence both in Bristol and beyond. The merchant, a former ally of Robert of Gloucester, had been one of Henry II's financiers during the Anarchy. He was well rewarded for his support of the Plantagenet monarchy after Henry became king. He held a grant for the lordship of Berkeley[6] and the right to rebuild its castle.[7] FitzHarding had the contacts, influence and wealth necessary to set about assisting Diarmait to regain his lost kingdom. In turn, the merchant recognised the prospect of profit and political influence when he saw it. The reeve welcomed his unexpected guests and began to plan a way forward for Mac Murchada. Both men realised that a return to Ireland required more than correspondence between the Irish king and his followers at home. It would require an army and gold to pay the men who joined it or something equally as lucrative.

The reeve arranged to accommodate the Irish, for the longer term, in the nearby monastery at Billeswick which he founded in 1140 on land purchased from the Earl of Gloucester. The Augustinians, or Black Canons (named for their long black cassock and hood), modelled their lives on poverty, chastity and obedience. They regarded the duty of hospitality as an essential part of their monastic obligation. Diarmait and his immediate family were shown to the guest accommodation reserved for important visitors, perhaps the abbot's own house, behind a gateway beyond the busy outer courtyard. The rest of their small retinue were admitted only to the more basic guest quarters.

Politics in Ireland were complicated. The seeds of Diarmait's removal from power were sown in 1152. He assisted Derbforgaill, the daughter of Dairmait's ally the King of West Meath to escape from her husband Tigernán Ua Ruaire, King of Bréifne, taking her cattle and the rest of her belongings with her. Historians have speculated that she was unhappy with the union made to cement an alliance between the kings of Meath and Bréifne and sought to escape from it with Diarmait's help. Derbforgaill returned to her family in Meath by the end of the following year and ended her days in a nunnery. However, for the wife of one king to elope with another was a shameful business whether she went voluntarily or not. Gerald of Wales, not known for his sympathy towards women, commented that it was a great evil and blamed Derbforgaill as 'a fickle and inconstant creature'[8] for the troubles that ensued. Gerald may have wanted to paint the picture of a war being fought because of a woman but Derbforgaill was no Irish Helen and the King of Leinster was not swept away with desire for a beautiful princess. It was much more likely that Diarmait and Tigernán's rivalry sprang from their shared aspiration to rule over the kingdom of Meath.[9]

To begin with, fortune favoured the King of Leinster. By 1161 Diarmait was recognised as one of Ireland's strongest petty kings allied to Muirchertach Mac Lochlainn, the High King of Ireland. In 1162, the Norse population, or Ostmen, of Dublin reluctantly acknowledged Diarmait as its overlord. It was a moment of sweet triumph for Mac Murchada whose father, Donnchadh, was king of both Leinster and Dublin. Donnchadh was murdered by the men of Dublin in 1115 and according to Gerald of Wales, they insulted the mortal remains of the dead king by burying his corpse with a dog. Other sources state that the king was killed in battle.

Diarmait had a reputation for being a brave and warlike man. He had consolidated his position in the Ui Chennselaig clan homelands of his family and risen to prominence following the unexpected death of his brother in 1126. As king of Leinster, his ruthlessness was well documented. He even arranged for the abbess of Kildare Abbey to be violated so that his own candidate could be instated to the post; making the point that traditionally it was the kings of Leinster who appointed Kildare's abbesses. In 1141 he had men who rose in rebellion against him killed or blinded. Gerald remarked that Diarmait, 'preferred to be feared by all rather than loved'.[10]

Tigernán could only bide his time and hope that luck would turn against his rival or that he could de-stabilise the hierarchy sufficiently to weaken Mac Murchada. The King of Leinster's power was tied to the continuing rule of the Irish High King, Muirchertach Mac Lochlainn. His murder, in 1166, by Tigernán, destabilised the balance of power. The sudden vacuum of authority provoked a sequence of events that toppled Diarmait from his throne. Ruardrí Ua Conchobair, King of Connacht, seized the chance to gather an alliance against Diarmait which included the king's reluctant subjects in Dublin: Domnall Mac Gilla Pátraic, King of Osraige who was the most important sub-king of the region controlled by Leinster; the other, lesser kings of Leinster; and, of course, Tigernán Ua Ruaire.

Diarmait retreated to the heartlands of the Ui Chennselaig but his choice was either death or flight. The *Annála Ríoghachta Éireann* (1632–66), more commonly known as the *Annals of the Four Masters*, or just the *Four Masters*, compiled from earlier Irish annals, recorded that the men who led the army against Diarmait demanded that he should pay Derbforgaill's honour price of 100 ounces of gold to her wronged husband and having ousted him from his throne, set up Diarmait's brother, Murchada, as the new king in his place. Safely in Bristol, Diarmait had no intention of remaining an outcast for long whatever his opponent might think.

Gerald of Wales's account written some twenty years after the episode recorded that the Irish king listened to advice provided by FitzHarding at the beginning of his exile. This view of events is supported by *The Song of Dermot and the Earl*, a thirteenth century poem that chronicles proceedings. The merchant understood that when Henry II first became king of England, he planned a conquest of Ireland. The matter was discussed at a council meeting held at Winchester in September 1155. Henry mooted the idea with a view to making his younger brother, William, Ireland's king but their mother, Empress Matilda, was not in favour of the project. At about the same time Pope Adrian IV, the only Englishman to have ever been elected as pope, issued a papal decree, called the *Laudabiliter*, permitting the king to regularise and reform the Church in Ireland by means of an invasion. Historians are divided whether or not the pope really did authorise the invasion of Ireland. The original letter written by Adrian to Henry II is now lost. Gerald of Wales used the *Laudabiliter* as a justification for the invasion of Ireland but at the time he wrote *Expugnatio Hibernica* and *Topographia Hiberniae* he was seeking promotion from the king. Besides which, his family, the FitzGeralds, were closely involved with the settlement of Ireland. It was in Gerald's best interests if it was recorded that the papacy approved of the annexation.

In 1166, FitzHarding considered that the time was perhaps right for Henry II to be reminded of his original plans for Ireland. It is less certain whether or not Diarmait understood what the consequences of his agreement with the land hungry Plantagenet might be. The Irish king went first to Aquitaine, according to Gerald of Wales, and possibly from there to Saumur Castle in the Loire Valley[11] to seek Henry II's backing for his planned return to Ireland. It is likely that the two men had previous dealings. In 1165, England's king led an army into Wales and used fleets of mercenaries from Irish ports including Dublin and Wexford which were part of Leinster to support his campaign. This could only have been done with the King of Leinster's permission. Now though, Diarmait had no land, no wealth and no power. With little in the way of bargaining chips at his disposal, the ex-king of Leinster offered to become Henry's liege man in return for assistance in regaining his kingdom.

The two kings represented different concepts of kingship and vassalage. Ireland was divided into petty kingdoms, each with its own king. High kings were men who achieved the most power but it did not mean that they were the head of a state or viewed as owning the whole of the island of Ireland by right. Nor was the hierarchy a static one. High kings might aspire to supremacy over neighbouring petty kings but power was based on a network of coalitions, marriages, and clientship. Rather than being vassals owing military duty to an overlord, petty kings of Ireland were autonomous rulers in their own right. Politics and stability in Ireland depended on a shifting tide of alliances.

The security behind the agreements between kings was underpinned by the giving and taking of hostages; some were more expendable than others. Hostages were regularly exchanged in medieval Ireland as guarantors of good faith. They were chosen, or demanded, either for their political importance or relationship with the people making the agreement. High kings took hostages from petty kings to assure their continuing submission and as a statement of their own power. In 1156, for instance, Diarmait gave hostages to the new High King of Ireland, Muircheartach Ua Lochlainn, when he acknowledged Muircheartach as his liege lord, and in return Ua Lochlainn recognised Diarmait as King of Leinster. Petty kings also took and gave hostages depending on the alliances they formed and the power they wielded. Diarmait took hostages from the King of Osraige, equating to modern Kilkenny, which became a sub-kingdom to Leinster. At times the situation was more akin to a system of fostering with sons being sent to and from one household to another to be raised and educated.

Kings who broke their agreements or sought to change the balance of power faced penalties visited, in the first instance, upon their hostages. Consequences might include killing, blinding, mutilation, or ransom for the safe return of the hostage being levied. Nor was hostage taking unique to Ireland. Hostages were used in Europe throughout the medieval period. King Henry II took political hostages and enforced death or mutilation upon them if his terms were unmet or broken. For example, in 1165 at Shrewsbury, in the aftermath of his unsuccessful campaign into Wales against Owain ap Gruffydd and his brother Rhys, Henry ordered the blinding of twenty-two hostages. It was a strategy designed to remind the Welsh of his continued dominance over them. Owain might have inflicted severe losses on Henry that summer at the Battle of Crogen, a bloody skirmish, near Chirk but two of the prince's own sons were among the men who were mutilated on the English king's orders.

The feudal system that placed King Henry II at the apex of a hierarchical pyramid in England was very different to Diarmait's understanding of kingship and vassalage. Henry was deemed to own all the estates in his realm by right of birth or conquest. He granted land to his tenants-in-chief who were his vassals owing both loyalty and military service to him. It was the king's duty to protect his vassals from armed aggression from other rulers and from injustice within his domains. The earls and barons, in their turn, subinfeudated their estates and manors to their own followers, creating tenant relationships with their own vassals who did homage to the barons and earls as overlords. They provided a set number of men on the battlefield for their lord depending upon the size of the estates they held for him. It was for this reason that a medieval manor was often described as a knight's fee. It encompassed the smallest parcel of land needed to provide for one knight, his family, equipment and the men he would need to do military service for his overlord. Feudal overlords and vassals were bound together by reciprocal military, financial and legal obligations to one another.

If Diarmait, a former king of Leinster, became Henry's liege man he would be a vassal who could request and expect to receive the English king's support regaining his kingdom. However, once Diarmait was restored to Leinster he would no longer be autonomous. He would have to answer Henry's summons for men at time of war, pay feudal fees and fines, and most importantly of all, the relationship would not end with either of their deaths. Except, of course, Henry did not demand hostages when he accepted Diarmait's proposition. The Irishman may well have thought he could shrug off his oath to a distant king who resided on the other side of not one but two seas, whether or not he achieved his own goal.

That summer, Henry had no troops to spare. He was embroiled in controversy with his former friend Thomas Becket, Archbishop of Canterbury, the papacy and King Louis VII of France. There was unrest in Brittany and in Aquitaine. Instead, Henry expressed sympathy and gave Diarmait permission to recruit men if he could find them from within England, the Marches and Wales. He issued letters allowing any of his subjects to go to Ireland to help the King of Leinster. It is very likely that the king expected that younger sons without titles or land of their own would find Diarmait's call to arms attractive. He did not anticipate that the Lord of Netherwent, kept on a short leash by lack of funds, would find the proposition appealing or that Mac Murchada would make de Clare an offer that he was unlikely to refuse.

It is plausible that FitzHarding, who was owed money by Strongbow, facilitated the meeting between the deposed king and the impoverished lord. According to Hamner's *Chronicle of Ireland*, written during the sixteenth century, Diarmait carried Henry's letter back to Bristol and 'caused them to be read several times in public and made liberal offers of pay and land'.[12] In this version of events Strongbow made the journey to Bristol where he reached an agreement with Diarmait. In other versions, the deposed king visited Striguil to outline his plans.

If Dairmait did visit Strongbow at Chepstow during a recruitment tour of the Marches and South Wales, he saw a border fortress perched high on a cliff above the River Wye. Strongbow welcomed his guests into the keep accessed by an external stairway. It consisted of a single large room built over an undercroft. During the negotiations that followed, Mac Murchada promised his daughter's hand in marriage and succession to Leinster's crown if Strongbow would come to Ireland and help win Dairmait's kingdom back for him. The Irishman chose to ignore Brehon law[13] on female inheritance and the fact that in addition to Énna and another illegitimate son named Domhnall Caomhánach, Aoife's full brother, Conchobar, was his intended heir.

Under Brehon law, codified in the seventh century, Diarmait could not arrange for Aoife to marry without her consent. She had the choice of who she would wed although in reality there were no other options. In addition to which, the status of a formal Irish marriage was dependent on the social standing of each partner and the property that each brought to the union. Aoife was equal to any husband she might marry with all the legal rights that equality brought. It meant that she would be able to assert more control over any land than if she was a Norman bride. Strongbow would not be able to sell any of her patrimony without her permission for instance. She had the right to be consulted on important matters and if Strongbow ever beat her so badly that he scarred her she would be entitled to reparation. Brehon law also permitted a woman to seek divorce from any husband she might take. Among the grounds listed were impotence, obesity and indiscreet adultery. It was only at the end of the sixteenth century that the law stripped married women in Ireland of the status that they enjoyed until that time.

Aoife expected to retain control over her own movable property which included household goods, valuables and herds of cattle, as well as any estates settled on her at time of their union by her husband or his family. Dower rights provided a bride with a life interest in estates belonging to the groom to support her should she be widowed. Women like Aoife were independent and, although they were permitted no formal political authority, their wealth gave them power within a marriage and beyond that was contrary to the legal and religious position of the State and Church in England.

The proposal was an opportunity that Strongbow could not afford to ignore. He discussed the matter with his most trusted knights before arriving at a decision. It was well known that Strongbow often sought advice before committing himself. Gerald of Wales inferred this was a weakness in a leader but it suggests a man who liked to weigh the different options. Here was a chance of power and wealth beyond the immediate control of Henry II. There was also a risk of incurring the king's wrath if Strongbow acted without obtaining royal permission. De Clare knew that he was gambling his future on the venture but he is unlikely to have been aware that Leinster was not Diarmait's to give away with his daughter's hand.

The story of the arrangement behind the marriage of Isabel de Clare's parents was told in the Song of Dermot and the Earl:

> His daughter he offered him to wife,
> The thing in the world that he most loved:
> That he would let him have her to wife,
> And would give Leinster to him,
> On condition that he would aid him
> So that he should be able to subdue it.[14]

Diarmait and Strongbow took an oath of equals to seal their agreement with the proviso that King Henry II must first agree to de Clare's part in the campaign and marriage to Aoife. Diarmait swore that as soon as Strongbow and his men arrived in Ireland and retook Leinster that the wedding would be celebrated. For de Clare it meant that in addition to land which equated to power he would have the opportunity to sire legitimate heirs to inherit his estates in England and Wales as well as the kingdom of Leinster.

It's unknown whether or not Aoife accompanied her father to Striguil in 1168 but it's likely she did. Diarmait would have wanted to show Strongbow his beautiful daughter as a lure for de Clare's agreement to the plan. Aoife, no more than 15-years old when she first met Richard, saw a man who was taller than average, with a short neck, a quiet voice (Gerald of Wales described it as a weak voice), and grey eyes.[15] As their stay continued, she might have learned first-hand his 'courteous manner'[16] and 'gentle words'.[17] She might also have discovered that de Clare kept a mistress and was a father to two daughters. Aoife's own father had two wives, besides mistresses, under Brehon law so it did not dismay her.

There is even less information about Aoife herself other than her education which would have befitted the daughter of a king. A wife, even a royal one, was expected to be able to run a household effectively. *The Triads of Ireland* first published in 1906 but drawing on early Irish literature, required women to have 'a steady tongue, a steady virtue, a steady housewifery'.[18] In Ireland, a wife's value, were she to divorce her husband, was based on her industry and housewifery. Idleness was grounds for divorce so Aoife knew how to run a household, manage her cattle, and prepare, comb, spin, dye and weave both flax and wool. As the daughter of a king, she was required to have good manners and to be modest. She would have been able to play a musical instrument, sing, dance and play popular court games. Education in its widest sense equipped Aoife to both run her household and to ornament her father's court. Before Strongbow could gather his men, fulfil his agreement with Diarmait, and claim his bride, he needed to raise finances to fund the adventure and gain King Henry's approval for the expedition.

In the meantime, Diarmait continued to search for potential recruits in South Wales. An encounter with David FitzGerald, Bishop of St David's in Pembrokeshire, shortly before his return to Ireland provided Diarmait with another recruit with little to lose by joining the venture. The bishop, a son of Nest of Wales and her husband Gerald of Windsor was the half-brother of a knight named Robert FitzStephen who had been the Constable of Ceredigion Castle before it fell, in 1164, into the hands of the Welsh prince Rhys ap Gruffydd. The Welshman swore to release FitzStephen, who was his cousin, only if he would take up arms against King Henry. FitzStepthen refused the terms and remained a captive in Ceredigion. The bishop persuaded FitzStephen that a campaign in Ireland was a more attractive alternative to imprisonment. The proposition also had the benefit of offering Rhys a chance to free his cousin without loss of face. Additionally, ap Gruffydd may have concluded that other members of the FitzGerald family were likely to join the campaign and, in their absence from South Wales, the Norman hold on territories he wished to reclaim for the Welsh might be weakened.

Diarmait made similar terms with the bishop's family to those he made with Strongbow. The king offered FitzStephen and, another half-brother, Maurice FitzGerald, the Norse town of Wexford if they would help him. As with his offer to de Clare, the agreement was not one that the king had any right to make.

Mac Murchada returned to his kingdom in August 1167 with a handful of mercenaries rather than an army at his back. It was an ill-considered journey even if he was welcomed by the people of Ferns. Diarmait and his followers were quickly defeated by Conchobair, Ua Ruaic and the Ostmen of Dublin. The handful of mercenaries who accompanied Mac Murchada were forced to leave Ireland. That winter Diarmait's family and followers were only allowed to remain in the monastery at Ferns after the humbled ex-king paid 100 ounces of gold as compensation for the abduction of Ua Ruaic's wife and provided hostages into the hands of Ua Conchobair who was now Ireland's High King.

Across the Irish Sea in England, King Henry made Strongbow play a waiting game that stretched from 1166 to 1170. Without Henry's acquiescence, de Clare risked losing his estates in England if he fulfilled his oath to Diarmait. Strongbow, tired of waiting, went to court to ask for permission in person. Once there, he was denied access to Henry and forced to kick his heels. But then the king unexpectedly gave his unfavoured earl the responsibility of escorting his own eldest daughter, 12-year-old Matilda, to Germany where she was to marry Henry V, Duke of Saxony as part of an alliance with the Holy Roman Emperor in opposition to the French. Negotiations surrounding an alliance between Henry and Frederick Barbarossa, the German Emperor were at their conclusion when de Clare first sought permission to join Diarmait in Leinster and to marry Aoife. Perhaps it was the mention of a marriage that implanted the idea in Henry's mind or the king wanted to be rid of the troublesome man with the grey eyes and quiet voice? There is no reason why the king should have selected Strongbow for the task. Perhaps even more likely, Henry sent de Clare to Germany simply to prevent him from fulfilling his oath to Diarmait. It was a double blow for Strongbow who, like the rest of Henry's tenants-in-chief, was required to pay towards the cost of Matilda's dowry.

Matilda accompanied by her mother, Eleanor of Aquitaine, left Dover on 29 September 1167. The wedding party spent the Christmas season in Normandy where de Clare is likely to have joined them. He travelled with the bridal retinue to its destination in Germany. The wedding took place on 1 February 1168 at Minden Cathedral. The embassy delayed Strongbow from fulfilling his oath for more than a year but he may have used the time to consider how he would raise funds for the venture and to seek the advice from men with an allegiance to the de Clare family.

William de Chesney, Sheriff of Norwich was among the party escorting Matilda to her wedding. He was another man who had supported King Stephen rather than the Angevins during the Anarchy. He was also a tenant of the Lords of Clare in East Anglia, with property links to Gloucestershire and to Strongbow himself. It is possible that it was from de Chesney that de Clare learned the full details of the blood libel perpetuated against the Jewish community in England starting with the murder at Easter 1144 of a boy named William of Norwich. No one was ever charged with the crime. By 1150, Thomas of Monmouth was able to rework the story as a slaying made in mockery of Christ's crucifixion. He described the boy's body discovered with a crown of thorns on its head. Thomas claimed to have been provided with an insight to the ritual nature of the killing by a former Jew named Theobald of Cambridge. He wrote that the death was an annual Christian sacrifice. Coincidentally, or not, the story of a boy ritually murdered by the Jewish community would resurface in Gloucester after Strongbow returned home and while his mind was turned to raising funds from Gloucester's Jews for his Irish adventure.

De Clare needed to borrow large sums of money to pay for soldiers, equipment and provisions. The only people legally able to lend the amount of money that de Clare needed were England's Jews. 1168 was a bad year for Gloucester's Jewish population. In March, as Strongbow hurried home from Germany, a child, named Harold, was found murdered in the River Severn. The Benedictine monks of Gloucester Abbey, who had their own links to East Anglia, claimed that the boy was kidnapped on 21 February that year and tortured to death by crucifixion on 16 March. Harold was about to become part of Gloucester's blood libel against its Jewish population. No one was ever arrested for Harold's murder and the story was much less well known than the similar tale relating to the death of William of Norwich. The monks tried to establish a cult around Harold in an attempt to raise funds to repair the abbey which had been damaged during the Civil War, to recoup money demanded from the abbey by Henry II and to repay a debt of £80 to Robert FitzHarding. However, the monks were largely unsuccessful in their endeavours.[19] The accusation of murder may have helped convince Gloucester's Jews that it would be wise to lend Strongbow the money he needed. The story has been described as 'a tool for extortion'.[20]

As well as raising funds for the Irish venture there were other calls on Strongbow's time and cash when he returned to England in the spring of 1168. He is thought to have joined Reginald, Earl of Cornwall on campaign in Wales with the earls of Gloucester and Hertford if the *Brut Y Tywsogyon* is to be believed. At least going to war against the Welsh avoided the necessity of paying Henry II yet more scutage fees.

In Ireland, Diarmait could only wait for Strongbow's promises to be fulfilled. Mac Gilla Pátraic, King of Osraige took the opportunity to blind Aoife's half-brother Énna even though Ruaidrí Ua Conchobair and Tigernán Ua Ruaire's authority seemed unchallengeable. It was vengeance for Diarmait's execution of hostages belonging to Mac Gilla Pátraic before his flight to England in 1166 and a warning for the humbled ex-king not to recruit more mercenaries to his cause.

Chapter 4

Winning Aoife

I t had been a winter of sorrow and waiting for the ex-king of Leinster who was reliant on the monks of Ferns Abbey for shelter and food. His spirits lifted when three ships carrying the first Norman, or more correctly Cambro-Norman, contingent of mercenaries led by Robert FitzStephen arrived in Bannow Bay at the beginning of May 1169. He was accompanied by 30 knights, 60 men-at-arms and 300 Welsh longbowmen. A smaller force of men led by Maurice de Prendergast, a man of Flemish descent recruited by Diarmait from the area around Milford Haven arrived the following day. Contemporary Irish chroniclers seeing only an army of invaders did not differentiate between English, Norman or Welsh. They described the heavily armed foreigners who arrived on Irish shores at Diarmait's invitation as Saxons,[1] or English.

There was no sign of de Clare despite his agreement with Mac Murchada. Strongbow still required permission from King Henry II before crossing the Irish Sea. Gerald of Wales implied that Strongbow dallied in Striguil while his own relations, more mindful of their solemn oath to Diarmait, were at the van of the Irish conquest. It was not entirely true. Strongbow's uncle, Hervey de Montmorency, arrived with FitzStephen as de Clare's representative and advisor. Gerald described Montmorency as a spy and an informer rather than a warrior: a 'man of broken fortunes'.[2] Diarmait, on hearing the news, gathered his own men and placed his illegitimate son, Domnall Caomhánach, at their head. The Irish and the foreign mercenaries marched on Wexford where they burned the port's suburbs. The combined force, led by FitzStephen, secured the town with little bloodshed. Its Norse inhabitants were dismayed at the thought of fighting on foot against heavily armed men on horseback. The lines of Welsh bowmen were another deterrent.

In a show of good faith, Diarmait fulfilled his promise to Nest's son by granting him Wexford itself and an additional two cantreds of land which equated to four knights' fees or 7680 acres.[3] Contrary to Gerald of Wales's derogatory description of Montmorency, Diarmait was careful to honour Strongbow's uncle with land between Wexford and Waterford at the same time in recognition of his own deeds. The tenure of land gave the Cambro-Normans a reason to continue fighting. They were not mercenaries in search of loot. They wanted land, towns and manors to call their own. Several local Irish clans returned to Diarmait before the confrontation at Wexford having heard about the arrival of the foreigners. More submitted to Diarmait after the victory. The men of the town offered their allegiance to him as part of the negotiations afterwards.

The King of Leinster's reputation was such that everyone knew that he would take his vengeance for both the humiliation of 1166 and the mutilation of his son Énna. Most petty kings and leaders in the orbit of Leinster preferred to be on Diarmait's side while he had the advantage. Mac Murchada directed his own men, the so-called Saxons, and the Ostmen of Wexford in a campaign against Ua Conchobair's allies in West Leinster before advancing on the kingdom of Osraige.

The southern half of Ua Páitraic's kingdom buckled under the onslaught but he decided that he could make a stand in the north. He selected a pass between two heavily wooded hills and ordered his men to build three fortified ditches across the pass itself. The first phase of the battle was said to have lasted all day. Diarmait's combined army was forced to retire as night approached and the risk posed by Ua Páitraic's light cavalry became more apparent. The Normans were temporarily deserted by their Irish allies when it appeared as though they might be defeated.

Maurice de Prendergast ordered his remaining men to feign a retreat and Ua Páitraic made the mistake of following them into open ground. The Osraige army was caught in a trap between hidden archers and the force of a heavy cavalry charge. The Irish returned to join battle when they realised that Ua Páitraic's men were losing. They began to lop the heads from the bodies of the Osraige soldiers. Following the victory, it was said, Diarmait danced for joy after he was presented with the severed heads of his enemies. In a show of vengeance, for the blinding of Énna, he bit the ears and nose from one of the bloodstained trophies of war. The *Annals of Clonmacnoise* simply stated that Diarmait's army 'preyed and spoiled the territories of Osseery'.[4]

More men submitted to the King of Leinster. In view of Osraige's collapse, they preferred not to oppose Diarmait. The Ostman ruler of Dublin reluctantly recognised Diarmait as his overlord. Other kings knew that reconciliation was impossible. Diarmait's desire for vengeance was too great. Relatives of the Abbess of Kildare had their own reasons for refusing to bow their heads to the man who ordered the rape of a nun. Mac Murchada launched a second raid upon Osraige that culminated with a battle that lasted for three days. It looked as though Diarmait was unstoppable and that Strongbow was not required.

However, Maurice de Prendergast and his Flemish mercenaries were not satisfied with the course of events. They received a share of the booty but unlike

Nest's sons and Montmorency they had not been gifted land. They decided to return to Wales. When Diarmait refused to give Prendergast transport, he took his troops into the lines of Ua Páitraic. At about the same time Ruaidri Ua Conchobair decided to prop up Ua Páitraic in an alliance against the King of Leinster. Diarmait was forced to recognise that without more men he could not defeat the high king. He and Ua Conchobair came to an agreement that Diarmait would once again be accepted as King of Leinster in return for recognition of the high kingship, the departure of the Cambro-Normans and the giving of hostages. The latter included Diarmait's son, Conchobar, Diarmait's grandson by his illegitimate son Domnall Caomhánach, and the eldest son of Diarmait's foster brother. All of them knew that if Strongbow arrived in Ireland to fulfil his oath that their lives were forfeit.

Ua Páitraic refused to accept the agreement. He never believed that his enemy intended to keep his word. Aided by Prendergast and his allies, he raided Diarmait's kingdom. Eventually Ua Páitraic's men plotted to kill Prendergast because of the high payment that he and his men were exacting in return for their services. The Flemings, on learning of the scheme, made a forced march to Waterford with the agreement of the king of Osraige, returning to Wales from there. Once they were disembarked, Prendergast hurried to Striguil where he gave Strongbow a full report of his exploits and the political situation in Ireland adding to the information that de Clare received from his uncle, Hervey de Montmorency, who was still in Ireland.

Soon after Prendergast's departure, Maurice FitzGerald, FitzStephen's half-brother, who had met Diarmait at St David's in 1167, arrived with more men aboard two ships. Diarmait, despite the assurances he gave the High King that he would not bring more foreign mercenaries to Ireland and the importance of the hostages that he gave Ua Conchobair, seized the opportunity to lead a raid into Osraige and against Dublin where he forced the city to accept him as it's king. Ua Conchobair might have executed Diarmait's hostages for breaking his oath but Aoife's father had not ventured beyond the bounds of what was his before he was toppled from power in 1166. Osraige was a recognised petty kingdom of Leinster. The High King was content to spare the lives of his hostages for the moment.

As Leinster found itself embroiled in a series of skirmishes, attacks and counter attacks, Strongbow, still in England, was forced to rely on Hervey de Montmorency's reports for information about the progress of the campaign. It was not good news. If Gerald of Wales is to be believed, Diarmait tired of waiting for de Clare offered Aoife's hand and the succession of Leinster's throne to Robert FitzStephen and Maurice Fitzgerald if they would put him back on his throne and rid him of his enemies. Nest's sons, already married, declined to become bigamists and advised that Diarmait should summon Strongbow. The Irish king wrote to de Clare reminding him of their agreement noting:

> 'the summer birds have come, and are gone again with the southerly wind; but neither winds from the east nor the west have brought us your much desired and long expected presence.'[5]

Gerald of Wales believed that Strongbow was unwilling to honour his commitment rather than lacking in the funds or having royal permission for the venture, although even Gerald recorded that when Henry II did allow de Clare to fulfil his promise it was more in jest than approval. As answer to Diarmait's rebuke, Strongbow sent a vanguard of men to Ireland led by Raymond FitzWilliam, another member of the extended FitzGerald clan. FitzWilliam, known as Le Gros, was one of Nest of Wales's grandsons as well as being part of Strongbow's *mesnie*, or military household, of knights.

De Clare turned his attention to the defence of his existing domain before venturing to Leinster. He gave orders for the wooden motte and bailey castle at Usk, which his men recaptured from the Welsh, to be rebuilt in stone. It would avail him little as it would be in the hands of Hywel ap Iorwerth within four years. As spring turned into summer, Strongbow, believing he had Henry's consent, travelled south through the Marches gathering troops as he advanced towards Milford Haven where he intended to embark for Ireland. In total his force numbered 200 knights, including Maurice de Prendergast who remained ambitious for land to call his own, and 1,000 foot soldiers. The *Annals of Clonmacnoise* called it 'a great armye of Englishmen'.[6]

On 23 August 1170, Strongbow was aboard his vessel about to set sail for Leinster when a royal messenger arrived. King Henry II, having heard about de Clare's preparations, had second thoughts about granting his permission for the venture. Strongbow ignored the threat that his estates in England and Wales would be confiscated if he persisted. The Lord of Netherwent was fully committed to making the journey. Among the passengers waiting for the boats to slip their moorings that summer's morning were de Clare's two natural daughters who were of an age when they might be married off to best advantage. Also there was Strongbow's sister, Basilia, who either travelled with the rest of the women folk or as soon as her brother summoned her to Ireland.

Isabel's father began his campaign to recapture Leinster for Diarmait by attacking Waterford on 24 August 1170, having landed unopposed the day before. Waterford was enclosed by a stone wall on top of a bank surrounded by a wide ditch. The wall was guarded by two towers. Twice Strongbow's men were thrown back but there was a weakness which the Normans, led by

Raymond le Gros, exploited. A house had been built up against the wall. The main beam of the dwelling, if that indeed was its purpose, was inserted into the wall. Le Gros cut through the beam causing the house to collapse. When it fell, it also pulled down some of the town wall. The Normans rushed into the breach and a massacre followed in the hand-to-hand fighting in the streets. The town's defenders made a last stand in Raghnall's (or Reginald's) Tower at the eastern end of the quay but were subsequentially captured and the majority of them executed before Diarmait arrived and interceded on behalf of the remaining survivors while the Cambro-Norman victors busied themselves looting, pillaging, and despoiling.

Aoife was part of the entourage that came with Diarmait to view Waterford's fall. It was a town in mourning for its dead. Rubble littered streets stained with the blood of its fallen defenders. Gerald of Wales wrote of the Normans 'slaughtering the citizens in heaps'.[7] Soon after her arrival in the ruined town, Aoife was married to Strongbow at the steps of Christchurch Cathedral, Waterford, where everyone could see that the King of Leinster honoured his oaths. Daniel Maclise, the Victorian artist, chose to romanticise Aoife's wedding by depicting a demure, pale skinned girl with flowing red hair and downcast eyes, dressed in white and laden with golden bracelets so that she fulfilled his society's cultural ideals about what beautiful Irish princesses might look like.

It was important too that Aoife's agreement to the wedding was seen to be freely given. Brehon law was not alone in giving the Irish princess an element of choice in her union with de Clare. The Catholic Church, under the papacy of Alexander III, was forming new ideas about the nature of marriage and the importance of consent. Aoife and Strongbow were married at a time in history when the practical transfer of land between families upon marriage was being juxtaposed with the spiritual aspect of a union between a man and a woman. Secular courts may have retained control of the former but the Church intended to regulate and direct the latter.

Aoife understood that the only means for her father to regain his kingdom was through the marriage that had been agreed in 1167. Irish women had married Normans before but Strongbow was different because he intended to remain in Ireland and hold Leinster by right of Aoife even if it was contrary to Irish law. Diarmait's sons were dwindling in number. Aoife's brother, Conchobar, was a hostage, and her half-brother, Énna, having been blinded was no longer able to claim the crown after his father's death. A proclamation recognising Strongbow's position as Dairmait's heir *de jure uxoris*, made at the time of the wedding ceremony meant that her other half-brother, Domnal

Cáemánch, who also had a claim to the crown despite the uncertain status of his mother, was excluded.

None the less it was not a foregone conclusion that Strongbow would inherit Leinster by right of his wife. Aoife was not an heiress in the way that the Normans understood it. Under Gaelic law a woman could not receive land if there was a male heir who might inherit. Brothers, uncles and male cousins were preferred to a female claimant. And, even if Aoife should inherit her father's domain, her interest was only a lifetime one. Strictly speaking, any children that Aoife bore Strongbow would not be eligible to make a claim on the kingdom inherited by their mother. Under Brehon law the only exception to this was if the woman's husband, and the father of the children, was also her kinsman with an existing entitlement to the property. It meant that land always returned to the original clan network rather than being transmitted to a new family through marriage. Where there were male heirs from within the family kinship network, as there were in Aoife's case, she was entitled only to a share in movable assets such as herds of cattle and household goods.

Diarmait's agreement with Strongbow, Aoife's marriage to the baron and subsequent proclamation meant that all the Irish King's extended family and Leinster's nobility would be required to ignore existing Brehon laws and submit to de Clare rather than recognise the males of Diarmait's own bloodline. The offer of succession that Diarmait made to Strongbow gave Aoife, styled the Lady of Leinster, a unique place in the kingdom and presented de Clare with the long-term problem of how he was to hold the land which he had won by fulfilling his oath.

As soon as the wedding was over Strongbow gathered his men and held a council meeting with Diarmait. Together they agreed to march on Dublin as soon as the king raised his troops. The Ostmen had already recognised Diarmait as their overlord but Strongbow intended to exert the same control over the city and its port as he now wielded in Waterford. Without complete domination of Dublin, it was impossible to rule all of Leinster effectively. Strongbow also knew that without more men to back him, holding Leinster would be a difficult business.

When news of Waterford's fall and the ensuing bloodshed arrived in Dublin, the Norse warrior elite appealed to the high king for assistance. Ruadri Ua Conchobair set about raising a new army; among them was Diarmait's old enemy Tigernán Ua Ruairc. Realising that the town was heavily defended and that Ua Conchobair would place his army in their path, Diarmait and Strongbow marched across the Wicklow mountains rather than taking the more obvious lowland route. Recognising that he was out manoeuvred, Ruadri Ua Conchobair withdrew and the siege of Dublin began.

Aoife's uncle who was the Archbishop of Dublin mediated between the different groups. Eventually the men of Dublin agreed to provide Diarmait with thirty hostages as a show of the town's intention to recognise Diarmait as its overlord. Strongbow understood that the town might retract its submission even though it was likely that Diarmait would kill his hostages. On 21 September 1170 matters were, seemingly, taken out of de Clare's hands when one of the Norman freebooters, Miles de Cogan, ordered his men to storm the town. Gerald of Wales believed that the band was 'greedy for plunder'.[8] It is impossible to be sure whether de Cogan acted from his own initiative or on orders from Strongbow. In either case, it was an opportune moment to attack.

The men of Dublin were not guarding the walls as they should have been. They were arguing about who should be sent to Diarmait. In the chaos that followed, the Ostmen ran for their longboats or were cut down as they fled. Having re-established order, Strongbow left de Cogan in charge of the city as its Constable and continued his pursuit of Ua Ruaic. The high king, furious that Diarmait was now declaring that he would become High King of Ireland with Strongbow's help, ordered the immediate execution of all Diarmait's hostages.

It is unknown what King Henry II might have thought of de Clare's military success in Ireland or the beautiful young bride he claimed. The Lord of Netherwent certainly did not have enough men or equipment for a wholesale invasion of the country and, besides which, Henry could confiscate all of de Clare's estates in England, the Marches and Wales if he so chose. Diarmait, who had sworn to be Henry's liege man, was still Leinster's king so Strongbow was not free from Plantagenet intervention.

Before the English king could take decisive action, fortune's wheel turned swiftly against the monarch and in favour of de Clare. On 29 December 1170, Thomas Becket, Archbishop of Canterbury was murdered by four knights from the king's court acting on an ambiguous remark made by the king himself. Henry found himself at the centre of a religious and political maelstrom which threatened his throne. His gaze turned from Ireland and back to the problems at home but it did not mean that he forgot the troublesome Marcher lord.

Just when things could not look more politically difficult for Henry II, in May 1171, Aoife's father died. The *Annals of Clonmacnoise* stated that the king died from unknown causes but that he died 'without doing penance, shrive or Extrem Unction'.[9] Diarmait, according to Christian belief of the time, passed away unpardoned for his many sins. He would be remembered as one of the most loathed names in Ireland's chronicled history. It was at his invitation that Strongbow and the FitzGeralds came to Ireland. The *Irish Chronicles* recording the death of the last king of Leinster blamed his end upon the vengeance of God and his saints for inviting the Cambro-Normans into Ireland:

'After having done extensive injuries to the Irish, after plundering and burning many churches...died before the end of a year, of an insufferable and unknown disease; for he became putrid while living, through the miracle of God, Colum-Cille, and Finnen and the other Saints of Ireland whose churches he had profaned and burned some time before'.[10]

Diarmait left a brother, Muirchertach Mac Murchada, and his own natural son Domnall Caomhánach, who both had a claim to the kingdom of Leinster under Irish law. Aoife must have wondered whether her male kinsmen and her father's nobility would accept her Norman husband as their king or whether he and she would be killed.

Strongbow, the earl who King Henry II kept on a tight leash, was the de facto ruler of his own kingdom on the English king's doorstep. How long would it take for men dissatisfied with their lot in Henry's realm to make common cause with the new Lord of Leinster? It must have seemed as though de Clare was taking his vengeance for the long years that Henry kept him impoverished and without the right to enter the earldom of Pembroke which was his by right.

Chapter 5

Pawns and Players

Strongbow claimed Leinster but he did not have enough military support to hold out against Henry II if he chose to mount an invasion of his own backed by the full might of a royal army. To avoid this outcome, de Clare took the precaution of sending Raymond le Gros and Maurice FitzGerald to Chinon where they were tasked with convincing the king of de Clare's loyalty to the Crown. Later he also sent his uncle, Hervey de Montmorency, to reassure Henry and confirm that all of the Norman gains in Ireland were the king's to do with as he wished. It was a risk. Henry might choose absorb the territory into Crown lands or hand it piecemeal to his own favourites.

To the king, who had always distrusted de Clare, it looked as though Strongbow intended to set himself up as a ruler in his own right. Henry had no intention of permitting an independent Norman kingdom to take root adjacent to his own realm. He issued an edict forbidding any trade from England to the island and also demanded that anyone who had departed his realm for Ireland should return by 4 April 1471. If they did not comply, their lands would be forfeit to the Crown. Many Cambro-Normans heeding King Henry's orders returned to Wales or England for fear of losing their estates there. Strongbow ignored the proclamation and hoped that the men he sent to court would be able to persuade the king to change his mind.

Henry was not the only one who thought that Strongbow was now effectively the first non-indigenous king of Leinster. The Irish rose in revolt against their foreign neighbours. Strongbow did not have the resources to conquer the whole of Ireland. Instead, he and the other settlers had to rely on holding what they had already succeeded in annexing and making alliances with the Irish. Domnall Caomhánach, Aoife's half-brother, recognised Strongbow as his overlord and was rewarded with the office of de Clare's justiciar for Leinster.[1] MacGilla Páitraic, King of Osraige submitted to the new ruler. The peaceful resolution to a potential confrontation was unexpected. Even so, Strongbow's hold on Leinster looked tenuous at best.

There were attacks on Waterford and in Dublin, Miles de Cogan was besieged by the Ostmen who were driven from the city the previous year. De Cogan was victorious but the frequent raids and sorties reduced the already limited number of men at his disposal. Muirchertach Mac Murchada, Aoife's uncle, opted to declare himself a petty king of Ui Chennselaig, from where his family originated. In this guise he joined forces with the High King to drive the Normans out of Dublin. If this end was achieved the kingdom of Leinster was his for the taking. The King of Man, who had his own aspirations to rule the city, sent a fleet to blockade the port.

Gerald of Wales states that Strongbow was besieged there for two months. Aoife, who was representative of her husband's claim to Leinster, is likely to have been with de Clare facing starvation. They sent Aoife's maternal uncle, Lorcán Ua Tuathail, Bishop of Dublin to negotiate with Ua Conchobair on Strongbow's behalf. He was prepared to recognised Ruardri as High King if, in return, Ua Conchobair accepted de Clare as a ruler of Leinster. Ua Conchobair refused the terms stating that the Norman could keep the Ostmen ports of Dublin, Waterford and Wexford but the rest was forfeit. The High King's dismissal of the Normans and his assumption of victory galvanised them into action. The Irish were caught off guard at their camp at Castleknock. Strongbow was triumphant.

At Carrick, near Wexford, Robert FitzStephen's wife and children encountered a similar predicament when they were besieged by the men of Wexford and their allies from Kinsale but their plight, 'surrounded by the enemy, were in a very ill-fortified hold, constructed of only turf and stakes'[2] was better recorded by Gerald of Wales who was their kinsman. FitzStephen was tricked into believing that Dublin had fallen and that his half-brother Maurice was dead but that he, his family and his men would be permitted to return to Wales if they surrendered. When news of the Norman victory at Dublin arrived soon after, FitzStephen's captors burned the port and withdrew, taking their prisoners with them.

By the end of 1171 Strongbow chose to recognise Muirchertach Mac Murchada's title to the Ui Chennselaig homelands removing the threat of Aoife's uncle at a stroke. De Clare recognised that if he was going to achieve his goal of settling Leinster, that a lasting peace was required. It meant that he began a policy of building alliances with the Irish that were not always favoured by his own land hungry countrymen.

King Henry II would be more difficult to placate. The blockade on exports to Ireland began to have an effect. It appeared as though he might have gambled his ancestral lands on winning the king's approbation and lost. Fortunately for de Clare, the murder of Thomas Becket, the Archbishop of Canterbury the previous year meant that Henry faced humiliating public penance and atonement, or even excommunication, for his suspected complicity in the archbishop's death. The situation in Ireland suddenly became a positive boon to the king who sent Hervey Montmorency back to Ireland with the message that if Strongbow was as loyal as he said he was, then he would meet with the king and make his submission in person. To do otherwise would be a sign of treachery. It would, the king added, go badly for Strongbow and his Cambro-Normans if Henry was forced to cross the Irish Sea to address the matter.

The meeting between king and subject took place at Newnham, near Gloucester.[3] Henry demonstrated compromise laced with finely tuned threat. He was also preparing a large army to accompany him to Ireland. Strongbow was confirmed in possession of Leinster but the strategically valuable and economically important ports of Wexford, Waterford and Dublin would belong to the king. Even Henry recognised that he could not take from de Clare what had been won by his own sword; to do so would have the reek of tyranny. Besides, too many of the king's subjects were intent on extending their lands by the same method for it to be a politically adroit outcome. The accord did not stop Henry from summoning the princes and lords of south Wales to Pembroke where he chastised them for permitting Strongbow to recruit men and take passage to Ireland.

Henry II's decision to travel to Ireland was not unexpected. He would claim what was rightfully his as de Clare's liege lord and expand his empire in the process. The plan provided the wily monarch an opportunity to avoid a meeting with the papal legates on their way to Normandy to discuss the conditions that the Pope wished to impose upon Henry as part of the process by which the king would be forgiven for his part in Becket's murder. It also meant that he would avoid having to undertake a pilgrimage as part of his personal atonement for the crime. Instead, he would claim that he fulfilled his obligations by regularising the Irish Church's relationship with the Archbishopric of Canterbury and with Rome as requested in 1155 by Pope Adrian IV.

In October 1171, King Henry II crossed the Irish Sea from Milford Haven with 500 knights in 400 ships[4] to land at Crooke, near Waterford. The next day Strongbow formally surrendered his new territories, including Waterford, to him. Having accepted his submission, the king returned Leinster to Strongbow as a fief. Aoife's role in the transition of the land from her father to her husband was trumped by the Norman system of feudal tenure whereby all land came from the Crown. The men of Wexford seeing a chance to win the king's favour arrived at Waterford with FitzStephen declaring that he was the first of the Normans to invade Ireland without royal licence to do so. The theatre of the moment did not escape Henry who 'loudly rated him, and threatened him with his indignation for his rash enterprise, at last sent him back loaded with fetters, and chained to another prisoner to be kept in safe custody'.[5] It was to be inferred that the new Lord of Leinster was fortunate to avoid a similar fate, or perhaps even a worse one.

Henry stayed in Ireland for the next six months to inspect the newest part of his realm. He rarely remained long in one place. He was a king known for his ferocious energy. The royal retinue travelled from Waterford to Cashel, where the king called a synod to meet at the beginning of 1172. The king's official reason for being there was to reform the Irish Church to fit the conventional pattern of diocesan bishops which in turn helped placate the papacy who still sought to punish him for his part in Thomas Becket's death.

The king journeyed from Cashel to Dublin where he celebrated Christmas and met with Aoife's uncle, Lorcán Ua Tuathail, Archbishop of Dublin. Henry gave Dublin a charter that made it a royal city and granted its citizens the same liberties as Bristol. He made sure that he established a system of administration in the bustling ports that were now in his possession so that they would yield profitable returns.

The majority of the Irish petty kings, seeing the impressive number of warriors who accompanied Henry and the splendour of the royal retinue, submitted to him during his progress and were rewarded with generous gifts for their voluntary recognition of his overlordship. The kings of Meath, Bréifne and Desmond were among the men who became vassals to the English king in the belief that they would then be safe from the foreign invaders if they accepted him as their overlord. They were lavishly entertained in Dublin by the king during the winter of 1171-1172. Noticeable by his absence was Ruaidrí Ua Conchobair of Connacht, the High King of Ireland. There is some indication that Henry intended to attack Connacht during 1172 but European matters were more important and the campaign was never launched.

Strongbow and Aoife stayed at Kildare. Henry did not fully trust de Clare even now. He gave orders that Dublin and its garrison were to be placed into the hands of Hugh de Lacy who was a favourite of the king as well as being a Marcher lord based at Ludlow. He was also granted the lordship of Meath, which Strongbow claimed as part of Aoife's patrimony, to govern in Henry's name. De Lacy began to settle the region with men from England and Wales who would be loyal to him and to fortify his estates. The process of conquest and colonisation was under way. It changed the balance of power in Ireland. Like Strongbow, de Lacy held lands in Normandy, England, Wales and now Ireland. Henry ensured that there was a magnate of similar status who would prevent de Clare from becoming a king in his own right. The grant also meant that de Lacy held land of strategic importance to the control of Dublin and its trading networks.

De Lacy compounded Strongbow's loss by recruiting men who were part of his own retinue with the promise of lands of their own as his vassals in Meath. In effect the king had devolved his authority upon de Lacy and men like him. At the same time, Maurice FitzGerald gained estates at Uí Enechglaiss, Inch, and Kilgorman further contributing to Henry's overall control of the area around Dublin. In the years to come aristocrats and men well versed in border warfare would be at the centre of a piecemeal conquest of Ireland.

Before he left Ireland, Henry created de Lacy *custos*, or keeper, of Ireland. It meant that as time passed Strongbow's importance in Ireland decreased. Henry's intervention shifted the balance of power in his favour but it also meant that the momentum of the conquest of Ireland stalled.[6] Instead, the Cambro-Norman lords of Ireland were left to fight for the land that they held and to intermarry with the Irish creating their own identity.

King Henry II returned to England after the winter storms were over. He arrived in Normandy in May 1172 where he was absolved from the murder of his former friend Thomas Becket. Later in the year Henry's eldest son, Henry known as the Young King, travelled to Winchester where he was crowned alongside his wife Margaret, the daughter of King Louis VII of France and his second wife, Constance of Castile. It was a stratagem to ensure the succession but as was often the case, fate took a hand, with unforeseen consequences for both the king and Strongbow the following year.

Strongbow returned to Ferns after the king's departure but took steps to build alliances of his own, based on gifts of land to his retainers and also by the device of building an extended family network to consolidate support for his rule. In addition to the associations he formed with Aoife's kinsmen, he also arranged for his illegitimate daughter, Basilia, named after his sister, to be married to Robert de Quincy who he appointed Constable of Leinster.[7] Some historians state that the marriage was to Strongbow's sister, others to his daughter. In either case, it was a short-lived union. De Quincy was killed in 1173 in a battle against Irishmen loyal to Aoife's brother-in-law, Domnall, but Basilia gave birth to Strongbow's granddaughter, Maud de Quincy who would have her own part to play in Irish politics.

For de Clare's plans to be successful, he needed a legitimate child to inherit his lands. Without an heir the fief which he won by his sword and a canny business deal would be forfeit to the Crown after his death. Aoife gave him a daughter, Isabel de Clare, born in 1172 or thereabouts. She had one brother named Gilbert, described by Hamner as 'a gallant stripling'[8] who was possibly born in 1173. Aoife had fulfilled her duty as a wife. There was plenty of time to beget more sons. Strongbow, who was born in 1130, was 43-years of age but in good health.

Both Isabel and her brother were subject to the strictures imposed by the Synod of Cashel which demanded the same observances in Ireland as in England. They were baptised soon after birth in a font that was consecrated. Gerald of Wales reported that in Ireland infants were not swaddled or placed in cradles. It is difficult to know whether or not this was an extension of Gerald's critical view of the Irish but there have been very few wooden cradles discovered in archaeological sites of the period. It was more likely that as a baby Isabel slept in a hazel and willow basketwork cradle and was soothed by the sound of Irish lullabies.[9] It is impossible to know the extent to which Isabel's infancy followed the pattern of Irish childrearing or whether Aoife chose to use Norman methods including the use of a wet nurse so that she could return to the business of providing her husband with a male heir as soon as possible. Certainly, if Gilbert was born within a year of Isabel, it suggests that Aoife found a reliable woman, perhaps a member of her own extended family, to act as a wet nurse for Isabel.

Sheltered in her nursery, Isabel was too young to know the dangers that faced her family in Ireland. Her father did not have enough men to conqueror it; he was unable to keep his troops sufficiently well-equipped and he was not always able to pay them. The arrival of the so-called Saxons and their military successes had also destabilised the existing political structure in Ireland. Ruardri Ua Conchobair was no longer able to exercise the control over the petty kings that he had before the arrival of King Henry II. The pale of Leinster and the lands that the Cambro-Normans held were in a constant state of guerrilla warfare characterised by raids, ambushes and surprise attacks.

On the other side of the Irish Sea, Henry II's son, the Young King, became frustrated that his father kept him short of funds and offered him no real political power despite the fact that he was crowned a king of England. Henry compounded his eldest son's resentment when he arranged, in 1173, for his youngest son John to marry the daughter of Count Humbert of Maurienne. John was granted the castles of Chinon, Loudun and Mirebeau as part of the agreement. The fortifications were vital to the defence of Anjou but were also part of the territories granted by Henry to the Young King in 1169. As John was still a minor, the castles reverted to the Crown.

The marriage came to nothing when John's intended bride, Alais, died but the damage was already done. The Young King rose in revolt taking his brothers Richard and Geoffrey with him to the court of King Louis VII of France. In Aquitaine, Henry's wife, Eleanor, roused her duchy to rebellion in support of her sons. Across his realm barons including Hugh de Kevilioc, 5th Earl of Chester, Robert de Beaumont, 3rd Earl of Leicester, Roger de Mowbray, and Hugh Bigod, 1st Earl of Norfolk joined in the insurgency against the king believing that he had withheld land and rights from them during his reign. William the Lion of Scotland, taking advantage of the unrest, invaded the north of England. In Brittany, Hugh of Chester raised an army to oppose the king. Henry gave orders that the troops he had left in Ireland should return to his side. De Clare, a man whose earldom of Pembroke was still withheld from him, was summoned to fulfil his feudal obligations by a king who had never trusted him and who had diminished him with every opportunity that arose.

For de Clare it meant leaving a fragile situation in Ireland to support his feudal overlord. His absence from Ireland raised the possibility that his brittle control over Leinster might shatter. The problem of his departure was compounded by the fact that his constable and son-in-law, Robert de Quincy, was dead and that Raymond le Gros, a man admired by the troops, had returned to Wales following an argument with Strongbow.

Le Gros aspired to de Clare's sister's hand in marriage. By 1173, Basilia was 25-years-old at the least, her father, Gilbert, having died in 1148. It is unclear whether the couple formed an attachment or whether the pragmatic scion of the FitzGeralds saw an opportunity to win promotion and land by binding himself more closely to Strongbow. Le Gros wanted to take de Quincy's place as official miliary commander and perhaps reasoned that if he was de Clare's brother-in-law that the role would be his. However, his suit was initially rejected. It is possible that Strongbow was either jealous of Raymond's popularity with his men, did not regard le Gros as having sufficient status to wed Basilia, or was wary of allowing the FitzGerald clan more power than it already held in Ireland.

De Clare's own troops demanded the knight's reinstatement and the pressure from the Irish was such that Strongbow needed a commander that his men could trust. Recognising that he had no choice following Henry II's summons, Strongbow recalled Raymond and granted both Le Gros' requests for his sister's hand in marriage and Constableship of Leinster. Basilia and Raymond were married in Wexford soon after the knight arrived back in Ireland from Wales but not before Ruardri Ua Conchobair's son, Conchobar, took an army into Leinster and razed the castle at Kilkenny.

Meanwhile, the rebellion that spread through Henry's realm took two years to quell. Robert Beaumont, 3rd Earl of Leicester, Strongbow's cousin, was defeated by Richard de Lacy, the king's justiciar in England, during October 1173. William the Lion was captured at Alnwick in July 1174. Strongbow provided military service for Henry in Normandy at Gisors. It was his task to control the road between Rouen and Paris. As a result of his loyalty to the king, the port of Wexford was returned into de Clare's keeping as was the castle at Wicklow. Strongbow was back in favour – if still not entirely trusted.

The situation in Ireland remained uncertain. To many of the Irish princes it looked as though the foreigners hold on Leinster was weakened. The situation was compounded when, as well as the conflict between the Irish and the foreign invaders, Le Gros had become caught up in a dispute between Ua Conchobair and the petty kings of Munster. A peace settlement needed to be established by the political and religious authorities in Ireland as soon as Henry II reasserted his control over his realm and Strongbow returned to his fief.

In 1175, Henry sought to reach an agreement with the Irish High King of Ireland. The Treaty of Windsor codified the lordship of Ireland and partitioned it in an attempt to limit its continued conquest. Ua Conchobair agreed that he would recognise Henry II's overlordship on terms familiar to the Irish. He would pay annual tribute but he would not become Henry's vassal. In return he would be recognised as High King but only in those parts of Ireland that was still ruled by the Irish. The pact proved ineffective in the longer term as Ruardri Ua Conchobair could not control his kinsmen or keep the other petty kings of Ireland from attacking the Norman settlers whenever an occasion arose. Henry could not regulate the men who settled in Ireland and who resented the halt that was called on their land grab.

Chapter 6

The Irish Countess

The arrangements that Henry II made for the administration of Ireland prevented de Clare from aspiring to the high kingship but he consolidated his position by coming to terms with the Irish and abiding by agreements that he made with them. Strongbow also forged links with the FitzGeralds who were a dominant force in the region's politics. He married his sister, Basilia, with great reluctance to Raymond le Gros and arranged for his one of his illegitimate daughters, Aline, to marry William the son of Maurice FitzGerald.[1] He became Lord of Naas in Kildare, a central position within the English pale and only 15 miles from Dublin. The *Song of Dermot and the Earl* describes how Strongbow made grants to his followers using the existing framework of Irish lordships but transformed them into a more familiar Norman feudal structure. De Clare offered Wicklow and its castle as a fief to his son-in-law as part of this strategy. Hervey de Montmorency, Strongbow's uncle, married Nesta one of Maurice's daughters although Gerald of Wales stated this was from envy of Raymond's enhanced status rather than any plan of Strongbow's to ally the two families more closely.[2] By the end of 1175 de Clare was free from the danger of King Henry's wrath, had regained power over Wexford, and the possession of Wicklow Castle gave him control of the coastal zone from Dublin to Waterford.

The problem of Irish hostility did not disappear even if Tigernán Ua Ruaire died at the hands of Hugh de Lacy in 1172; his head stuck above Dublin's city gates as a warning to others. Some Irish princes recognised the Normans and pretended friendship but made their long-term decisions based on the calculated risks of challenging the men Diarmait invited to Ireland. Domnall Mór Ua Briain, King of Thomond in the province of Munster, Strongbow's brother-in-law by marriage to Aoife's half-sister Órlaith, weighed the political situation carefully.[3] Ua Briain offered his submission to King Henry II at Cashel in 1171 in the expectation that he would be safe as a vassal of the English king both from the foreigners and the hostility of the high king, Ua Conchobair. He also made alliances of his own with a new generation of Irish princes including Ua Conchobair's son, Conchobar Máenmaige Ua Conchobair, who was intent on pushing the foreigners back into the sea. His decision cost him the town of Limerick in 1175.

That winter passed quietly but, in the spring, word came that le Gros was to return to England to perform military service for King Henry II. Before he could obey his orders, news arrived that le Gros' cousin, Miles FitzDavid, who had been left in control of Limerick after its capture the previous year, was under siege. If the town was to remain in Norman hands, there was no time to waste but Strongbow's troops were reticent about following anyone apart from le Gros. Under the circumstances, the King's envoys, sent by Henry to tighten royal control on the region, agreed that Raymond need not leave Ireland until the crisis was under control.

Having raised the siege on Limerick, Raymond marched on Cork at the request of the King of Desmond to intervene in a dispute with his eldest son who was also his main rival. They were still enroute when a message for le Gros arrived from his wife, Basilia. The letter she sent contained an innocuous enough note 'let it be known to you my true and living husband, that that large molar tooth, which caused me so much pain, has now fallen out'.[4] The cryptic note was a code. Strongbow was dead from blood-poisoning. Raymond returned immediately to Dublin.

De Clare's foot became infected either through an unspecified wound, cut or even crack in the skin. The diseased foot became painful and hindered Strongbow's mobility as it festered and went septic. Strongbow became fevered. The poison spread rapidly despite any treatments that Aoife and Basilia tried. His life still might have been saved if his foot was amputated but the sepsis spread into his bloodstream infecting his whole body before this could be done. Even if the operation was performed there was every chance that de Clare would have died from loss of blood. A priest was summoned when it became clear that the Lord of Leinster would die in his bed rather than on the battlefield or caught in an ambush. Strongbow needed to make his final confession, to be shriven of his sins and prepare for his death.

Isabel de Clare was not yet in her sixth year. Her brother Gilbert was a year younger at most. The news of their father's death placed them in grave danger because the Irish were likely to try and force the so-called Saxons from Ireland in a general uprising. Basilia, in sending the letter to Raymond and summoning him and his army back to Dublin, showed that she was more than a pawn to be moved around the marriage board. She either acted on her own initiative or Strongbow relied upon her to secure his legacy. In either case, Basilia played a key role in securing Leinster. She also placed her husband in a position where he could make use of the lack of stability and uncertainty following de Clare's death to take the fief for himself if the possibility arose.

Strongbow, whose passing was kept secret until le Gros' return to Dublin, was buried in Christ Church Cathedral on 20 April 1176. The *Annals of Ulster* were jubilant, 'the Saxon Earl died at Athclaith of an ulcer he got in his foot, through the miracles of Brigit and Columcille and the saints besides, whose churches he destroyed'.[5] All the Irish chroniclers shared a general delight that Aoife's husband was dead. No one missed him. Raymond le Gros, married to Basilia de Clare, intended to fill the void left by his overlord. The majority of men who came to Ireland at King Diarmait's request never agreed with Strongbow's policy of peaceful interaction with the Irish. They wanted to make the green hills and fertile lands of Ireland their own. King Henry II never fully trusted de Clare, even after his service in Normandy.

Without de Clare to protect her, Aoife's future in Ireland looked uncertain. Under Brehon law the Kingdom of Leinster was hers for her life only, after which it should have reverted to Aoife's male kinfolk of the Ui Chennselaig, even if her father's pact with Strongbow ignored those rights. The agreement made between King Henry II and de Clare in 1171, effectively changed him from an invited guest into an invader. Basilia's husband Raymond le Gros took control of Strongbow's troops and the administration of his lands in Ireland until Henry II made a decision about the future governance of Leinster. Aoife was left only with her dower rights and the hope that one day Gilbert would inherit what remained of his grandfather's kingdom.

In the meantime, King Henry II had no intention of permitting the FitzGeralds any latitude. He sent William FitzAldelm as his justiciar to Ireland attended by ten of his own household knights to ensure that his orders were carried out. He also dispatched a supporting commission to Ireland composed of Miles de Cogan, John de Courcy and Robert FitzStephen, each arrayed with their own retinue of fighting men. Raymond met them with his cavalry behind him, perhaps intending to intimidate the king's men. He had won the land by his sword, was married to de Clare's sister; his Fitzgerald relations formed a dominant faction in Ireland, and he was popular with the troops that he commanded. In the end though, le Gros had no choice other than to deliver Strongbow's fief into FitzAldelm's keeping as well as all of the hostages that de Clare had taken from Ireland's petty kings to ensure that they would abide by their agreements with him. It soon became clear that FitzAldelm and his fellow commissioners intended to scatter the Geraldines rather than permit them to assume the status of overmighty subjects.[6]

Henry II took Leinster for himself during the minority of Strongbow's son. William FitzAldelm was appointed to administer the fief. He was also granted temporary responsibility for Aoife's children. This does not mean that Gilbert and Isabel were immediately removed from her care, simply that legal responsibility for them now rested with the king's representative. As guardian, not only did Henry take control of the land, he also held the right to award

Gilbert's marriage where he chose. While her younger brother was still alive Isabel was not an heiress, although a suitable husband would have to be found for her as she grew towards adulthood. The king also had some say as to whom Aoife, styled the Irish Countess as a reminder of her own right to Leinster, might take for a second husband.

That same year King Henry transferred his rights as Lord of Ireland to his own youngest son, Prince John. FitzAldelm was restyled custodian of Leinster and given Wexford at the Council of Oxford in May 1177. At the same time Henry granted Ua Briain's kingdom of Thromond to Philip de Braose, one of three captains left in charge of Wexford in 1172. Ua Briain was determined that de Braose would neither take nor hold the lands that the English king granted to him. What was more significant, was that until that time Henry had refused to grant Ua Briain's land to any of his own men stating that Limerick and its environs were unconquered territory. His grant to de Braose signalled the start of a new policy. King Henry claimed the whole of the island, and authorised the men who sought to make their fortunes to conquer more of its land.

Hugh de Lacy, appointed by Henry as a counter balance to Strongbow's authority before the king departed from Ireland in 1172, resumed his role as Ireland's governor after the meeting at Oxford. The grant of Meath was reconfirmed and de Lacy was also awarded new territory in Connaught. It was de Lacy's job to secure both fiefs. De Lacy's stewardship of Ireland was described by Gerald of Wales as 'indefatigable'.[7] He built castles and alliances with the Geraldines as well as conducting military campaigns. He also recognised that he needed to reach an accommodation with the Irish if he was to maintain his hold on the pale of land that the settlers had carved out. In 1180, imitating Strongbow's example, he married Rose, a daughter of the deposed High King, Ruaidrí Ua Conchobair, without first asking King Henry's permission. The union resulted in him becoming subject to the king's paranoia. Did de Lacy aspire to the high kingship of Ireland? He was summoned to England the year after his wedding to explain himself. De Lacy was better able to persuade Henry of his loyalty to the Crown than Isabel's father had ever been and was allowed to return to Ireland and to retain custody of Dublin. In future though, he would be closely monitored by Robert of Shrewsbury, a royal clerk, appointed by the king.

Aoife and her children left Ireland soon after Strongbow's death. Crossing the Irish Sea was not for the faint hearted. The men and women who travelled upon it lived with the fear of shipwreck. Aoife made her farewells to Ireland, in all likelihood, from Wexford or even the royal port at Waterford. The bulk of Anglo-Irish trade made landfall in Chester or Bristol with which she was more familiar. Unfortunately, there is little record of the ships that left the Irish harbours or their destinations. It is possible that Aoife's boat docked at St David's or Milford Haven and that she travelled from one of those to Striguil.

Isabel's mother remained a woman of power and influence because of the dower land, including Striguil Castle, which she now held in the Marches of Wales. The king placed the lordship of Netherwent and the castle under the guardianship of Ralph Bloet but the income from the estates was Aoife's. The Bloet family held land in Wiltshire for the de Clare Earls of Hertford. Ralph's brother, Walter Bloet, was rewarded for his services to Strongbow with the vill of Raglan, as a knight's fee, in 1171. Raglan guarded the road from Abergavenny into Wales. Henry had travelled to Gloucester in 1175 to reassert his authority in the Welsh Marches in the aftermath of his sons' rebellion against him. It is thought that Ralph Bloet's wife, Nest, conducted a brief affair with the king during his expedition. The child that resulted from the union, Morgan, was raised in Bloet's household. The brief encounter may have been enough to ensure that Henry looked favourably upon the knight. Bloet retained the position of castellan throughout the remainder of the reign. His accounts for the profits of the Honour of Striguil were submitted in the first year of Richard I's reign before he transferred his service to the new lord of Netherwent. It raises the intriguing possibility that Isabel's first acquaintance with the Plantagenet brood was in the nursery playing with Nest Bloet's son who was probably born in the same year as Strongbow died.

Aoife's dower rights were in England rather than Ireland because those were the lands that Strongbow held at the time when the settlement was agreed in 1166. It is also probable that the king did not want her or her children in Ireland where it would be much easier for an unscrupulous freebooter to marry Aoife or her daughter and claim Leinster by right of his bride. The concept of the *morgengifu*, or 'morning-gift' paid in both land and money by a groom to his bride evolved through the early medieval period. The woman held control over this gift herself in pre-conquest England. In addition to the *morgengifu*, marriage agreements specified what estates a woman would hold in the event of her husband's death. After the Norman conquest it was usual for a woman to receive a *maritagium*, or marriage-portion, from her father and a dower from her husband. In time the dower settled at one third of a man's estates to be held by his widow for her lifetime.

The agreement placed Aoife in a position of independence so long as she did not remarry. Under the terms of King Henry I's coronation charter which Henry II reissued when he came to the throne, the monarch promised not to give widows in a new marriage against their wishes. On this occasion it may have suited the king not to furnish Aoife with a husband because of the strategic value of the lands which the countess held in the Marches and because of the claim it would give any spouse to the kingdom of Leinster. There is no existing evidence to suggest that Aoife paid a fine to the exchequer so that she would not be compelled to remarry.

The king's own familial problems did not moderate with the passage of time. Another quarrel with his sons arose in 1182 when the Young King invaded Poitou which was part of his younger brother, Richard's, domain. The real problem was that Henry II remained determined not to share any real power with his heir. Henry and Richard found themselves at war with the Young King and Henry's third surviving son, Geoffrey of Brittany. Only the death of the Young King from dysentery in the summer of 1183 halted the crisis. As he lay dying, the Young King took the cross and begged that one of his knights, William Marshal who began his service to the Plantagenets in the household of Eleanor of Aquitaine, would fulfil a crusader's vow on his behalf. Marshal, having said his farewells to his family in England, presented himself to the king before setting off on his journey. The knight spent the next two years in the Holy Land but when he returned was granted a place in Henry II's household. Marshal's activities during his time in Syria and Palestine are largely unknown.

Decisions made by Aoife during her widowhood are also absent from documentary evidence although she is mentioned as 'the Irish countess' or the 'countess of Striguil' in the records.[8] If she chose the former title herself it was because she had no intention of permitting the king or the apparatus of State to forget that she was her father's designated heir and that it was through her that Strongbow claimed Leinster. She was also demonstrating political foresight. The king did not always honour the rights of heirs if his own interests could be better served elsewhere. Aoife had no intention of her children being denied what was rightfully theirs. It has also been observed that the countess sometimes simply referred to herself as the 'wife of Earl Richard'. Aoife was keeping Strongbow's claim to the earldom of Pembroke alive for her children by the very fact that she gave no geographic appellation to the title.[9]

Aoife first appears in the Pipe Rolls in 1176-1177 when she received a payment as part of her inheritance rights valued at sixty shillings.[10] There is no indication of how Aoife managed to negotiate receipt of her dower with Henry II or to hold continued custody of her children. It was usual to leave children with their mother until their more formal education began at 7-years of age. Nor is it clear if she travelled to court to speak in person with the king. In all likelihood she initially made her home at Chepstow with her children although she received payments from dower manors in Essex, Hertfordshire and Cambridgeshire. In 1183-1184 she received an advance of £20 from the king.[11] It is probable that the money was for the defence of Chepstow and corresponds to similar payments made to other castellans in the region. Ralph Bloet was appointed castellan from 1184 onwards and he received the same amount from the Crown.[12]

The Welsh Marches were never long without hostilities and 1183 saw a major uprising throughout South Wales. The unrest was triggered in Glamorgan, by the death of William FitzRobert, 2nd Earl of Gloucester. Morgan ap Caradog led the fighting which concentrated around Neath and Kenfig. Cardiff and Newport were both damaged by the Welsh and in Kenfig, the castle along with the town went up in flames. Entries in the Pipe Rolls reveal a number of grants being allowed for both the maintenance of castles and the payment of castellans throughout the region. The records for 1184-1185 show the king's expenditure of £10 38s 0d on repairs to Chepstow Castle.[13] Seen against the backdrop of rebellion, the funding which Chepstow received helps create a potential picture of Aoife engaged in the defence of the castle which was both part of her dower and her son's birthright. Isabel, aged 12-years, learned from her mother not only how to be run a castle and its estates but how to oversee the defence of one.

Isabel was familiar with the castle at Chepstow from early childhood onwards. The keep remained the same as it had been during her father's life time with the great hall on the first floor. It might have looked splendid with its band of Roman tiles and formidable façade but even with the line of windows that looked across the River Wye it was a dark and cold place. Aoife and her children lived near the keep in a timber building, with a roaring fire in the winter as well as rugs, tapestries and hangings to keep cold draughts at bay. From here Aoife wrote to Ireland on occasion and dealt with business arising from the management of her dower lands.

Isabel was cared for on a day-to-day basis by her nurse. Her education was overseen by her mother. It is likely that it was from Aoife and the women who cared for her during her childhood that she learned Irish. She could also speak French, English and Latin. Isabel was also taught the essential elements of Christianity including the *Pater Noster, Ave Maria* and the *Credo*. Aoife ensured that Isabel began her day with Mass in the castle chapel and communicated to her daughter the importance of making gifts to monastic houses to secure the prayers of their inhabitants as well as the saints they represented.

A poem written in the fourteenth century entitled *How the Good Wife Taught her Daughter*, was directed at women of Aoife and Isabel's rank. Its content was not much different from earlier expectations of female education. Alongside piety, it focused on the importance of obedience, virtue and chastity:

Daughter, if thou wilt be a wife,
Look wisely that thou work;
Look lovely and in good life,
Love God and Holy Church.
Go to church whenever thou may.[14]

The advice included the importance of not being seen to gossip in church, to be meek and not shrewish and to be honourable in all things.

Isabel learned comportment and good manners. A virtuous young woman did not smile too much or laugh immoderately. She was to maintain a pleasant expression on her face and behave demurely. The idea of proper conduct was something that all gently born children were required to learn. During the twelfth century so-called courtesy books began to make an appearance providing mothers like Aoife with a model to draw upon. These books contained advice on how courteous ladies should behave, eat and even speak. The ideas contained in the books grew from the culture of courtly love and chivalry that took hold of European courts while King Henry II was on the throne. It was important for Isabel to demonstrate temperance at the table, not to eat with her mouth open or to chew bones, pick her teeth or to eat all the best things. As well as manners, Isabel learned to sing, to play a musical instrument, to dance, and to play popular games including chess, draughts and backgammon. She may also have learned how to play *merelles* better known today as Nine Men's Morris. She was also expected to be proficient at horse riding, hawking and archery.

In Ireland a girl was prepared for marriage so that she was able to run a household efficiently. For a woman to do otherwise was a reason for a union to be dissolved. Aoife knew about dyeing processes, spinning and weaving, as well as the care of herds of cattle which often formed the basis of a woman's movable assets. She could sew and cook, manage dairy work and knew the rudiments of medical care to look after her family and her household. Good housecraft was an essential for women whatever their social rank. Isabel learned all that she needed to manage an estate, to be self-sufficient and to plan ahead for any purchases the household might need that could not be provided from her own lands. Even her toys, which are likely to have included a doll dressed according to Isabel's own rank in society, was an early form of preparation for motherhood.

Aoife might also have taught Isabel the importance of managing a garden. Herbs provided flavour to food and were also an essential requirement for medicine. Fruit trees were often also grown in gardens. A late thirteenth century poem, The *Treatise of Walter de Bibbesworth* written for Dionysia de Munchensy[15] who died in 1304, covers aspects of estate and household management in twenty-three parts. One of the consequences of the loss of Normandy during the reign of King John was that while the court still spoke French, it was no longer the mother tongue of the nobility by the end of the thirteenth century. The book was designed to be used to help children learn the French they needed to run a typical estate as adults. The vocabulary it contains helps to create a picture of day-to-day tasks that a medieval woman required to run a household. The vocabulary encompassed baking, spinning and brewing as well as horticulture.

At some point between the end of 1184 and 1186, Gilbert de Clare died unexpectedly. By the sixteenth century a story grew up that the boy's death was at his father's hands as a result of cowardice on the battlefield during his eighteenth year. It was said that Gilbert, unaccustomed to the wild yells of Irish warriors fled the field of battle:

When his father was in cruel fight, gave back with his company, to the great discouragement of the host, yet the Earl got the victory, and commanded with the tears in his cheeks, that his son should be cut in the middle with a sword for his cowardice in battle.[16]

The dates do not add up and the death of an only son was something to be avoided. The purported tombs of Strongbow and his son at Christ Church Cathedral, Dublin, perhaps lent something to the tale. Both effigies were damaged when the roof fell in 1562. The sculpture alleged to be Gilbert's likeness was cut in half. Both Hanmer and Richard Stanilhurst, writing in 1854, claimed that the tomb corroborated their farfetched tale of filicide. Medieval sources make no reference to the story.

It is more likely, assuming he survived infancy, that Gilbert died unexpectedly after falling ill. Study of medieval skeletal remains reveals that dysentery, malaria, flu, typhoid, smallpox, tuberculosis and leprosy were common. 'Diseases that caused diarrhoea and that led to rapid dehydration and death'[17] were much feared by parents. The truth was that life was fragile even in aristocratic households where there was better food and care.

Isabel was Strongbow's only remaining legitimate heir. Whoever married her would claim her father's lands in England and Wales as well as the lordship of Leinster. To ambitious men, Isabel was representative of titles and estates that might be secured through marriage. For Henry, it was essential that Strongbow's legacy be placed in capable as well as trustworthy hands. The king who was occupied with rearranging his plans for the succession and dealing with another rebellion, this time orchestrated by his son Richard who refused to hand the duchy of Aquitaine to his brother John, was at Westminster at the end of 1184. He arranged for his ward to be sent to London to be placed in the care of Ranulf de Glanville, the chief justiciar in England, where she was less likely to be stolen away and forcibly married by an adventurer seeking to enrich himself

Henry's own queen, Eleanor of Aquitaine, was subject to two attempted abduction attempts to claim her and the duchy she represented after the annulment of her marriage from Louis in 1152. As Eleanor travelled from Paris to wed Henry at Poitiers, two lords attempted to seize the newly available duchess and marry her so that they would gain control over her domains. One of the would-be rapists was Henry's own younger brother, Geoffrey. Abduction of heiresses, and coercion to marry, was well recorded not only in Henry's realm but elsewhere in Europe. In France the kidnap of an heiress was not only illegal but subsequent marriage between the victim and her abductor was forbidden.[18] The Statutes of Westminster in 1275 and 1285 made rape a capital offence. During the later Middle Ages, the laws on *raptus* were muddied by the fact that the definition of abduction included elopement or secret marriages made against the wishes of the woman's guardian. There were other acts passed in the fifteenth century but these seem to have been in response to notorious examples and they served the best interests of an heiress's guardians rather the wishes of the abducted woman.

Henry had no intention of allowing Isabel or her assets to be seized but the court was not always a safe place for a royal ward who caught the king's fancy. Ida de Tosny, a cousin of Strongbow's through Ida's mother Margaret de Beaumont, was one of Henry's charges but he made the girl his mistress and she bore him a son, named William Longspée, who was born c.1176. Ralph the Black, a supporter of Thomas Becket, once described the king as 'a corrupter of chastity'.[19] Isabel's wealth, as a sole heiress, was too great for seduction to be his aim. He would provide a husband for Isabel. The strategic value of the lands she represented were too great for him to sell her wardship to a third party. She was a pawn in the king's strategy to control his kingdom and to keep the Welsh under control in the Marches. A reminder of the importance of her domains, if one was needed, occurred in 1187, when Tenby Castle, which was part of Isabel's inheritance, was besieged by Maelgwn ap Rhys and his brother Hywel. The town was destroyed. The legal element of choice which Aoife had in her own marriage would be denied to her daughter although the Church insisted that consent should be freely given by both parties.

It is unclear to what extent Aoife oversaw her daughter's education during Isabel's wardship in London. There is some evidence to indicate that Aoife took up residence at one of her dower manors in Essex at Chesterford or

Weston in Hertfordshire which would have enabled her to visit her daughter more readily. As Isabel grew towards adulthood, she would have learned courtly pursuits essential to an aristocratic woman who was expected to be an ornament in her husband's hall and at court.

Having secured Isabel, the king turned his attention back to Ireland. He intended that his youngest son, often known as Lackland because of the paucity of his possessions, would rule there. Before Henry sent John to his new domain, the king sought approval from the papacy. Pope Urban III ratified the decision to have the boy crowned king of Ireland and sent him a crown that included peacock feathers. In April 1185, Henry's son arrived on his first visit to Ireland at Waterford. He met several Irish kings soon afterwards and received their submission. Instead of respecting their rights, he, and other youths who formed part of his household, were rude to them. Even worse, John began to issue their lands to his own followers. Gerald of Wales was with the prince's retinue and reported the way that their new lord alienated the Irish. The original Norman settlers were also unimpressed by John's antics especially when he failed to support them against Irish sorties into the territories they considered to be their own.

Even worse from Aoife and Isabel's perspective, among the grants given to John's favourites were estates in Osraige which were part of the lordship of Leinster. Strongbow's inheritance in Ireland was being eaten away by John and by the settlers who lived there. In England, Aoife maintained her claim to Leinster and when she confirmed a charter in Ireland in 1188/89 it was as the Countess of Hibernia. She had no intention of permitting anyone, even a Plantagenet prince, to claim what was rightfully hers. It was a position she bequeathed to her sole remaining child. Isabel would need a husband capable of facing down the Angevin monarchy and the barons who lived in the Irish pale by their swords.

King Henry II's realm faced troubled times in the final years of his life. In Ireland, Hugh de Lacy was murdered on 25 July 1186 at Durrow in County Offaly. William of Newburgh, a contemporary chronicler, described the king's delight at de Lacy's death as it provided a new opportunity to attempt to assert royal control over the territories that his freebooting subjects had won for themselves.

Before Ireland could be pacified and its lands made secure, Henry was faced with an attempt by the French to benefit from Plantagenet family discord. The relationship between Henry II and his remaining sons did not improve with the death of the Young King. Geoffrey of Brittany, a friend of King Philip II of France, planned an uprising with the French against his father during the summer of 1186. Treachery was only averted because the prince was trampled to death during a jousting tournament in Paris on 21 August. He left a posthumous son named Arthur who was the Duke of Brittany from his birth.

Of Henry and Eleanor's five sons only two survived. The king arrived at a plan to divide his possessions to allow his youngest son John to inherit territory in addition to the lordship of Ireland. He ordered Richard, who was his own successor since the death of the Young King, to relinquish the duchy of Aquitaine to John. Richard, who had been sent to Aquitaine in his youth as his mother's heir, was deeply attached to both Eleanor and her duchy. The end result was that John invaded Aquitaine and Richard retaliated by assaulting Brittany. Peace was restored but in 1187, still fearful of his father's intentions, Henry's heir rose in rebellion against him once more. Philip of France played on Richard's fears ensuring that Richard did homage to him for his territories in France. Henry, increasingly unwell, had no option other than to defend his territories from his own family once more but found himself deserted by all but the most loyal of his magnates and knights.

Chapter 7

A Valuable Prize

The concept of female succession to estates and the heritability of title was established in post-conquest England to 'ensure the transmission of blood line and land'.[1] By 1130 more than twenty baronies had descended by a direct female line rather than a collateral male one.[2] Isabel was representative of the land and titles she inherited and the king, whoever he was, would arrange to marry her to his own advantage in exactly the same way that any other father or guardian might be expected to do. Marriage was permitted by Church and State from puberty onwards; 12-years of age for girls and 14-years for boys. Isabel's prospective husband needed to be experienced in warfare and to be able to command the respect, or fear, of the men he commanded.

Under English law, girls and women were considered legally incompetent both before their marriage and after. Both Christian theology and the science of the time considered women as weaker, more fragile and less morally able than their male counterparts. In the eyes of the law when Isabel took a husband she and her spouse would become as one. She would be under the protection or cover of the man that the king chose for her to marry, rendering her largely invisible to the apparatus of State and the written record. Theoretically the majority of women were without power. In most cases, it was only when a wife became a widow that she attained a legal status of her own. Of course, in reality aristocratic women wielded both the power of their status in a feudal society and the responsibility of running their estates in the absence of their husbands. They were also recognised as having influence within their kinship and social networks.

Isabel's education continued while she was in de Glanville's care. Her new guardian, both literate and well educated, was an efficient administrator as well as the presumptive author of a legal treatise described in a list of texts by Roger of Howden as the *Glanvill*. His household was a good place to learn how to administer a large estate. There is no indication whether Isabel could read or not before she arrived in London. Glanville was critical of barons who failed to teach their children to read;[3] if she could not do so before, Isabel knew her letters by the time she left the justiciar's care. It is less likely that she could write. A scribe could be employed for such activities. Women of Isabel's rank were not expected to have inky fingers. They could employ scribes to write what was required; far better to be able to check the contents of a page or account book for accuracy.

It was de Glanville's business to be well informed about what happened in England and to dispense justice. Isabel knew that when she married, she would be expected to dispense justice among her tenants in the absence of her husband. Her time spent within his household was an opportunity to learn about the laws and customs of land ownership and tenure as well as understanding the fees and fines associated with manorial overlordship. She learned about the men who ran the kingdom, met their wives and daughters, listened to the gossip that circulated London and heard the news about Henry's ongoing war with his own heir.

On occasion she also heard more about the dangers of angering a king. De Glanville was Queen Eleanor's custodian. She was kept confined in Windsor or the castle at Old Sarum. Her imprisonment was one of the reasons that Isabel was not at the royal court. Until her confinement in 1174, Eleanor's household was home not only to her ladies-in-waiting but to royal brides and aristocratic wards like Isabel. De Glanville had charge of the disgraced queen and monitored her household, which was composed of a maid named Amaria and, after 1180, two chamberlains. Eleanor was almost entirely absent from the record. She might as well have been forgotten but in de Glanville's household the queen remained a matter of concern. Isabel could only hope that she would not be married to someone as despotic and overbearing as King Henry II.

In 1189, shortly before he died, the king offered Isabel as a bride to William Marshal, the man who went on pilgrimage to Jerusalem on behalf of the Young King. He was a knight famed for his skill on the tournament field and his loyalty to the Plantagenets. Marshal, a younger son of John Marshal and his wife Sibyl, started his career in to the household of his uncle Patrick of Salisbury. The marriage between John and Sybil had been designed to end a feud between the two families. William's presence in Patrick's household was both familial and a continuation of an aim to bring peace between the belligerent families. In April 1168, Salisbury's retinue, which was escorting Eleanor of Aquitaine, was ambushed by the Lusignan family in Poitou. Although Patrick perished, Marshal rode to his uncle's defence and then fought on with his back to a hedge until a Lusignan soldier thrust a lance through the undergrowth and brought William down from behind. Eleanor was able to escape to safety while the young knight held off her enemies.

Marshall was wounded and captured but ransomed by the queen whose household he then entered before joining the retinue of her eldest son, the Young King, Henry. Following the Young King's death on 11 June 1183

Marshal undertook a pilgrimage to Jerusalem on behalf of his royal master. When he returned from the east, he became a captain in Henry II's military household. He did not have land or titles of his own but he began to receive royal rewards. Among the first of these grants was the wardship of John d' Earley who became Marshal's squire. In 1186, the king settled him with an estate at Cartmel and the custody of Heloise of Lancaster whose inheritance included the barony of Kendal following the death of her father William the previous year.

It might reasonably have been expected that Marshal would take the opportunity to make Heloise his bride, effectively turning him into a northern baron at the same social level as his own eldest brother, John Marshal, who inherited their father's Wiltshire lands in 1165. Instead, Marshal's biography written soon after his death in 1219, records that Heloise and William remained 'just good friends'. The knight chose to wait for another heiress. The wardship of Heloise passed from William's hands with his agreement. She married Gilbert, son of Roger FitzReinfred who was one of Henry II's justices as well as the Sheriff of Berkshire. The marriage was an exceptionally good one for Gilbert, a friend and colleague of Marshal, who did not inherit his father's estates, there being some suggestion that he was illegitimate.[4]

In 1188 the right circumstances for being rewarded with marriage to a wealthier bride than Heloise arose. Marshal remained loyal to the king when Henry's heir rebelled against him. The king promised Marshal the hand of Denise, heiress of the honour of Châteauroux in Berry in return for his military support. The previous year King Philip II of France led an army into the region and attempted to capture Châteauroux but was unsuccessful in his endeavour. But, in June 1188, Philip's army defeated the castle's defenders. Henry II, who was increasingly ill, made his offer to Marshal in the hope that William would secure the region and drive the French out. The following year, during Lent 1189, King Henry, who was sick both in body and heart, raised the stakes even further. He offered Marshal Isabel de Clare as a wife and with her the possibility of receiving the earldom of Pembroke which he had denied to Isabel's father.

Spring turned to summer. Henry's health did not improve and nor did his relationship with his son Richard. Henry was forced to fall back as Philip II, in alliance with Richard, advanced through Maine towards Le Mans. Marshal saw action on 11 June 1189 against the French at the gates of Le Mans. It was to no avail. The king and his knights were obliged to break out of the trap in which they found themselves. As the king fled, Marshal remained behind to delay the king's pursuers, of whom Richard was one. William's ambush was such a success that he killed the next king of England's horse from beneath him. It allowed Henry time to arrive in safety at Fresnay and to travel from there to Chinon. Marshal, who did not attempt to kill the heir to the throne when he had the advantage, must have considered what his loyalty to the old king would cost him when a new monarch sat upon the throne.

Marshal was given responsibility by Henry for the defence of southern Normandy. He was still reliant upon retaining the king's favour, on him being true to his word and on him living long enough for William to marry his promised bride. King Henry's undertaking was not immediately followed by a binding betrothal between Isabel and Marshal. The king was in the middle of a war: Tours fell; Henry's health continued to deteriorate; and John deserted his father for Philip II. Of all his sons, it was an illegitimate one, Geoffrey, who remained loyal to his father. When the king died on 6 July 1189, he was on his own apart from the servants who looted everything of value in the chamber including the king's bedding. The new king of England was the man whose horse Marshal killed outside Le Mans.

The proposed match with William was not the best one that Isabel might have expected. Although Marshal was more than twenty years older than Isabel, he was her social inferior having no title or inheritance of his own. As a younger son he earned his living as a professional soldier and tournament champion. During his lifetime, Henry II recognised the value of Marshal's abilities and loyalty but it was not a foregone conclusion that he was so indispensable that the marriage to Isabel would go ahead. If Marshal married Strongbow's daughter the union would increase his standing in society and render him independent of the Plantagenet monarchy. It would be the medieval equivalent of winning a lottery jackpot. For Isabel, the union with Marshal might mean that her patrimony in Leinster was more secure from John's predatory attentions if he was able to outwit the prince. Aoife had written to the Archbishop of Dublin as 'the heir of King Diarmait'[5] asking for information about the possessions which John had granted to the cathedral from estates which were part of her husband's fief and now part of Isabel, Countess of Striguil's inheritance.

Chapter 8

A Safe Husband

After Henry's death, despite the fact that Marshal unseated and killed his horse on the field of battle, Richard confirmed his father's offer of marriage to Isabel. Roger of Howden noted that the new king, despite his own rebellions against his father, retained the service of the men who remained loyal to Henry II. Marshal's allegiance to both the Young King and to King Henry II was well attested. Eleanor of Aquitaine, in whose household William first served, was known to be fond of him. In confirming his father's decision to allow Marshal to marry Isabel, Richard was taking the necessary steps to ensure that Marshal transferred his loyalties to him.

As soon as William received written confirmation of King Richard's permission to claim his bride as well as a letter from his new master for Queen Eleanor and orders for her release, Marshal rode north. He stopped to take possession of Longueville which was part of the Giffard lordship which Richard transferred to William for a fee of 2,000 marks[1] at the same time as granting permission for him to marry. It was part of the inheritance Henry II withheld from Strongbow in 1164 and signalled Marshal's intention of consolidating Isabel's patrimony.

From Dieppe, where in his haste to board the boat the knight slipped from the gangplank, Marshal crossed the Channel. He spurred his horse to Winchester where he met with Eleanor who had already been released from the captivity in which her husband placed her. Marshal also gave her the welcome news that she was to be Richard's regent in England until he arrived on its shores. Roger of Howden recorded that Eleanor moved quickly to secure her son's kingdom for him and to win over its nobility who knew little about their new master.

Marshal hurried to London, still covered in the dust from the road, to the home of Ranulf de Glanville. Travel stained and weary, he presented King Richard's writ permitting his marriage to Isabel. De Glanville was not convinced that it was anything more than a ruse to snatch a wealthy bride, so suddenly had authorisation been granted. He did not want to risk rousing the king's wrath by losing a valuable asset. He must have realised his role as Eleanor's goaler during her long imprisonment already inclined the king to disfavour him. Eventually de Glanville was persuaded and Marshal was able to lay out his plans for a speedy wedding.

Richard FitzReiner, who was Henry II's financial agent in London as well as its sheriff since 1187, provided a warm welcome and accommodation for the groom at his own home in Cheapside. He was even persuaded to lend his friend enough money to pay for the nuptials since Marshal had little of his own. The course of a betrothal and subsequent wedding might, in most instances, have included a discussion between the families of the bride and groom about a financial settlement. A woman was expected to bring a dowry with her when she married that usually reflected her share of any inheritance. It was anticipated that she would bring valuables and household goods as well. In return the groom would provide a dower for his bride, that was hers for her lifetime in the event of her new spouse dying before her. Marshal was the fourth son of an unimportant knight. He inherited nothing from his own father's patrimony and the lands he was gifted by King Henry II were not extensive. It was not a match of equals so the formalities were different on this occasion. By the terms of Marshal's will, Isabel was dowered with the estates that were hers by right of birth and which she had brought to her husband when she married him. There is no existing record of a betrothal ceremony or any of the legal agreements before the wedding took place. The *Histoire* makes it clear that the knight had no intention of losing the right to marry Isabel. As the sole heir to her father's estates and titles, the Countess of Striguil's marriage turned William Marshal into one of the richest men in the kingdom.

On the morning of her marriage, without yet having met her intended husband, Isabel bathed and washed her hair with scented water. Her ladies helped her into a fine linen chemise over which she wore a figure hugging bliaut with a full pleated skirt and sleeves which were tight to the elbow before the fabric flared out to her wrists. The bliaut was laced either at the side or the back and was belted at the waist. Since it was summer Isabel is unlikely to have worn fine furs but sable, ermine and even squirrel fur, known as miniver, were fashionable at the time. Isabel wore her hair flowing over her shoulders. It was symbolic of her femininity and her virtue. She might have worn a chaplet of flowers for the occasion. Once a married woman she would have kept her hair hidden beneath a wimple since a woman's hair also symbolised promiscuity. The only females who appeared in public with their hair uncovered were either brides or prostitutes. In the medieval world it was only one short step from virtue to vice.

William, freshly shaved, and dressed in his best tunic, hose and cloak, collected his young bride from the Tower of London where she was then resident. Isabel's first sight of her husband to be was of a professional soldier in his early forties, possibly scarred from his many encounters on the tournament field and in the service of the Plantagenets. He was burned brown from the time he spent outdoors training and on campaign. In his turn, he saw a fashionably dressed young woman with a pale complexion and her father's reddish gold hair and, perhaps, grey eyes. Although she was curious about him, manners dictated that Isabel remember to maintain a demure and serious expression when she was introduced to the man who was about to become her husband. She did not want him to think she was forward or frivolous. She must have wondered what kind of man he would prove to be, how much independence she would be permitted and whether she would soon return to the Welsh Marches and her childhood home at Striguil.

Prior to the twelfth century, literature did not describe standards of feminine beauty but by 1210 men like Geoffrey de Vinsauf, a noted rhetorician, were creating written expressions of the ideal of loveliness. Beauty criteria for women included long hair, a neck like an elegant column and long, thin white hands. Aristocratic ladies were expected to have milky complexions since they were not required to labour in the sun. Some females resorted to regular bleeding to achieve the correct pallor. There were also various recipes that some women applied to their faces to lighten their complexion. Typically, the most innocuous contained egg whites or even ground lily roots; others were more toxic involving the application of lead paste as a skin whitener. Fortunately for Isabel, light hair was in fashion but high foreheads were considered to be beautiful so many women plucked their hairlines. Slenderness was admired but plumpness, associated with good food, was a better indicator of a lady's status in society. *Le Roman de la Rose*, a medieval poem written in about 1230, by Guilaume de Lorris was able to create a personification of beauty recognisable to his readers.

Introductions complete it is likely that the couple went to St Paul's Cathedral which was near FitzReiner's residence where they were married. Marshal was fortunate that he was granted permission to marry in July. There were certain times of the year when the Church prohibited weddings including Advent and Lent because sex, even between married couples, was proscribed as sinful at those times. The countess was somewhere between 16 and 18-years old when they married and Marshal was more than 42. No one asked Isabel what she thought about the union. Norman society demanded filial obedience to the head of the household – in Isabel's case as a ward of the Crown this was the king. Love, desire or even liking had nothing to do with the marriage of an heiress. It was sufficient that she would do her duty to her husband and provide him with heirs although the Church took the view that a marriage was only valid if a couple gave their free consent to a union. Few elite women of the period had any real choice as to who they would marry or an opportunity to build a relationship before the wedding unless theirs was a cradle marriage which gave the couple the opportunity to grow up together in the same household. Little thought was given to the compatibility of the bride and groom. Marriages were made for the political and financial benefit of the men and the families who arranged them.

Isabel made her marriage vows in front of witnesses standing at the door of St Paul's Cathedral although with so many medieval churches in London it is impossible to be completely sure. Witnesses were not necessary for a marriage to be valid but Marshal would have wished to ensure that the king could not change his mind at a later date and arrange for the union to be annulled. A priest officiated at the wedding adding an extra layer of validity to the event. The preliminaries to the exchange of vows included a confirmation that both parties were of an age to be married, that they were not related within any of the forbidden degrees of consanguinity and that they both gave their free consent to the union. It was important that Isabel and Marshal were not related by blood or through the marriages of their extended family networks. Consanguinity and affinity within four degrees of kinship, counting back up the respective family trees of the bride and groom would have required a papal dispensation if a common ancestor was found. Canon law for medieval marriage was still evolving. It was only in 1215 at the Fourth Lateran Council that marriage became a holy sacrament and adopted the need for banns to be called three weeks prior to the wedding ceremony, although even then they were not a legal requirement for a marriage to be valid. It was sufficient for a man and woman to exchange vows that they intended to marry one another.

The same council described a ceremony which included the exchange of rings and an injunction against men presenting a ring to a woman unless they intended marriage. It cannot be certain that Isabel received a wedding ring from her husband. Classical cultures adopted the tradition of giving rings and since it was believed that the fourth finger of the left hand contained a vein that led to the heart the Romans wore wedding rings on their ring finger. Although there are various contemporary medieval tales involving wedding rings and even court cases testing the validity of marriages that involve witness statements attesting to the exchange of rings during the interchange of vows there is no account of Isabel receiving a ring from Marshal. It is only during the later medieval period that the giving of precious rings as love tokens or as symbolic of marriage is more substantially evidenced.[2] If Isabel did receive a wedding ring, it may have been one belonging to her own mother as it is assumed that such rings were often reused within a family. Rather than a plain gold band it may have been adorned with precious gems many of which were regarded as having their own beneficial medical properties and protective powers. The notion was one derived from the Ancient Greeks and grounded in the medical beliefs of the time. Some stones were more suitable than others for a wedding band. Sapphires, for instance, were said to douse the flames of passion while a pearl was symbolic of fertility.

After Isabel and her new husband exchanged their vows, they entered the cathedral to hear a celebratory Mass. Marshal is also likely to have arranged to give alms to the poor as an act of thanksgiving. Afterwards the couple returned to FitzReiner's home where they celebrated their wedding with a feast. The meal was an important part of the marriage but since neither Marshal nor FitzReiner's household had time to organise its preparation, it was not as lavish as some documented banquets, including for example the feast celebrating the marriage of Henry III's daughter Margaret to Alexander III of Scotland in 1251 that took five months to prepare.[3] FitzReiner's servants had cleaned the hall, decorated it with tapestries and hangings, and hurried to the market and purchased what was available for a meal which would be remembered if it was insufficiently splendid. William FitzStephen, a Londoner, described the capital in the late twelfth century. He said that everything was at hand including exotic spices.

As Isabel, sitting next to her husband, looked around the assembled gathering, she recognised the justiciar Ranulf de Glanville, FitzReiner, and other influential Londoners. She also began identifying faces from within her new husband's household who would become very familiar to her over the coming years. John d'Earley who was a similar age to her. He was William's squire and would be an important part of the household for the rest of their lives. Today he stood behind his master carving the meat, serving food and wine.

At the end of the evening's entertainment a priest blessed the bed, in the hope that the union would prove fertile, and Isabel's female companions prepared her for her marriage night. Isabel's clothes were removed, her hair brushed and she was put into bed where she was given a spiced wine to drink. Bedding rituals were another important part of the wedding. Usually, the groom's friends, having enjoyed the feast, put him into bed beside his bride and then toasted the couple amid singing and bawdy jokes. The room was often full of drunken wedding guests. The curtains were drawn around the bed, the symbolism of the bedding having been witnessed and the couple were finally left alone. Alternatively, Marshal, a chivalrous knight, might have preferred a more private start to married life.

Marshal knew that until such time that the union was consummated, the wedding was not complete even though vows were exchanged. Marriage was regarded as validated in two parts: through verbal consent and physical consummation. Without the act of physical lovemaking there were grounds for annulment. In addition, William only retained a life interest in his wife's inheritance subject to Isabel's survival and the birth of at least one child, even if it only lived for a few minutes, which would allow him full possession of the countess's estates in his own right even after her death. Otherwise, Strongbow's titles, lands and castles would revert to his collateral heirs, in this case the senior branch of the de Clare family, and Marshal would be left with nothing.

A carnal marriage based on desire or a union grounded in love was neither expected nor desirable throughout the medieval period and beyond. Instead, the Church taught that affection binding a couple was to be looked-for but not essential. Intercourse, an essential part of married life, was recognised as marital debt. The idea of husbands and wives being entitled to sex with one another arose from St Paul's instruction in 1 Corinthians 7:3-4. Congress for the procreation of children and in payment of marriage debt was without wickedness. In all other cases lust and carnal knowledge were regarded as sinful. The Church laid down other rules including the need for abstinence at certain times of the year: during fasting days; when a woman was deemed unclean during menstruation; or while she was pregnant and for forty days after she gave birth. If either Isabel or Marshal refused one another sex at other times, or even during prohibited occasions, it was a matter that required confession. None of this meant that sexual activity was to be regarded as a pleasure. Thinking lustful thoughts about a spouse was almost as sinful as adultery. Intercourse was for the begetting of children and for good health but not gratification. This raised some problems as medical opinion largely agreed that for conception to happen a woman needed to enjoy lovemaking.

Public theory and private realities are two very different things. It is impossible to understand how Isabel's relationship with her husband evolved or the complexity of their feelings for one another. Isabel was bound by a duty of wifely obedience to a stranger shortly after her first meeting with him. William Marshal was one of the most celebrated knights of the period. The *Histoire*, commissioned by his eldest son as a chronicle of William's life, expands on Marshal's career as a tournament knight as well as the rewards he garnered through loyalty to the Plantagenets, starting with service to Eleanor of Aquitaine. Henry's queen was credited with bringing the ideas of romantic love to her husband's court. He understood the concept of courtly love which placed an unattainable, and idealised, woman on a pedestal. It was an extension of the cult of the Virgin Mary which elevated women as the embodiment of purity and, grounded in the principles of self-restraint, had more to do with spiritual attainment than physical love. A man might love a woman who was unattainable and dedicate his chivalric deeds to her without hope of recognition or reciprocation. It was more normal for the object of the courtly lover's desire to be someone else's wife. It would have been unusual for a knight to dedicate himself to his own wife. Courtly love, as understood by the fashionable society in which Isabel and Marshal moved, held that the devotion of a knight for his lady was not possible for a married couple. The rationale was that sentimental love and the affection between a married couple were mutually exclusive. The kind of love described by troubadours was something to be found outside the feudal requirements of landed and political interest.

William was a practical man but played the role of courtly knight because it was expected of him. He might even have been rather too good at it. As well as being a champion tournament knight he was known for his courtesy, generosity of spirit and kindness. As a young man, if such things had existed then, he was something of a pin-up. His success and popularity made other men jealous. In 1180, Marshal was accused of exceeding the bounds of courtly love by taking Prince Henry's wife, Margaret of France, as his lover. The scandal reached its peak during the Christmas of 1182 when Marshal appeared in front of King Henry II and demanded the right to trial by combat to prove his innocence, against not one but three of his accusers, in order to prove that he was indeed a chivalric knight though Margaret was no Guinevere.

It is very likely that Marshal treated his new bride with the habitual humility and courtesy of a chivalric lover. It was, after all, the form of courtship with which he was most familiar. He also recognised that theirs was not a marriage of equals. Marriage might have made Isabel subordinate to Marshal but it was her wealth and status which elevated him to a comital rank.

In addition, Isabel's husband was known to be a pious man. Matrimony was a contract but it was also a sacrament. It was only in 1215, at the Fourth Lateran Council that the Church enshrined the idea of the union of a man and a woman imparting divine grace. Prior to that date, earlier theologians including St Augustine described it as a sacrament while St Paul entitled it a great mystery. He added that it was better to wed than to commit sin but it was a second best to celibacy. Marshal had no known mistresses after his marriage to Isabel. It would seem that Isabel married a virtuous man for whom love was part of honourable nobility.

After the wedding celebrations there was a brief opportunity for the couple to become better acquainted with one another before Marshal returned to the service of the king. One of the knight's friends, Enguerrand d'Abernon, leant the newlyweds his home at Stoke d'Abernon in Surrey.[4] The *Histoire* noted that it was a quiet and pleasant place. D'Abernon had his own links with the senior line of the de Clares being one of their major tenants in Surrey and in Kent. During lazy summer afternoons Isabel and William may have considered what the future held for them.

Isabel's wedding to Marshal did not legally deprive her of her father's estates scattered across Richard's realm and in Ireland where John was the feudal overlord. However, she would have been exceptionally strong minded, not to mention politically powerful, to wield independent control over her domain as the State and the Church regarded women as emotionally, morally and intellectually inferior to men. William became the holder of Isabel's titles and estates, *jure uxoris*, by virtue of his marriage.

In theory Isabel's life would be restricted to a domestic role under the protection, and in the shadow, of her husband. During her marriage to King Henry II, Eleanor of Aquitaine a woman known for her intellect and strong will was mentioned only sporadically in the chronicles of the period before her sons Richard and John each became king in their turn. There are only sixty-six known charters issued by Eleanor in her capacity as duchess prior to 1189 but many more recorded during her widowhood.[5] For the first thirteen years of her married life to Henry II she was almost constantly pregnant and besides which Henry II had no intention of anyone besides himself determining how his realm should be administered. His domination of politics was one of the reasons his own sons revolted against him. Eleanor's situation was not unique. Documented evidence across the social spectrum demonstrates that widows had greater agency than married women throughout the medieval period.

Marshal proved to be an exceptional husband. He was not required to give his young bride an overt administrative role in the management of the estates which were her birthright but he chose to recognise the debt that he owed her by working in partnership with Isabel in matters of writs and charters. Although he was sometimes described in official records as an earl during Richard's reign it was a courtesy and nothing more. He signed his charters plain William Marshal. It was his wife who was the Countess of Striguil. What evolved in the case of Isabel and William's marriage was a union that combined a business partnership and love. Isabel in her turn was pleased to have a personal seal which bore the legend '*uxor*'; wife.

On 13 August, the king and his brother, John, arrived at Portsmouth and journeyed from there to Winchester where they were reunited with their mother. Isabel and Marshal began to consolidate their possessions and look to the future. On 29 August John was to be married to Isabel of Gloucester, at Marlborough. The castle there had once been held by William's father John but which was lost to the family in 1158 when King Henry II alienated it and the manor of Wexcombe returning both into the custody of the Crown. Territorial ambitions aside, Isabel and Marshal recognised that the union between John and Robert of Gloucester's granddaughter turned the prince into an important landowner on the Marches. Overnight he was turned into their neighbour. And with Richard intent upon taking the cross, his brother was likely to be a powerful influence in the coming years. The king also gave his brother the county of Mortain as well as the earldom of Cornwall among a clutch of other important honours that strengthened the new count's political hand.

Of more immediate importance, was the news that John was given the honour of Lancaster. It meant that Isabel's husband, not only became Prince John's vassal for the lands that he held in Leinster *jure uxoris* but also for the land which he held in his own right in Cartmel. The occasion of his oath giving was an opportunity for Marshal to begin discussions about Leinster. As Lord of Ireland, John should have held Strongbow's fief on Isabel's behalf and handed it back to Marshal when he married Isabel. The prince was disinclined to return the fief and, besides which, he had made substantial grants out of the estate to his own followers. When negotiations stalled, Marshal asked the king to intercede on his and Isabel's behalf. John finally, reluctantly, returned the fief to Strongbow's heir but insisted that the estates which he had already given away remain in the hands of their new custodians.

By the beginning of September, Isabel was back in London. Roger of Howden described 'a vast multitude of knights,'[6] nobility and churchmen who descended on England's capital. The streets thronged with men and women. For Isabel it was a chance to meet with kin and to become acquainted with the wives and daughters of the realm's elite. On 1 September the king and his mother rode through the capital's streets which were hung with tapestries. William and Isabel were among the nobility who escorted them to St Paul's Cathedral and from there to the palace at Westminster.

King Richard I's coronation took place two days later at Westminster Abbey. His magnificent crowning ceremony, chronicled by Roger of Howden, would be the model for English coronations for generations to come. Marshal, described as 'Earl of Striguil'[7] carried the king's sceptre and his elder brother John Marshal also played a role in events but Isabel was not there to witness them or the evil omen presented by a bat which flew around the king's head. Women, excepting the king's mother and her attendants, and Jews were prohibited from attending the investiture. Marshal and his brother attended the lavish festivities which followed the coronation. The celebrations lasted for three days but because Richard was unmarried there were no women present to enjoy the king's hospitality, not even Eleanor of Aquitaine. There is no record of whether the wives and daughters of the king's barons joined with the king's mother for their own celebrations. It is certain that Isabel, Countess of Striguil, made the acquaintance of Eleanor during this period.

On 17 September, or soon afterwards, Isabel learned that her former guardian, Ranulf de Glanville, had been summoned before the king, pardoned for releasing Eleanor of Aquitaine without direct orders but that he had been dismissed from the post of justiciar. De Glanville's misfortune did not end there even though Eleanor sought no vengeance for her long incarceration. The king imprisoned him until such time as he paid a ransom of more than £1000 for his release. The men who replaced him as co-justiciars were the Bishop of Durham and William de Mandeville, 3rd Earl of Essex who, like Marshal, had remained loyal to King Henry II until his death. De Mandeville did not have long to enjoy his promotion. He died two months later in Normandy.

In the weeks that followed, King Richard I, whose plans for joining the Third Crusade were underway, created William Marshal as one of many associate justiciars[8] to support two senior co-justiciars to oversee England in his absence. Isabel, at 18-years of age, was wife to one of the most important men in the realm. Marshal remained with the king while Richard prepared to join the Third Crusade. William's brother John Marshal was also present. He was appointed the king's chief escheator in England, the estates at Wexcombe were returned to him and he assumed the shrievalty of Yorkshire resigned by Randulf de Glanville. John's new post, in addition to the hereditary title of king's marshal, meant that he was responsible for overseeing the lands of men who died without adult heirs or with no heirs at all. For Isabel it was an opportunity to learn more about her new husband's extended family, to become better acquainted with the wives and daughters of the men who would be at the heart of government in Richard's absence and perhaps, if Aoife was resident in one of her Essex or Hertfordshire dower manors, to spend some time in her mother's company.

Chapter 9

Wife and Chatelaine

While Isabel was in London, she had occasion to ensure that both herself and her husband were dressed according to their rank. Marshal's clothing was largely functional but Isabel recognised that what they wore was an indicator of their status and wealth. Richard I's Pipe Roll for 1189 includes an account of £9 12s 1d[1] (approximately £14,000 in November 2022) for new clothes provided at the king's expense for the daughter of Richard de Clare. Given that William claimed Isabel as his wife with no notice, it is probable that the royal gift was made in the autumn of that year. Isabel visited Cheapside, the heart of London's mercantile community, where she bought lawn and linen for shifts, fine silks, woollens and furs.

She was able to afford woollen fabrics dyed with vivid colours including scarlet, green and blue. Men intending on joining the Third Crusade were prohibited from wearing fashionable miniver and sable or cloth dyed crimson but Isabel's winter mantle was lined with fur to keep the cold out. She may have chosen Flemish cloth for gowns destined for everyday wear. The wool came from England but was woven in Flanders. It was known to be exceptionally good quality. Gloves and belts, essential for a countess, were often decorated with embroidery. Fine veils were also selected to wear over her wimple. Her expensive clothing made the statement that Isabel was the Countess of Striguil. She might have been legally hidden in the shadow of her new husband by the patriarchal society in which she lived but that did not mean that she was unable to make a statement about her rank or wealth; both of which equated to power and influence.

Isabel's personal seal, a plaster cast of which is held at the British Museum, depicts her wearing a tight-fitting dress, which was fashionable at the time of her marriage but by the time of her death had been replaced with looser attire; a long mantle and a pointed wimple. Both the earlier and later dress fashions with which Isabel was familiar dictated that a woman's arms were respectably covered.

On a more practical level the Countess of Striguil's identity lay in her function as wife and landowner. During the twelfth and thirteenth centuries the role and status of a noblewoman revolved around the efficiency with which she ran her household. In Marshal's absence in service to the king, Isabel was expected to run their estates and defend their domain. It was essential for her to have a thorough knowledge of her territories and to be able to work in partnership with a trustworthy steward. She needed an understanding of the feudal laws and dues associated with medieval manors and manor courts in order to administer justice to her tenants and serfs, deal with crimes and legal disputes, and access the resources to which she was entitled. If the monarch levied a feudal tax on her domains, the countess needed to know the amount she owed and for what she was paying. Together with her stewards, it was her responsibility to raise the required funds. It was her duty to ensure that her estates were both productive and economically stable. And, as an aristocratic woman with a lordship in the Marches, she was required to be able to defend her possessions should the need arise even though men like Ralph Bloet were official castellans. During times of war, it was Isabel who ensured that Marshal and his men were outfitted and provisioned. If her husband was so unfortunate as to be captured by his enemies it was Isabel's charge to raise the ransom demanded in return for his freedom. In the event of his death, it would be her responsibility to care for any children they might have besides an heir who would become the ward of the king.

Much can be learned about the household management skills required of a countess from the account book of Isabel's daughter-in-law Eleanor, Countess of Leicester or her granddaughter, Joan de Valence and from later books containing advice for ladies with large households. Robert Grosseteste, Bishop of Lincoln drew up a list of rules in 1240 so that the recently widowed Margaret, Countess of Lincoln could govern her household efficiently. Two centuries later, Christine de Pisan, the widow of a French nobleman, set down a list of skills that women like Isabel needed and what should concern her in *The Treasure of the City of Ladies*. The accounts and the bishop's regulations together with books like Christine de Pisan's provide useful insights. The daily rhythms of Isabel's life were not so different from the lives of other aristocratic women throughout the medieval period.

It was Isabel's responsibility to oversee her own household, manage its finances and ensure that her army of servants were both virtuous and sober. It was easier said than done since the management of a baronial household included oversight of bakehouses, brewhouses and dairies as well as the kitchen and the laundry. She was expected to understand the process by which linen was cleaned, bread was baked, and how ale was brewed. She also needed to know how butter was churned and cheese made, how meat and fish were preserved and salted, and how herbs and fruit were grown, prepared and best used. It is very likely that Aoife shared the skills that she herself was required to learn as a child in order to be a competent wife in Ireland which including dyeing, spinning and weaving. Isabel was expected to be able to sew her clothes, to decorate garments and other belongings with embroidery, and to stitch altar cloths and vestments as an outward demonstration of her own piety.

Aided by the steward, Isabel knew which estates yielded which crops, how her flocks of sheep and herds of cattle should best be managed, the production and sale of wool and meat, and quarrying and timber management. She knew the calendar of the farming year; the use of ponds to farm fish, and the value of her warrens and the best places to site them. Her house-keeping included overseeing the management of supplies from her own estates and their distribution around her domains in a timely fashion. Other necessities, that could not be harvested from her estates, had to be purchased well in advance of when they were needed. Her scribes needed vellum, and linen and wool cloth was required not only for her family's clothes but also for her servants' liveries and for those of Marshal's *mesnie*. Candles were another essential as was salt which was needed to preserve meat.

Given her wealth, Isabel's household also enjoyed foods flavoured with herbs and spices from the Middle East and Africa. The countess could afford saffron, cloves, pepper, ginger and cinnamon. When the Countess of Striguil's cooks were called upon to provide food for her guests they were able to produce aromatic tasty dishes, accompanied by spiced wine, that demonstrated the wealth and power of the family. Laying in stores was not just a matter of keeping a household clothed and fed. The commodities that Isabel purchased and the way they were presented were reflective of social status and power.

As well as catering, a medieval woman was expected to have a basic understanding of medicine: to grow and prepare herbs; to be able to treat common ailments; sooth scalds and burns; set broken bones; and stitch and bind wounds. Isabel may have employed an apothecary or consulted, on occasion, with either a doctor or a local monastic infirmarian but knowledge about medicinal plants and the best kinds of food to eat to treat specific ailments was a housewifely duty. Herbs were also a source of sweet smells as well as fungal or insect repellents. Common Fleabane, for instance, which is found throughout England and Wales could be used as a fumigant once it was dried or hung in bunches to keep fleas away. Rosewater, in a household of comital status, was another essential at mealtimes. It was used to wash hands during feasts and was also the basis of a perfume.

A well-run household was a regimented one with set times for attending divine service and eating meals. Dinner was at 11 am during the thirteenth century, supper at 6 pm. Sweetmeats and spiced wines were readily available for guests. During feasts, Isabel oversaw the seating arrangements that placed her and Marshal at one end of the great hall with their guests in descending order of rank on either side of them. Trestle tables placed down two sides of the hall accommodated everyone else, also in descending order of importance. It was Marshal's task to supervise the pages and squires who held the basins filled with rose water, and other aromatics, so that their most honoured guests could wash their hands. As well as servants, squires and pages were required to bring each dish to table and present it before carving if required. They also acted as cupbearers. Isabel was expected to help teach Marshal's wards, pages and squires, good manners and courtesy as well as helping them to acquire courtly refinements such as playing a musical instrument and dancing.

Cleanliness and hygiene were another imperative. Even the whitewash that was used on the walls to kill off bacteria, because of its lime content needed to be reapplied regularly. Isabel ensured that the floors of the important chambers, the solar and the great hall, were kept covered with sweet smelling herbs and grasses that deterred vermin and, when it was fresh, provided a pleasing fragrance. She may have preferred woven rush mats which were more expensive. Both types needed to be replaced seasonally. Garderobes, or toilets, needed to be maintained. Often, waste emptied down a chute directly into the moat. Other latrine shafts emptied into a pit or chamber which needed to be emptied regularly and even moats, had on occasion, to be dredged and cleared. The business left the smell of sewerage throughout the castle. Isabel, having made her plans, moved her household to another residence and gave orders for the dwelling from which she departed to be thoroughly sweetened. At least in Striguil, some of the garderobes emptied over the cliff into the River Wye below.

Isabel's diverse duties did not end with the physical wellbeing and comfort of her family and household. Their spiritual wellbeing was also her business. It was for this reason that great households had rules restricting gambling to the Yuletide festivities and required servants to be sober, industrious and clean living. Society required the countess to lead by example. Records show that her household had its own chaplain to lead divine service; to hear the household's confessions and to provide spiritual counsel. He also assisted with the spiritual education of Isabel's children. The countess, a woman of faith like the rest of the society in which she lived, provided a visible display of piety for the men and women who looked up to her as well as for the benefit of her own soul. She attended mass at least once every day along with her household as well as celebrating all the important festivals of the church calendar.

Giving alms to care for the sick and the needy was an important part of Christian duty and baronial households fulfilled this with daily gifts of food. A servant known as an almoner, who was in official charge of charitable giving, collected anything left over from meals including the trenchers made from bread that served as plates to feed paupers who assembled at the castle gates. Money might also be given to provide food and care for the poor and the sick. As well as daily charitable offerings it was also usual to provide alms to celebrate weddings, births and to commemorate the dead. Open-handedness might also include the care of elderly servants as well as the widows and orphans of the men and women under Isabel's charge.

It was Isabel's day-to-day task, even though she was a countess, to ensure that her husband, their family, their household and the *mesnie* of knights who followed Marshal had everything that was required from food to footwear. To achieve this, she oversaw the work of an army of servants, labourers and tenants. Aoife's education of her daughter and the time spent under the guardianship of Ranulf de Glanville equipped Isabel with the management skills necessary to supervise stewards and bailiffs as well as household servants, and to be able to oversee the accounts. Living with William, she also learned about generosity of spirit and being at ease with people. As a feudal overlord and domestic manager, Isabel learned that she could not simply impose her will upon her servants and tenants. She had a duty of care towards them in exactly the same way that they were obliged to serve her.

As chatelaine, Isabel was both seneschal and quartermaster making use of the services of a clerk, named Walter, to keep track of everything. Unfortunately, it is often difficult to find surviving documentary evidence specific to Isabel's management of domestic matters. Her presence can be discerned in charters and gifts to monastic houses but, more often than not, it was William's signature and seal that attested to the authenticity of the transaction. Even so, like many of her female predecessors she was in possession of her own seal. De Clare women used their seals to show their ancestry and status. Interestingly their seals often depicted their matrilineal descent.[2] Isabel's seal depicts a full-length figure of a woman holding a falcon by its jesses in her left hand. The bird, a popular choice of design for elite females[3], is symbolic of Isabel's status but may also have been a chosen because Ireland was a source of birds of prey viewed by falconers as being the very best. Existing fourteenth-century records held at Kilkenny Castle show that raptors were used for payment of rents. The depiction of a woman with a bird of prey may also have been a frequent choice during the thirteenth century for women's seals, perhaps because of their active participation in the sport.[4]

De Pisan's writing, from which she earned a living, was critical of the patriarchal system. Even so, she emphasises the complimentary nature of a marriage partnership. It is worth remembering that the banners that flew at Striguil and wherever the countess was in residence depicted the de Clare three chevrons *gules* (red) on a field *or* (gold) as well as Marshal's rampant lion gules on a field per pale (divided vertically in two) of *vert* (green) and *or*.

Isabel's marriage to William Marshal secured her inheritance for the next generation. He began the business of administering the estates he gained by right of his wife at the same time as helping to prepare the realm and an army for the forthcoming crusade. Ralph Bloet, whose father Walter held Usk for Strongbow and was the castellan of Striguil before Isabel's marriage, transferred his service to the new earl and continued in his role at Chepstow. Isabel knew his family from her own childhood. He died in around 1199 but his son, also named Ralph, continued to serve the Marshal family.

It was Bloet who oversaw Marshal's plans for the rebuilding of the castle when Isabel's husband began the process of upgrading the fortifications there. Striguil, was the *caput* of Marshal's new lordship. Dendrochronology demonstrates that the huge and intimidating gatehouse doors, which can still be viewed, date from this period.[5] The name Chepstow was first recorded in 1306 and is likely to have referred to the town with its bustling market rather than the castle which was known as Striguil in the Domesday Book of 1087.[6] The reference to the market is an indication of the way that Marshal and Isabel developed the commerce of their lordships both in the Marches of Wales and later in Ireland.

The honour of Striguil included land in nine counties and the manors of Weston in Hertfordshire, Chersterford in Essex and Badgeworth in Gloucestershire. Part of these holdings were among Aoife's dower lands. In addition, Marshal found himself holding Usk Castle, its town and estates between the rivers Wye and Usk. The lordship of Leinster included Kildare, Kilkenny, Wexford and Carlow. As well as extensive lands in the Marches and in Ireland, Isabel retained a claim to the earldom of Pembroke by right of her grandfather Earl Gilbert. For the moment, Isabel was the daughter and granddaughter of an earl but her husband remained plain William Marshal although men like Roger of Howden called him the earl or lord of Striguil as a matter of courtesy.

Marshal's new position as a landowner meant that he needed to expand his household to assist with the administration of Isabel's estates, especially if he was expected to achieve the tasks that the king asked of him. He was often at court following the coronation as evidenced by the 109 charters he attested to, from September 1189 to April 1190.[7] In the years immediately following his marriage William's household expanded to include a chaplain, an almoner and five clerks[8] so great was the administrative load which he took on as a landowner and servant of the Crown. He also had a chamberlain named Walter Cut who was responsible for receiving funds and paying out money. The revenues and income from Isabel's estates as well as the fees resulting from Marshal's new administrative roles passed through Cut's hands. Richard I's Pipe Roll for 1189-1190 shows that despite the knight's new-found wealth that he was heavily in debt to the crown for £1,460.[9] This was accrued because Marshal was allowed to purchase Isabel's half of the honour of Giffard, the wardship of Elias Giffard, and the shrievalty of Gloucester.[10] The Pipe Rolls of 1193 show that Marshal was excused payment of 500 marks and had finished paying the fine for Isabel's Giffard inheritance. A record in the Pipe Roll dating from 1203 indicated Elias was in arrears for scutage owed from Richard's reign but a note was added to the effect that the boy was in his custody and had a writ acquitting him from the debt signed by Geoffrey FitzPeter, 1st Earl of Essex who served in various posts under the Plantagenet kings including as a justiciar during Richard's absence on crusade.[11]

Fortune, and King Richard I, favoured Marshal who continued to call himself plain William Marshal. His recognition of all he owed to Isabel is reflected in his description of his wife as a countess. She was the daughter of Aoife, the Irish Countess and her husband Earl Richard de Clare, Lord of Leinster and Netherwent. It was an expression of the courtesy and respect with which he treated her throughout the rest of his life.

Chapter 10

Motherhood

Following the death of William de Mandeville, a mere two months after his appointment as co-justiciar alongside Hugh du Puisset, Bishop of Durham, the king assigned his chancellor, William Longchamp, Bishop of Ely to the post. He also gave him custody of the Tower of London and the royal seal. The two bishops did not work together harmoniously, so in March 1190 Richard changed the terms of their offices, giving du Puisset, who already held Windsor Castle on behalf of the king, jurisdiction north of the Humber as well as permitting him to hold Bamburgh Castle as Earl of Northumberland. Longchamp became justiciar for the rest of England. With hindsight, Longchamp's selection was a poor choice but the records showing the attestation of charters from 1189 to the spring of 1190 suggest that the bishop and the other men who Richard chose to govern the realm in his absence worked well together.

On 11 December 1189, King Richard crossed from Dover to Calais. The bishops of Durham and Ely remained in England in their capacity of chief justiciaries but Marshal was with the king. Isabel was beside her husband. It was the first time she crossed the Narrow Seas or visited Normandy. For many women the most common reason to travel was to make a pilgrimage to a local shrine or to somewhere further afield like Walsingham or Canterbury to visit the shrine of Thomas Becket who was canonised within three years of his death. Travelling long distances was something that required careful planning and must have been associated with physical discomfort. Isabel might have ridden, travelled by carriage or used a litter. By the seventeenth century carriages had turned into the coach with chain or leather strap suspension and improved methods of harnessing and driving but suspension was a luxury not afforded to similar vehicles in the twelfth or thirteenth centuries. The equipage that medieval queens and other aristocratic ladies used were more akin to covered carts with curtains that could be pulled back so that the traveller could see out.[1] In order to keep the carriage moving a servant was responsible for greasing the wheels during long journeys. Not only was a carriage expensive to buy it was also costly to maintain. If Isabel and Marshal invested in one, Isabel made herself as comfortable as she could on a mattress and cushions and held on to a loop of cloth when the jolting over roads, that were narrow and rutted, became too great. Four wheeled vehicles, often dragged by a team of oxen, were an indicator of wealth but the un-sprung body on its iron rimmed wheels was not a comfortable conveyance. Carriages were relatively rare during Isabel's lifetime although she was wealthy enough to afford one if she chose. The more likely mode of transport was a litter. These were made from two long poles supporting a seat covered by a pod-like canopy. One horse was harnessed between the two poles in front of the seat while another followed behind. Although it did not jolt like a carriage, the litter rocked from side to side.

Crossing the Channel was fraught with its own difficulties. As well as the hazards of bad weather and shipwreck there was also the possibility of piracy. Nothing could disguise the roll of the vessel, the ingress of water in winter, boiling heat during the summer months, or the stench of vomit and other bodily fluids. Jean de Joinville who was born in 1224 described the perils of a sea crossing, 'for at night you fall asleep without knowing whether you will find yourself the next morning at the bottom of the sea'.[2] It would have been easier to leave Isabel in England either with her mother or at another of the couple's estates. Isabel, who conceived soon after her marriage to William, was pregnant with their first child. Expectant women were advised not to travel for fear of a miscarriage caused by the rigours of the journey. Physicians feared that embryos might be shaken loose from the womb. As a first-time mother, she may not have known for sure that she was expecting a child until the baby quickened by which time her pregnancy was already at between seventeen and twenty-two weeks but if her child was born in the spring of 1190, she and William decided that they wanted to be close to one another despite the associated risks.

Women and their unborn infants were in God's hands throughout pregnancy and childbirth. Gynaecology was based on the works of Galen and Aristotle but practical understanding was a feminine preserve grounded in experience. Women were viewed as physically inferior copies of men. Aristotle explained that a man's seed imposed itself on menstrual blood and created an embryo. If the blood was fresh and the woman lay on her right immediately after intercourse a boy would result. If the blood was less fresh, a girl would be conceived. It was also believed that if a woman lay on her left that she would produce a girl. According to this theory, a woman was no more than a receptacle. Galen, whose principles were of longer standing in the west, believed that both partners contributed to the developing infant and that menstrual blood nourished the foetus in the womb. In either case the mother was regarded as a weak vessel who faced the pains of childbirth as atonement for Eve's original sin of tempting Adam with the apple in the Garden of Eden. Despite this, motherhood, and its associations with the Virgin Mary, was also regarded as a sacred duty as both a woman and an aristocratic wife. A legitimate heir was essential for the transmission of both estates and titles to the next generation.

The dangers of miscarriage were not to be underestimated. Isabel was told to avoid bitter foods and overly spicy dishes as well as pungent ones containing onions and garlic. Her ladies provided her with meals that were easy to digest and that were devoid of superstitious associations. For instance: eating fish heads during pregnancy would result in the child having a more pointed mouth than was usual; mustard might cause the child to be self-indulgent; an excess of alcohol resulted in clumsiness. If Isabel consulted with a doctor during her pregnancy, he might have recommended a diet designed to enhance the stability of mother and child; several small meals a day and moderate quantities of wine. Hot milk was sometimes recommended. Other foods, including pears and pomegranates, were recommended as a means of strengthening the stomach against the nausea associated with pregnancy.

Medieval physicians were well aware of the desire some pregnant women have for odd or even indigestible foods including unripe fruit or even coal. This was assigned to an imbalance of humours. Classical medicine, defined in the works of Galen, declared that the four humours were bodily fluids necessary for good health: blood, phlegm, yellow bile and black bile. Any excess or deficiency of the humours resulted in illness or extremes of behaviour. Each of the four humours was associated with temperature and humidity. Black bile, for instance, was defined as cold and dry. Women were naturally cold. It was believed a woman's genitals were the same as a man's penis and testicles but without the hot humours of masculinity they remained inside the body. If a woman failed to conceive it was because she was too cold. In order to be healthy a person required their humours to balance.

Intercourse during pregnancy was discouraged for fear that it might damage the development of the child and because the Church regarded it as a sin. William may have been advised to eat less meat in order change the balance of his own humours and avoid the temptations of the flesh during the time that Isabel was unavailable for lovemaking. Meanwhile, if her humours became too hot and moist, indicated by a fever or she had an overly flushed complexion, it was because Isabel was suffering from an excess of blood in her body. She was not to be bled to rebalance the humours until she was at least four months into her pregnancy. It was believed that embryos did not have souls until they quickened. Miscarriage was more likely during the time before a child's soul was formed. The *Trotula* explained that a woman should not be bled until the danger to her unborn child was passed.

It is unclear the extent to which Isabel accompanied Marshal to court during this period. Eleanor of Aquitaine was in Normandy from February 1190 while

Richard arrived at an agreement with King Philip II of France about their roles, rights and protection of their territories during the crusade. It is possible that Isabel joined the queen while her husband fulfilled his obligations to the king. She may have learned, at first hand, how fortunate she was to be married to a man she could respect, and love. Hawise, Countess of Aumale was widowed in November 1189. Like Isabel she was a countess in her own right and far too valuable to be left unmarried for long. The king arranged, against her wishes, that she marry William de Forz, a minor member of the aristocracy who was to command Richard's fleet. When the crusaders departed Hawise was pregnant with her son; rumour credited the king's brother as being the boy's father.

As her own pregnancy progressed, Isabel and her women, neighbours and friends, as well as the wives and daughters who travelled with Marshal's *mesnie* may have speculated about the likely sex of Isabel's child. As might happen today, popular wisdom decreed that a woman with a large, rounded belly was more likely to carry a boy than a girl because of the belief that a male was carried on the right side of the body. A woman with a flushed complexion was also regarded as more likely to have a son because the redness was associated with heat. Another indicator of a male heir was if the mother favoured her right foot when she took a step forward. As the months passed, and Isabel made herself at home in Longueville (the estate given by Richard I to Marshal and which was part of her own father's share of the Giffard inheritance), she prepared herself for the birth. More experienced women advised her about what she needed including clean linens to be made ready for her bed as well as swaddling clothes for the infant.

It was thought that a mother-to-be became increasingly overtired by the movements of the child in the womb and that any sudden jolting actions might cause a miscarriage. Best practice dictated that women remained immobile and calm as their pregnancy drew to a close. For this reason, a lying-in was recommended. It was not an essential of aristocratic childbirth before the fifteenth century.[3] If Isabel did go into seclusion on the occasion of the birth of her first child, she attended a special church service to ask for God's blessing and make her confession. For thirty days or thereabouts Isabel's world contracted to the chamber, the ladies who visited her there and the gossip they shared.

The room in which the countess gave birth was hung with tapestries to block out lights and draughts. Too much light was said to damage an expectant woman's eyes. The sight of a full moon could affect the baby and if anything startled the countess, it was thought that it would have an impact on either the child's physical or mental health. A fire burned in the hearth to keep the devil from flying down the chimney and stealing her child's soul. The warmth and the darkness of the room was almost like another womb. Cold was something to be avoided. Heat was required so that a healthy baby would develop. Balance was essential. A woman near the end of her pregnancy should not be too hot, it was believed that overheating could cause a premature birth. Being too cold could result in a difficult labour. It was usual to keep one small window open to permit some ventilation. The darkened room was filled with soft furnishings, warmth and the scent of soothing herbs and the chatter of women's voices.

Marshal was not permitted to visit his young wife. No man was allowed across the door's threshold. If a doctor was appointed, he remained outside passing instructions to the midwife and women on the other side of the closed door. If he wished to check the balance of Isabel's humours, a flask of urine was handed to him by one of her ladies so that he could assess its colour and taste it before offering advice. All Marshal could do was keep himself busy and pray. Childbirth was life threatening for both mother and child. It is estimated that one in every forty women died in childbirth throughout the medieval period into the Tudor and Stuart eras.[4] Aside from ties of affection, the knight knew that if Isabel and their child died before it was born, all the estates that he gained upon their marriage would revert to his wife's collateral heirs and he would be left with nothing.

When her labour started, Isabel may have been encouraged to sneeze in order to stimulate the process. Isabel is likely to have been given a religious icon, a cross or even an amulet to hold; Marshal may even have arranged to borrow a holy relic. Many monastic foundations professed to hold such items as the girdle of the Virgin Mary which could be borrowed and laid on a woman's belly while she gave birth. Such items were thought to ease the pain of labour because of Mary's painless delivery of Christ. If not a holy relic, Isabel may have been given a semi-precious stone to hold. Eaglestones, a kind of iron ore contained in a hollow geode creating a form akin to an embryo within the womb (and thought to be taken by eagles to their nests during the breeding season) were a popular choice. The women in the room with Isabel opened any cupboard doors and unlaced Isabel's gown and her hair to symbolise an opening up and encourage a speedy birthing process. Isabel and the women with her, prayed to the Virgin Mary, Saint Anne or Saint Margaret. All women were encouraged to accept the pains and perils of childbirth because the Church regarded childbirth as women's atonement for Eve's original sin. Even so, she was carefully tended by the women around her and opiates may have been available if required.

The midwife oversaw the preparations for Isabel's labour, the birth and aftercare. She was a trusted and respectable woman known to be skilled as

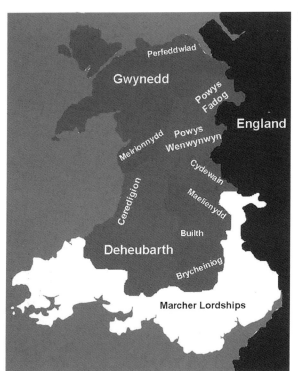

Principalities of Wales map. (*James Frankcom at English Wikipedia, CC BY-SA 3.0, via Wikimedia Commons*)

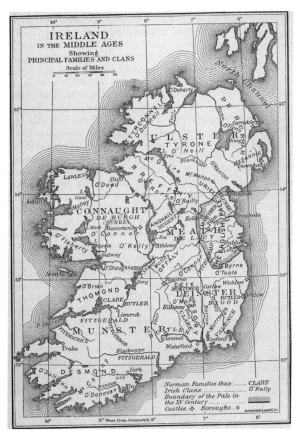

Ireland in the Middle Ages map, 1915 (*Internet Archive Book Images, no restrictions, via Wikimedia Commons*)

De Clare coat of arms, The Priory Church of St Mary, Usk. (*Photograph: Kyle Hewgill*)

Arms of William Marshal, 1st Earl of Pembroke. (*Zacwill16, CC BY-SA 4.0, via Wikimedia Commons*)

Effigy of Richard 'Strongbow' de Clare, Christ Church Cathedral, Dublin. (*Photograph: Sailko, CC BY 3.0, via Wikimedia Commons*)

Tintern Abbey. (*Photograph: Julia Hickey*)

Chepstow Castle, also known as Striguil Castle. (*Photograph: Julia Hickey*)

Chepstow Castle doors.
(*Photograph: Kyle Hewgill*)

Chepstow Castle keep. (*Photograph: Kyle Hewgill*)

Goodrich Castle. (*Photograph: Kyle Hewgill*)

Pembroke Castle. (*National Library of Wales, CC0, via Wikimedia Commons*)

Usk Castle. (*Photograph: Kyle Hewgill*)

Effigy of William Marshal, 1st Earl of Pembroke, Temple Church, London. (*Photograph: Adam Hewgill*)

Effigy of Gilbert Marshal, 4th Earl of Pembroke, Temple Church, London. (*Photograph: Rob Farrow, CC BY-SA 2.0, via Wikimedia Commons*)

Gilbert de Clare, 4th Earl of Hertford, 5th Earl of Gloucester, Tewkesbury Abbey. (*Photograph: Kyle Hewgill*)

De Clare Earls of Gloucester, Tewkesbury Abbey. (*Photograph: Kyle Hewgill*)

Llywelyn ap Iorwerth, St Mary's Church, Trefriw, Denbighshire. (*Photograph: Llywelyn2000, CC BY-SA 4.0, via Wikimedia Commons*)

Henry III's coronation, Gloucester Cathedral. (*Photograph: Kyle Hewgill*)

a midwife and with children of her own. It was expected that a midwife would have her own experiences of successful childbirth. It was her task to keep mother and child safe, or to deal with any unexpected complications. The woman may have been recommended by one of Isabel's extended kinship network or even by her Norman neighbours; she could even have been the mother of one of Marshal's *mesnie*. It is likely that the midwife was a woman of mature years, not tied to the care of her own family, able to stand almost as a mother to the woman in labour. Isabel's women and female relations also stayed with her throughout her labour, encouraging and supporting her as well as helping the midwife with practical tasks such as feeding Isabel, cleaning her after she gave birth and preparing the bath for her new child. In effect, all the women in the birthing chamber were part of an apprenticeship scheme that ensured a practical understanding of the parturition process.

At the time Isabel first became a mother, medical knowledge of female bodies was developing a better understanding of female needs. Information contained in books, arriving from university towns like Salerno, was often derived from Ancient Greek and Roman medicine but increasingly drew on the knowledge of the Arab world. *The Trotula*, a practical compendium specialising in women's health, was a text in three volumes written during the late eleventh and early twelfth centuries. The unknown author, Trota, who identified herself as a woman, advised encouraging labour at the end of pregnancy by the use of massage oils like laurel and linseed which stimulated the hot humours or to take a bath in water containing mallow, fenugreek and linseed.

The Trotula is regarded as the most important medieval text on female medicine. Its writer gave advice on everything from cosmetics to childbirth. The texts provided information about how to counterfeit virginity, the problems of infertility, skin complaints including symptoms of syphilis, and the difficulties of celibacy. Many of *The Trotula*'s treatments were based on Galen's principle of the four humours and the need for their balance. The remedies are often derived from herbs and the use of oils. After she gave birth, the midwife checked that the countess expelled the placenta; instructions for its removal ranged from a midwife using her fingernails to fumigating the new mother's vagina. The *Trotula* gave advice on suturing and should the need arise there were also instructions for repositioning an infant who was in a breech position before it was born.

With the birth of William, named after his father, Isabel had fulfilled the main duty, if the Church was to be believed, of a woman and an aristocratic wife. Marshal had a son and an heir who would inherit Isabel's patrimony. The transition of the estates and power which she represented into the hands of

Marshal was completed by the arrival of an infant whether he survived into adulthood or not. Unaware of his importance, William the Younger was cleaned and rubbed with salt, then his gums were smeared with honey before he was wrapped in a warm towel. Finally, the midwife wrapped William in swaddling bands, and handed him to his wet nurse. According to medical beliefs of the time, the use of honey and salt reduced excess warm and moist humours while the swaddling bands helped to maintain balance of the humours, keep the new baby warm, and replicated the womb.[5] Aoife might not have swaddled Isabel when she was a baby. Gerald of Wales reported that the Irish neither used swaddling bands nor cradles.

In England and Normandy, a wooden cradle was an essential. Given Isabel's wealth, young William's nursery was equipped with everything that might be required including a young girl called a rocker who kept the cradle moving and sang lullabies. Bibbesworth's treatise identified what Isabel needed to equip a baby's nursery. As well as a cradle he identified the need for the rocker, who might also have helped when William started to walk by following after the boy to make sure that he did not come to any harm.

In a period with high infant mortality rates, it was important for a woman of the countess's rank to give her husband more sons as soon as possible. According to medieval beliefs of the time, derived from Galen and other Greek writers, unborn infants were nourished by menstrual blood in the womb until it's birth. Once the child was born the blood from the womb travelled to the breasts where it became milk. Aristotle believed the transformation occurred through a boiling process inside the body which purified the blood, thickened it and turned it white. Breastfeeding was believed to prohibit pregnancy and if, by chance, a woman was to become pregnant while suckling a child the quality of the milk would suffer and the child's health deteriorate. Robert of Flamborough, in the *Liber Penitentialis*, warned that a second child conceived before its elder sibling was weaned risked deformity, leprosy, or lameness.[6] It was better for young William to be provided with a wet nurse, especially as weaning happened when a child was about two years of age. Isabel's ladies bound her breasts until the milk stopped flowing.

The wet nurse was selected before Isabel gave birth. The woman was chosen based on recommendation from family, friends and neighbours. An ideal wet nurse already had children of her own and had given birth to an infant, preferably a boy, within two months of becoming a wet nurse, was not too fat nor too thin, in good health, tranquil in temperament, and of good reputation. The woman moved into the nursery which Isabel oversaw and where the wet nurse's diet was carefully monitored. It was already recognised that the quality of a woman's milk reflected the quality of the food she ate.

Marshal was an uxorious husband. His countess would repeat the birthing process the following year with the arrival of another son, named Richard after her own father. She would give birth to ten children in all and it appears from the bonds that existed between the Marshal children as they grew to adulthood that Isabel was an affectionate as well as dutiful mother.

As a postpartum woman, Isabel, remained in her chamber during her forty days of lying-in that all women who could afford it were required to undertake after birth to enable their better recovery. Her women gave her wine and foods such as chicken broth, regarded as nourishing and warming, to help her rebalance her humours and regain her strength. Neighbours came to admire Isabel's new child and sit beside Isabel's bed and gossip. In addition, the Church regarded her as unclean. It forbade sex between a new mother and her husband but did allow that a woman might have intercourse with her spouse if her husband was in danger of falling into adultery in which case, she should seek purification before rendering the marriage debt. Women who had given birth needed to be ritually cleansed before being welcomed back into church.

It meant that Isabel was not present at William's baptism which was likely to have been performed very shortly after he was born. In theory a baptism should have taken place within eight days of birth, but in practice most families wished to baptise their newborn child as soon as possible for fear that it might die before receiving Christian rites. Baptism was the first of the sacraments and it admitted Isabel's son into the Catholic Church which in turn made salvation possible. Before baptism a child who died was destined to an eternity in limbo without ever being able to enter Heaven. After receipt of the sacrament, a child who died in infancy would be redeemed of its sins including the shadow of Adam and Eve's original sin that all humans carried with them. So alarming was the idea of death without salvation that anyone, including women, could perform the necessary rite of baptism in an emergency.

The countess's first public appearance after giving birth was at her churching. The ceremony included a ritual blessing and purification while she knelt at the entrance of the church with a lighted candle and gifts of thanksgiving. The idea arose from the Book of Leviticus that pronounced women as unclean for a week after the birth of a son and two weeks after the birth of a daughter. By the medieval period the ceremony in which Isabel took part signalled her return to the church and the resumption of marital relations. Then she entered the church and was blessed again, giving thanks for her safe delivery and offering a gift at the altar. Many women gave candles dedicated to the Virgin Mary in thanks for their safe delivery. It is likely also to have been the occasion for a celebratory feast wherever Isabel was resident.

When Isabel emerged back into the world, it was to the continued preparations of an army about to set off on the Third Crusade. She may have learned more about the wave of anti-Semitic riots that shook England's Jewish community that winter. Violence against Jews escalated in the aftermath of Richard's coronation, the slaughter of some of the population's prominent leaders who came with gifts for the king to London at the time of his crowning, and with his departure on the Third Crusade. On 16 March 1190 York's Jewish population sought refuge inside York Castle where they were besieged. That night many of them took the lives of their families before killing themselves rather than dying at the hands of the mob or being forcibly converted to Christianity. The following day the survivors surrendered and were massacred. One hundred and fifty men, women and children were killed. The entire Jewish community of York was wiped out.

In the massacre's aftermath, William Marshal's political opponent, the chief co-justiciar William Longchamp took the opportunity to remove Marshal's brother John from the office of Sheriff of Yorkshire which he gained in 1189 following Ranulf de Glanville's resignation. It was an indicator that Longchamp believed that in the king's absence he could do what he wished despite the terms of his appointment. By June 1190, the Bishop of Durham was denied the regency of the north and imprisoned in the Tower by his rival for overstepping the bounds of his authority.

Marshal was about the king's business in Normandy as events played out in England. On 27 June he was at Tours, on his way to see Richard and Philip II at Vézelay before they began the first stage of their journey to the Holy Land. After the two kings departed, Isabel's husband turned back for home and his new administrative roles as landowner, sheriff and one of the junior justiciars appointed by Richard to rule his realm in his own absence. Marshal who was more at home with a sword in his hand than as a baron of the exchequer must have wished that he was going with the king.

Before Richard's departure, when he was intent on selling offices and possessions to the highest bidder to pay for the crusade, Marshal acquired the shrievalty of Gloucestershire, took custody of Gloucester Castle, the Forest of Dean and St Briavels Castle.[7] It meant that William controlled the roads from England into Striguil and South Wales. In fact, the king had provided his loyal knight with enough power to rival Prince John who was the Lord of Gloucester and Glamorgan by right of his own wife Isabel of Gloucester. Richard made his brother swear that he would not set foot in England for three years during the time he was away on crusade. Both the king and his mother, Eleanor of Aquitaine, who was also part of Richard's regency council, with the right to rule as though she was a *de jure* monarch, understood the extent of John's ambitions for the throne. Inevitably, as soon as Richard departed, his younger brother broke his oath. The situation was not without its challenges for Marshal, who had not one but two feudal overlords. His role as justiciar meant treading a narrow path between maintaining order on Richard's behalf and obeying his feudal overlord in Ireland and also Cartmel: Prince John.

Of more pressing concern to Isabel was packing up her belongings and arranging their transport back to England. If she wanted a role model, the countess needed to look no further than Eleanor of Aquitaine who did not remain long in one place during the early years of her marriage to King Henry II, even when she was pregnant or a new mother. She crossed the Narrow Seas on a regular basis accompanied by a large household and, on occasion, a number of her own young children.

Chapter 11

Wife of a Junior Justiciar

Isabel's return to England rather than a lengthier stay in Normandy was prompted by William's role in the regency administration as one of the associate justiciars alongside Geoffrey FitzPeter or FitzPiers, William Bruyere or Bruer who was Henry II's Sheriff of Devon, Robert de Whitfield, and Roger-RizRainfrey or FitzReinfrid whose brother Walter de Coutance was the Bishop of Rouen. It was their duty to work with Longchamp to keep order and to dispense justice according to the laws and customs of feudal England. Marshal had much to learn if he was to fulfil the role. His colleagues were much more experienced royal administrators.

William Longchamp's intention of diminishing, even before the king's departure, the influence of the men whose task it was to work alongside him created problems, especially as he held the Great Seal which was needed to authenticate the king's business. Longchamp had already removed Marshal's brother, John, from his office in Yorkshire and in August he besieged Gloucester Castle. It has been speculated that the chancellor intended to strip Isabel's husband of the shrievalty of Gloucestershire before his return from Normandy as he stripped other junior justiciars of their power in an attempt to concentrate authority in his own hands.[1]

As William and Isabel's retinue made its way to Striguil, the couple considered the circumstances in which they found themselves. Government was destabilised without the king at its head. Longchamp aspired to total control of the country. He was not the only problem that faced them. King Richard's ambitious brother, John, was a presence who could not be ignored. Richard had given his brother the honours of Lancaster and Peveril among others as well as making him master of the castles at Marlborough, Ludgershall and the Castle of the Peak. It was a power base that could destabilise the kingdom if he chose to make trouble. Despite having made a promise not to set foot in England for three years, the Count of Mortain was quick to return to England as soon as the king's attention was focused on his own journey to the Holy Land.

Word of Longchamp's highhandedness reached the king in Sicily in September 1190. The Mediterranean state was a stopping off point enroute to the Holy Land. Richard's sister Joanna, the widow of King William II of

Sicily, was imprisoned by her husband's cousin and successor, Tancred who also refused to honour her inheritance rights under the terms of William II's will. When the new king failed to free Joanna or fulfil his financial obligations, Richard occupied the port of Messina. Buildings were burned, hostages taken and women carried off. The business did not sit well with Philip and it deepened the tensions that already existed between the two crusading kings. Their delayed departure gave Richard the chance to send letters to his justiciars in England, including William Marshal, and to appoint Walter de Coutance, Archbishop of Rouen as Longchamp's successor, should the need arise. There was also the issue of what might happen if the king was killed while he was in the Holy Land. Richard's young nephew, Arthur of Brittany, had a claim which many regarded as better than Prince John's own. Arthur was the child of Henry II's third son Geoffrey. When the king named Arthur as his heir in his correspondence, Longchamp's duty was to the boy rather than John. The news, when it finally reached England, meant that Marshal and his countess, even under the best of circumstances, had to navigate a difficult course through the winter of 1190-1191.

Coutance and Eleanor of Aquitaine, did not leave Sicily until February 1191, stopping in Rome before they crossed the Alps on their return journey. When the bishop arrived in England, he found that Prince John and Longchamp were at war with one another. The chancellor besieged Lincoln Castle which was held by Gerard de Caville who was loyal to John. The prince seized the castles at Tickhill and Nottingham which were both in Longchamp's custody before marching on Lincoln with the intention of raising the siege there. Coutance brokered a peace between the two men which was signed at the end of July 1191 but Longchamp was forced to agree that it was John, not Arthur, who would be the king's successor.

The agreement, unlikely to be lasting, collapsed when the chancellor forbade John's illegitimate half-brother, Geoffrey, newly consecrated Bishop of York, from coming to England. Geoffrey ignored Longchamp, landed at Dover on 14 September and outwitted the chancellor's men placed to keep watch for the bishop. He hurried to the safety of the priory church of St Martin but Longchamp's 'sinister satellites'[2] seized him in the act of celebrating Mass and imprisoned him in Dover Castle. Although the bishop was released before the end of the month, the indignation of the Church was enough for John to demand a meeting of the junior justiciars, as well as the realm's prelates and barons at Reading. Isabel could only watch as Marshal, at the head of his retinue, set off from Striguil. Her husband was about to become embroiled in the politics of government. He would be guided by the instructions given to him by the king and the orders of Eleanor of Aquitaine who was active on Richard's behalf.[3]

Isabel shouldered her duties in William's absence, spent time with their son and looked to the security of her domains. If it came to war, whether it was civil unrest or an attack by the Welsh, Striguil would have to withstand siege. The countess may also have been grieving for the loss of her mother. It was during 1190 that the countess received most of her mother's dower estates, suggesting that Aoife died at about that time, though the date of her death may have been as late as 1204.

If this was the case, it is possible that Isabel's mother took up residence at Goodrich Castle during her final years. The keep is known locally as the 'Mac-Mac' Tower, a possible derivative of MacMurchada.[4] It is often asserted that Isabel's father built the tower keep but there is little or no evidence of him as a significant builder in the Marches; his relative poverty prior to his arrival in Leinster and the architecture of the castle is not in keeping with the period in which Strongbow lived. Circumstantial evidence for Aoife's presence on the Marches lays in the fact that Marshal did not gain control of Goodrich until 1204.

What is certain is that Aoife's funeral cortege wound its way through the Marches to Tintern Abbey for burial. The mourners stood by Aoife's bier and lit candles before the monks began a Requiem Mass. The Irish Countess was buried in the church founded by Walter de Clare the first de Clare lord of Striguil as was her right. The *Visitation By the Heralds in Wales* undertaken in 1531, a short while before Henry VIII's dissolution of the monasteries, recorded that Aoife's tomb was in the northern section of the abbey church.

Medieval attitudes to mortality are best defined by the idea of what happened to the immortal soul after death. Without repentance from sin, people risked an eternity in Hell. Repentance and confession were an essential part of life. Prayer, almsgiving and the singing of masses were a form of penance. The de Clares were generous patrons to Tintern Abbey and Aoife's tomb was positioned accordingly. Placed close to the altar, it was thought to benefit a soul's journey through Purgatory to eternal salvation. Masses were said for the departed countess's soul and afterwards the Marshals distributed alms to the poor in Aoife's memory.

When Marshal returned to Isabel's side in 1191, it was with the news that Longchamp, having locked himself into the Tower, was deposed and in exile and that the Bishop of Rouen was now the senior justiciar as ordained by King Richard at Messina. Knowing the ambitions of both John and Longchamp, it seemed unlikely that would be the end of the matter. The former chancellor left England but he complained to Pope Celestine III demanding restitution. The bishop was also a papal legate whose authority should have been sacrosanct; the pope wrote to his bishops in England demanding that they should excommunicate the men involved with Longchamp's removal as justiciar. None of them complied with the pontiff's demand.

The Marshals gave orders for the remodelling of Striguil. The work was supervised by the castellan, Ralph Bloet. The castle's keep, as Strongbow and Aoife recognised it, was based on those found in Normandy before the conquest. Its builders incorporated a band of Roman tiles in the masonry that originated from nearby Caerwent. It was William who, at vast expense and with the agreement of his countess, strengthened the castles walls with the addition of a new gatehouse and gates, as well as adding circular towers to the walls imitating castles in France. The shape of both the towers and the intimidating new entrance meant Striguil could withstand projectiles launched by siege engines with greater efficiency.

It was during this stage of the castle's evolution that the private chambers in the southwest corner of the castle, in the upper bailey, were added for Marshal and Isabel's greater comfort. Marshal's Tower is a two-storey building that includes elegant windows and fireplaces. In an account of 1271-1272 they were identified as the *camera comitess* or countess's chamber.[5] In an era when privacy was something of a novelty it seems that Striguil was innovative in more ways than just military ones. The views from the windows looked across the Wye Valley beyond. The castle was a forbidding fortification but it was also Isabel's home.

From time-to-time news of the Crusade carried by men returning from the conflict and messengers on official business arrived on English shores. Isabel heard that King Richard and Duke Leopold of Austria quarrelled at Acre when Richard's men tore down Leopold's flag and threw it into the moat. The duke left shortly afterwards. On 31 July, King Philip II of France also returned home. Philip, always suspicious of Richard, was unhappy that the English king had refused to honour the terms of his betrothal to Alais of France made by King Henry II and, perhaps more importantly that Richard had failed to restore his sister's contested dowery lands in the Vexin. The men's quarrel over the spoils of Acre soured the relationship beyond repair. By Christmas, Howden reported, that Philip was intent on defaming Richard and seizing his kingdom. The chronicler claimed that the French king sought an audience with the pope on his way home to be excused from his oath not to attack Richard's realm in his absence. Philip boasted 'that he would before long lay waste the territories of the King of England'.[6] It was the start of a rancorous conflict that would last for the rest of the English king's life.

In 1192, with building work under way at Striguil and amid the likelihood of war, Isabel became pregnant again. Eleanor of Aquitaine arrived in Portsmouth in February. She summoned her son's justiciars so that they could back her demand that Prince John remain in England rather than returning to Normandy, or France, where Eleanor feared that he would ally himself with Philip to gain Richard's throne. She also demanded that all men renew their oath of allegiance to her son. From her, Isabel learned that if women were gaming pieces that they could be queens as well as pawns.

That summer Marshal was often absent from home. He travelled with the bishops of Hereford and Coventry to administer justice in his capacity of justiciar. The Pipe Roll for year five of Richard's reign shows that William visited Gloucestershire, Worcestershire, Herefordshire, Shropshire, Warwickshire and Staffordshire.[7] Isabel may have joined him on occasion but for the most part, as her pregnancy progressed, she remained at Striguil overseeing the household and managing their estates while William learned the intricacies of the law from his co-justiciars.

Isabel's eldest daughter, Maud, was born by the end of 1192 at the latest. The birth of each of her children was proceeded by withdrawal from the wider world into a chamber from which all men were excluded. Each successful delivery was followed by rejoicing; a time of recuperation, followed by ritual purification or churching at the end of forty days. All of the countess's children were baptised soon after birth to wash away the original sin with which all infants were thought to be born and to ensure their place in Heaven in the event of an untimely death. It was usually the midwife who carried the newborn baby to church. The priest welcomed the procession at the church or chapel door, where he blessed and gave salt to the baby to exorcise any evil spirits. It was usual to test the godparents' knowledge of the *Pater Noster*, *Ave Maria* and the *Credo*. Only then did the congregation enter the church. The priest baptised the baby at the font by immersing it in the water before one of its godparents lifted it from the font and wrapped it in its christening gown. The party processed from the font at the entrance of the church to the altar where the godparents made a profession of faith on behalf of their new godchild. Godparents could be called upon to testify at a later date to the baptism itself if required and witnesses often came forward if evidence needed to be provided at an inquisition post-mortem about a young person's age to ascertain whether they had attained their majority or not in order to inherit parental property or were more rightly wards of the Crown. The baptism ceremony concluded with a feast to celebrate the new arrival and the presentation of gifts to the new baby by its godparents.

Families tried to choose a godparent who was of a higher social status than they were themselves in the hope that they might help the child through life as well as to teach them about what it meant to be a good Christian. Marshal and Isabel selected the godparents of their children with great care although there were few men or women better placed than themselves. It was usual for a girl to have two godmothers and one godfather and for a boy to have two godfathers and one godmother. Children often took the name of the most senior of their godparents. Canon law codified relationships created by baptism in the *Decretum of Gratian* and the *Decretals of Gregory IX*, published in 1230. The baptism ceremony established ties between a child and their godparents that was considered to be familial because acceptance into the Catholic Church was a spiritual birth. The shared tie created a spiritual affinity which was an impediment to any future marriage between family members. The concept of a spiritual relationship was well established by that time. Emperor Justinian, living in the sixth century, disapproved of marriages between a godparent and godchild. It was a short step from there to prohibit the joining of a natural child with a godchild. The Marshals, planning baptisms for their children at the end of the twelfth century before the publication of the Church's complicated regulations, would still have been very careful not to ask someone to be a godparent from a family that they hoped to become more closely linked to through marriage. Instead, they would have chosen adults from families with which they were already related, to strengthen bonds within Marshal's *mesnie* and extend the influence of the Marshal affinity, with their neighbours, or to tie them closer to the political elite.

In the same year that Maud was born news reached England that the king had departed the Holy Land on 9 October having won a battle at Jaffa and forced the Muslims, led by Saladin, to permit unarmed Christian pilgrims and merchants to visit Jerusalem. Richard failed in his dream to recapture the city and by then news had arrived that John was attempting to usurp his throne. His return was prompted, in part, by a letter from his mother requesting his presence because she feared John and Philip's intentions.

Richard I was shipwrecked off the coast of Italy on his way home and forced to make his way, in disguise, over land through Europe with a small number of attendants. Among their number was one of William Marshal's friends from his days in service to the Young King and as a tournament knight, Baldwin de Béthune. During the journey Richard and his men were captured near Vienna by a servant of Duke Leopold of Austria who gave him into the hands of the Holy Roman Emperor, Henry VI who was aggrieved by Richard's treaty with Tancred of Sicily. Rumours gradually spread through England that the king was a prisoner. Despite the threat of excommunication which hung over his head for the imprisonment of a crusader, the Holy Roman Emperor demanded a ransom of 150,000 marks and kept the king in chains in Trifels Castle in Germany, from December 1192 until February 1194.

The Christmas season of 1192 passed without word of the king's whereabouts. Eleanor spent it at Westminster. When news of Richard's captivity did arrive it upset the balance of power that she and the justiciars had managed to maintain the previous year. During the time of his captivity, Richard's brother, John, held the ascendency in English politics. He was quick to proclaim himself as the heir to the throne, promise to marry Alais of France and to do homage to Philip II for the Angevin lands in France. It seemed as though England was on the cusp of another civil war.

In Normandy, Richard's barons refused to offer John the fealty due to a sovereign lord. Philip II led an army into the duchy but was resisted by Richard's loyal subjects including Isabel's kinsman, Robert de Beaumont, 4th Earl of Leicester who was recently returned from Syria. De Beaumont defended Rouen before attempting to reclaim his own domain at Pacy from French hands. He was captured by the French soon afterwards and held for ransom. In attacking Normandy, Philip II was breaking the oaths that bound monarchs not to invade the lands of crusaders in their absence.

When Prince John returned to England with an army of mercenaries, Marshal and his fellow justiciaries prepared to defy him even though the royal castles at Wallingford[8] and Windsor surrendered. Isabel, secure in Striguil with her children, could only wait while Marshal once again fulfilled his duty to the Crown. It is likely that the castle at Milford Haven was strengthened as Howden reported that seaports and 'all the maritime places'[9] were secured, and ever wary of the Welsh, the Marches prepared for attack from the west. The tensions of the South Marches were exacerbated by John's own status as a powerful Marcher lord. Men from John's lordship of Glamorgan would face Marshal's levies from Bristol and Gloucester if it came to armed confrontation.

Castles changed hands like gaming pieces on a board. Windsor, in the hands of John, was under siege by Marshal with his Marcher levies.[10] At home, Isabel and the senior household servants busied themselves ensuring that supplies and equipment found its way to the men who needed them; and that the regular cycle of the farming year was not affected. It has been suggested that the justiciars' army as a whole was made up largely of mercenaries from Wales.[11] The exchequer could not afford to pay the men and even though the royal treasury paid Marshal £400 in February 1193, the rest of the money had to come from elsewhere. Some of the army's pay was raised from fines exacted by Marshal in his capacity of Sheriff of Gloucester but he was also forced to divert his own revenues. Isabel knew that her husband was in debt to Bristol Abbey and, like her father, to Jewish financiers so that he could pay his men.

Thankfully for Isabel and Marshal the difficult position of owing allegiance to both Richard and John was side-stepped when Eleanor of Aquitaine and the justiciars managed to scrape together 70,000 silver marks as a down-payment on the whole ransom following a letter written by Richard in the spring of 1193 asking for help. Marshal was among the men who agreed that:

The clergy as well as the laity ought to give the fourth part of the present year's revenue for the ransom of our lord, and to add as much from their chattel property …They also exacted from each knight's fee twenty shillings.[12]

It is to be wondered what Isabel made of the amount when Marshal relayed the information to her. Payment of both scutage and carucage, a tax on the land they held, to help pay the ransom was a heavy duty. As chatelaine it was her task to raise the funds while he and his fellow justiciars tried to outmanoeuvre John. At least, unlike the canons and nuns of the Gilbertine order at Sempringham Priory, she did not have to sacrifice the whole of her estates' wool production for the year.

In November, following negotiations, John surrendered Windsor to his mother along with Wallingford and Peak Castle, as Peveril Castle in Derbyshire was then known. In December 1193, the ransom raised by Eleanor of Aquitaine and the justiciars arrived in Germany as did the men who were required to act as hostages as surety for the rest of the ransom including de Coutances and Longchamp. Negotiations for the king's liberty continued until early 1194 by which time King Philip II and Prince John made Emperor Henry VI a counter offer of 100,000 silver marks if he would keep Richard in confinement. On 4 February 1194, Richard did homage to Henry VI for his realm and agreed to pay an annual tribute to the Holy Roman Emperor.

As soon as Richard's freedom was assured the justiciars moved against the prince. Marshal was charged with seizing Bristol and other properties in the southwest. William's eldest brother, John Marshal, was Prince John's seneschal so he had been well placed to ask for the return of Marlborough Castle, former Marshal holdings, into his own hands when John first seized it. However, as its castellan he had to defend it against the new Archbishop of Canterbury, Hubert de Walter. The bishop was known to Isabel from the days of her wardship. Hubert's uncle was her old guardian, Ranulf de Glanville. Prior to Richard's ascent to the throne, he was Dean of York but was elevated to the bishopric of Salisbury in 1189.[13] Both men had accompanied Richard on crusade. De Glanville died at the Siege of Acre in 1190 but de Walter returned to Europe in time to help raise the king's ransom and to ensure that

Richard had a kingdom to which he might return. John Marshal was mortally wounded in the siege that followed and died before the end of March 1194.

News reached Striguil that John Marshal was dead and that King Richard had landed in England at Sandwich on 13 March 1194 accompanied by Eleanor of Aquitaine. Isabel's husband now inherited his elder brother's hereditary role as Marshal of England. Despite the fact that John was a traitor to the king, William Marshal met the funeral cortege at Cirencester on its way to Bradenstoke Priory and offered comfort to his sister-in-law, Joan du Port who had no children of her own to support her. It is unknown whether Isabel was with him at Cirencester. Marshal did not attend his brother's funeral. He was on his way to join the newly returned king at Huntingdon before besieging Nottingham which still held out for John.[14] It did not take long for the castle to surrender.

Joan du Port, John Marshal's widow, was a part of the kinship networks of both William de Braose and Earl Ranulf of Chester.[15] In 1200, Joan married for a second time to Richard de Rivers, one of King John's officials, who is recorded as paying the necessary fine to marry Joan, who was the daughter of the Lord of Basing in Hampshire.[16] The court links make it plausible that Marshal introduced John's widow to her second husband which in turn raises the intriguing prospect of Joan in Isabel's company. However, all that is known for certain is that Isabel welcomed John Marshal's illegitimate son John into her husband's household after her brother-in-law's death.

There were numerous nephews by marriage who served Marshal and who benefitted from their relationship to Isabel's husband either by employment or receipt of land. Among the men who could claim kinship to Isabel through marriage was Marshal's former ward, John d'Earley who was married to Sybil, another of William's charges. It is probable, given the family name, that she was another one of John Marshal's natural children. Sybil, even after her marriage, lived in Isabel's household as part of the countess's extended family and travelled to Normandy with her. It was usual for the women who served in an aristocratic household to be the wives and daughters of the lord's *mesnie*.

Following Richard's return to his kingdom in 1194 and a reconciliation with Prince John, Isabel and William spent most of the next five years serving the king in France. Evidence shows that Marshal arrived by the king's side each spring and remained throughout the campaigning season which concluded with the autumn rains. William should not have been exposed to the same dangers as his young household knights including John d'Earley. However, Marshal sometimes forgot his rank in the heat of the moment and behaved more like a young knight trying to make his fortune and his reputation rather than a respected commander. In 1197, when William was in his early fifties,

Isabel must have experienced some alarm as well as pride when she heard about her husband's exploits at the siege of Milli.

King Richard's forces were beginning to retreat from their attack on the castle walls when a knight, Guy de la Buryere, became stranded on a siege-ladder having been caught on one of the defender's pikes. He was at risk of being pulled from his precarious perch. Marshal ran fully armed across the castle ditch avoiding missiles and scaled the ladder to render assistance to Guy. Single handed, he reached the wall walk, beat off the defenders there and took a section of Milli's battlements. The constable of the castle, William de Monaceaux arrived to fight beside his men. By that time Marshal was breathing hard from the exertions of the last few minutes but took on his new opponent, hitting Monaceaux so hard with his sword that it cut through the constable's hauberk and felled him. The Marshal sat on the stunned man to keep him down and to regain his breath. Little wonder that Marshal, whose actions turned the tide of the attack in King Richard's favour was described as the greatest knight who ever lived, even if the king was furious that it was William who seized the moment rather than himself.[17]

Isabel, who understood that she was married to a career soldier, must have worried about what would happen to her and her children if anything happened to William. Her children would become royal wards as she had once been and it was entirely possible that, unless she was able to pay a fine to prevent it, that she would be required to take another husband. Hawise Countess of Aumale, who had been forced to marry William de Forz in 1191 was widowed in 1195 and required to marry Marshal's old friend Baldwin de Béthune who had become Richard's companion during the Third Crusade and been a hostage for the king when Richard was released from Henry VI's captivity. The marriage fulfilled a promise of a rich heiress made by the king to Baldwin but the king and her groom took no account of the Countess of Aumale's views on the matter. When she was widowed for a third time in 1212, she paid King John for the right to enjoy her widowhood unfettered by a fourth spouse who was not of her choosing.

Marshal is largely absent from court records during the winter months.[18] It is likely that Isabel spent two thirds of the year in Normandy managing her and Marshal's estates at Longueville, caring for her household and family and enduring the vicissitudes of repeated pregnancy on her own. During the time of year when military campaigning was halted, Marshal joined his family and managed his own affairs. For Isabel the years in Normandy were a time of nurturing her children, training them and overseeing their education. A household of nursery staff carried out the physical care while Isabel provided oversight and started the task of providing a Christian upbringing for her children.

During the months when William was at home the cycle of Isabel's year went on as it did for all women. By Martinmas, 11 November, the countess was prepared for the annual slaughter of cattle and pigs because of the lack of fodder in the cold season. She planned the purchase of salt to preserve the meat in advance of the event. The household knights went hunting to subsidise the larder and Isabel joined them on occasion to go hawking. The choice of a falcon on her seal suggests that she enjoyed the recreation that also provided for her larder.

The month long fast of advent heralded the start of the Christmas season. Isabel, married to a man known for his piety, ensured that rich foods were removed from the menu until 25 December. The holiday that began on Christmas morning lasted for twelve days and was a highlight of the medieval year. No one worked other than to feed their animals, homes were decorated with evergreens and a Yule log burned in the hearth of the great hall throughout the festivities to ensure good luck in the coming year. For Isabel and Marshal, it would have been an occasion to socialise with their household, neighbours and tenants; to feast, to dance and to play games until the feast of Epiphany, when the arrival of the three magi at Bethlehem was celebrated.

As well as being the end of the twelve days of Christmas it was a date with significance to Marshal. Previously in 1182, Marshal had been banished from the household of the Young King, following rumours that the knight was having an affair with Henry's wife Margaret of France. Marshal, denied the right to defend himself at Henry II's Christmas court that year chose to go on pilgrimage to the shrine of the Three Magi at Cologne. In 1164, the Holy Roman Emperor, Frederick Barbarossa, removed the relics from their home in Milan and gave them to the city. The goldsmith, Nicholas de Verdun, fashioned a specular shrine from gold and precious jewels after William's pilgrimage but he must have felt an attachment to the cult of the three kings and may have owned a pilgrim badge depicting the adoration of the magi as a souvenir of his visit and as proof that he undertook the journey.

There was little opportunity for Isabel or her husband to think of making another pilgrimage or even to visit Ireland to consolidate their claim to the land which Strongbow gained by marriage to Aoife. It was not safe to cross the Narrow Seas or the Irish Sea during the winter months and when the spring came Marshal would be required back at the king's side.

Chapter 12

Divided Loyalties

During the remainder of King Richard's reign, Isabel's time was spent mainly in Normandy, visiting the Welsh Marches only occasionally. The pattern of her existence changed abruptly with the unexpected death of the king, aged 41-years, on 6 April 1199. The news that he was killed by a wound from a crossbow bolt which became infected while besieging Châlus Castle in Limoges was a shock to the whole realm. As soon as word of the king's passing reached Marshal at Rouen on 10 April, he acted on orders given by Richard on his deathbed to secure the town, the castle and its treasury. He hurried from there to the nearby royal palace at Le Pré to consult the Archbishop of Canterbury, Hubert Walter, even though, according to the *Histoire*, it was late at night.

There were two possible candidates to succeed to the throne: Richard's brother John or their 12-year-old nephew Arthur of Brittany, the posthumous son of John's elder brother Geoffrey. Richard initially favoured John but, in 1191, named Arthur as his heir in a letter sent from Sicily to Longchamp. However, in 1194, Richard identified his brother as his heir and did so again before he died. The king's bequest carried weight but the realm's magnates were not bound to obey Richard's wishes. Rights of succession were not yet hard and fast rules. It was unclear whether John, the brother and son of a king, or Arthur, Henry II's grandson, had the better claim. Hubert initially supported Arthur because he was the son of John's elder brother. It was, however, a fact, according to contemporary chroniclers, that Eleanor of Aquitaine distrusted Arthur's mother, Constance of Brittany, because she wanted to end the rule of the Plantagenets in Brittany. Marshal and the archbishop knew that their own choice of monarch taken with Eleanor's preference would swing men in favour of one candidate or the other. Marshal eventually persuaded the reluctant archbishop to support John's right to the throne. Arthur was unproven in battle and still a child governed by his advisors. In the *Histoire's* account, the archbishop told Marshal that they would come to regret the choice.

John secured his brother's treasury and, on 25 April 1199, was invested as Duke of Normandy at Rouen. However, many of the nobility in Anjou and Maine swore loyalty to Arthur. Constance took steps to place her son under French protection. In return, Arthur recognised Philip II as his feudal overlord in Anjou, Maine and Poitou. Philip, delighted by the opportunity that care of Arthur afforded, exacerbated the succession crisis by invading Normandy.

Marshal sent a messenger to warn Isabel that he would have to go to England. William, who was unable to write, also dictated a letter to Geoffrey FitzPeter. He was one of Marshal's five co-justiciars while Richard I was on Crusade as well as being the Constable of the Tower of London. He sent his trusted knight John d'Earley to ensure that FitzPeter received the dispatch while he finalised arrangements for his journey before heading north. It is unknown whether or not he found the time to stop at Longueville to snatch a few hours with his family before he crossed the Narrow Seas. Hubert Walter accompanied Marshal to England to keep the peace there and to administer an oath of loyalty to the new king. Together with FitzPeter, the two men worked to ensure that the throne passed to John uncontested. Roger of Howden recorded that the leading magnates of the realm had their doubts about the new king despite the assurances of men like Marshal, Hubert and John's illegitimate brother William Longspée, 3rd Earl of Salisbury who was married to Marshal's cousin, Ela of Salisbury.

In the days that followed Richard's death, Isabel prepared to relocate her family to England. In choosing to move her household to be with her husband, Isabel was following a model adopted by Eleanor of Aquitaine during the childhood of her own children. Eleanor's daughter Matilda, who Strongbow accompanied to Germany for her wedding in 1167, crossed the Channel with her mother for the first time when she was only a month old in 1157. She and her elder brother, Henry, travelled through Normandy to Aquitaine where they celebrated Christmas that year. Travel with small children made journeys even riskier than usual but it was something that Isabel had done before. On this occasion her daughter Maud was aged 5-years, Gilbert was a toddler of 18-months and the countess was either pregnant with her fourth son Walter or he was a young infant. Her second son Richard was either 8 or 9 years of age and was likely to have already left the care of the nursery to join the pages and wards fostered by his father. They also needed to be transferred to England but their care was not Isabel's immediate responsibility.

It was probable that when Isabel departed Normandy for England that she left her eldest son, William the Younger behind. William, born in 1190, remained in his mother's care until he was 7-years old. It was normal for boys between the ages of 7 and 14 to serve as pages and then as squires in the households of families other than their own. It was considered part of their education. He might, like his brother Richard, have been part of his father's military household learning the path to knighthood alongside Marshal's wards. Circumstantial evidence provided by William's betrothal in 1203 to

Alice de Béthune, the daughter of Marshal's friend Baldwin and his reluctant wife Hawise, Countess of Aumale is suggestive of Marshal's determination to strengthen the bonds between the two families. This information, taken together with links to Richard Siward who served de Béthune and Hawise's son, William de Forz, before entering the service of William the Younger is enough to suggest that by the age of nine, Isabel's eldest son was already being fostered by Baldwin. There were few other men who Marshal might have considered as suitable tutors for his sons.

While Isabel and her younger children made themselves at home in one of their residences close to London in readiness for John's coronation, Marshal re-crossed the Channel and gave counsel to the king at Dieppe. He was still with the king when he arrived in England on the 25 May 1199, only two days before John's coronation. Marshal had crossed the Channel three times within a month. On this occasion his dedication to the monarchy won back the last of Isabel's patrimony. The king granted the earldom of Pembroke to Marshal when he was crowned. William de Broase, who played his own part in smoothing the king's way to the throne, was also rewarded. Like monarchs before him, John needed to secure the loyalty of his magnates and Marshal was a man relied upon by successive Plantagenets.

The addition of the honour of Pembroke to Marshal's portfolio of estates made him the most powerful lord in the Marches of Wales. The title originally belonged to Isabel's grandfather Gilbert de Clare and her father never ceased to petition for the title and its honour from King Henry II. It could be argued that John simply returned what was Isabel's by right of descent but it was her husband who recognised an opportunity for winning the lordship at a time when Eleanor of Aquitaine 'ensured that John endorsed various gifts to faithful servants and knights'.[1]

He was not the only member of the Marshal family to reap the rewards of his loyal service to the Crown. John Marshal, the illegitimate son of Marshal's elder brother, John, who had been part of Marshal's *mesnie* since 1194, was married to a co-heiress, Alice de Rie, in 1199 or 1200. She was the daughter of Hubert de Rie, or Rye, of Hingham and Hokering.[2] John received eighteen knights' fees belonging to the Norfolk barony of Rye by right of his wife as well as a small estate in Normandy. In 1204, John gave land at Foulsham to Walsingham Priory in order that masses could be said for the souls of him, his wife, his parents and for the salvation of William and Isabel. The inclusion of the earl and his countess reflects the depth of John's affection or gratitude to his uncle and aunt for their patronage. A household knight with no lands of his own was not the natural choice for an heiress. John's suitability as a husband derived from his association with his uncle and aunt.

For much of the next eighteen months, Marshal remained at the king's side in England, Normandy or Gascony. Isabel was in the Marches soon after her husband was granted Pembroke. It's probable that she went by sea from Chepstow to Pembroke as it was the easiest and most direct route. It is also likely that Marshal was eager to assess the defensibility of the fortifications contained within the lordship of Pembroke because, in 1200, or thereabouts, using his understanding of continental castles to good effect, he began to rebuild Pembroke Castle in stone rather than wood. It was under his orders that the huge circular stone keep with its domed roof began to take shape. Earlier improvements at Striguil included rounded towers along the outer walls and the introduction of more effective arrow loops. Marshal understood that curved walls were much better at deflecting missiles. He took the same approach to the protection of Usk on the Welsh borders and at Carlow Castle in Ireland. William transformed basic defensive structures into something more intimidating. In place of a wooden palisade at Usk, he gave orders for a stone wall behind which he commissioned the Garrison Tower and a nearby round tower.

By May 1200 John reached an agreement with Philip II in return for the much-disputed border region of the Vexin. Arthur agreed to give up his claims to Anjou and Maine. Having gained an empire and settled the matter of the succession in his own favour, the king turned his attentions to his rebellious subjects in Anjou and Poitou. In June, Marshal was in Normandy for the campaigning season. The patterns of William's service to the Crown appeared to be re-establishing their earlier shape. The countess is likely to have been resident in Longueville with her children for some of the time but dangerous currents swirled beneath the surface of the world in which the Countess of Pembroke inhabited.

The king who was crowned without his wife Isabel of Gloucester by his side secured a dispensation from his marriage on grounds of consanguinity. He took for his second wife Isabella of Angoulême in order to prevent her wedding to Hugh IX, Lord of Lusignan and Count of La Marche. Isabel understood that any proposed union between Angoulême and Lusignan posed a threat to the king's control of Poitou and to the stability of Gascony. She also knew that Marshal blamed the Lusignans for the death of his uncle, Patrick of Salisbury, in 1168. William may have briefly enjoyed Hugh's loss of face when the king, who was Hugh's feudal lord, abducted his betrothed bride. Rumours also reached South Wales that John was besotted with Isabella who was barely out of childhood.

As the summer of 1200 came to an end and the days began to shorten, Isabel and her much travelled household were at Pembroke Castle watching the new keep take shape. The countess was nearly at the end of her third trimester of pregnancy with her seventh child so did not travel to London to see Isabella crowned in Westminster Abbey on 8 October 1200. Instead, she waited in her chamber, swaddling clothes and midwife at the ready, for the new baby to arrive and prayed that she and her infant would both survive. Her neighbour in the Marches, Maud, wife of King John's favourite William de Braose, was reputed to have provided her husband with sixteen children. Each birth brought with it an increased risk of complications. Isabel may have spared a thought for Eleanor of Aquitaine's daughter, the unlucky Joanna, Queen of Sicily who, having avoided a diplomatic marriage during the Third Crusade to Saladin's brother, was married in 1196 to Raymond VI, Count of Toulouse. She provided her husband with an heir the following year and a daughter born in 1198 but died shortly after Richard I in 1199 as a result of complications arising from her third pregnancy and childbirth. Isabel, more fortunate than the Lionheart's favourite sister, gave birth to a second daughter, named Isabel, on 9 October.

By now the process of giving birth and handing the child to its wet nurse was well rehearsed. Isabel was either pregnant, caring for, or schooling young children for more than half her married life. She gave birth to ten infants in a space of fifteen to seventeen years. Her last child, Joan, was born between 1208-1210. In an era when numerous pregnancies and births were the norm for women, what was unusual was that all of Isabel's children survived to adulthood. It has been estimated that in medieval England half of all children died before their seventh year.[3] God, it seemed, was smiling on the Marshals.

At the time of baby Isabel's birth, the children's household was well established. There was a girl called a rocker to keep the cradle in motion and probably also to sing lullabies, as well as the wet nurse, a governess and the domestic staff needed to fetch and carry water and fuel. Some households employed older children to make sure that toddlers came to no harm as well as for domestic tasks. Isabel took responsibility for overseeing the education of all her younger sons and of her daughters as they grew from infancy to childhood but their day-to-day care rested in the hands of trusted servants.

At the end of 1200 when Isabel was recovered from the birth, Marshal who was home for the winter took the opportunity to visit Leinster. The children remained at Pembroke[4] but it was sensible for Aoife and Strongbow's daughter to be seen by Marshal's side, even if the *Histoire* did not mention it. The journey across the Irish Sea was fraught with danger. The wooden vessel Isabel and William sailed in was caught in a storm that threw the boat around like a toy. Seized by sea sickness and fear, all Isabel could do was pray that they would survive the journey. William swore to found a monastery in gratitude for safe deliverance onto Irish shores.

Until now, Isabel had spent most of her life in Normandy or the Marches. This was the first time she returned to Leinster since leaving it as a child. Her Irish kin were alien to her and she had nothing in common with the men and women who arrived in Ireland with her father three decades before. Her husband was not welcomed by the men who called Leinster home. Norman, Welsh or Irish, they were used to running their affairs without the interference of an interloper even if he was their overlord by right of marriage. They had heard of William's prowess on the tournament field and his service to the Plantagenets but in Ireland it counted for very little even if Geoffrey FitzRobert, Marshal's seneschal for Leinster appointed in 1192, was a 'capable administrator'.[5]

Undeterred, Marshal and Isabel began the process of creating a new settlement and port on the River Barrow called New Ross. The *Chronicles of Ross* date its foundation to 1189, soon after Isabel's marriage. They also founded two new Cistercian monasteries in fulfilment of William's oath at Tintern Parva or Tintern de Voto (of the Vow) as it was known, and Duiske. The former, built at speed, was a daughter house of Tintern Abbey in Netherwent and occupied by 1203. Their foundation was reflective not only of the inherent dangers of sea travel and the Marshals' piety but of their strategic business acumen. It has been argued that monastic links between Ireland and Wales 'were crucial to the ecclesiastical, legal, commercial and political exchanges between the two countries'.[6] The earl and his countess may not have had the leisure to consolidate their overlordship of Leinster in the winter of 1200-1201 but they recognised that groundworks needed to be established so that they could both strengthen and expand upon what was rightfully theirs just as they had already done in Normandy.

Isabel may also have made a closer acquaintance of her illegitimate half-sister Basilia.[7] Their formidable aunt was likely to have been the girl's godmother as it was usual for a child to be named after its chief godparent. Marshal arranged her marriage to his own advantage when he appointed FitzRobert, a trusted member of his own household, to the post of seneschal. By investing his representative with blood ties to de Clare through his marriage to Basilia, William continued a tradition begun by Strongbow. The marriage added lustre to Marshal's right to rule in Leinster. The ties of kinship, however, were short lived. Isabel would have other no opportunity to strengthen her relationship with her half-sister. Basilia was dead by 1204 whereupon FitzRobert remarried Eve de Bermingham, *suo jure* Lady of Offaly.

It was FitzRobert who began to rebuild Kilkenny Castle, almost thirty miles north of Waterford, on Marshal's orders and to develop commerce at New

Ross. The river was bridged to enable traffic from Kells and Kilkenny to access the new centre of commerce. The Marshals also moved the centre of Leinster's administration from Ferns to Kilkenny. At the same time, having been granted the barony at Kells by Marshal in 1192, FitzRobert was responsible for the foundation of the famous Augustinian priory. While FitzRobert tended to the administration of Leinster and carried out Marshal's policies for its economic and religious development the earl returned to support King John in his defence of Normandy from the predatory attentions of King Philip II of France.

In 1201 the fragile peace with France began to crumble when the Lusignans rose in rebellion. John was the overlord of Poitou but the Lusignans could petition his feudal master. Hugh appealed to Philip II against John's abduction of Isabella. The French king summoned John to Paris to answer the charges in 1202. John refused to go in person to the court, or to respond to the accusation, because he argued, as the Duke of Normandy he was relieved from the feudal obligation of attending Philip. The French used the response as a pretext to declare John's continental possessions to be forfeit and gave all of the Angevin territories that fell under the rights of their Crown to Arthur.

Philip's invasion was a blow to Isabel and Marshal who had spent the last decade consolidating their lordship in Normandy. They even granted some of Marshal's English estates to Roger d'Abernon, son of their friend Enguerrand, in return for the fief of Abernon near Orbec in 1200.[8] This suggests that the earl believed the Treaty of Le Goulet signed in May 1200 to be a lasting one. It had given Philip overlordship of most of the Angevin Empire as well as the Vexin region between Normandy and France, with the notable exception of the castle at Gaillard that guarded the eastern side of the duchy. But now, in the spring of 1202 Marshal needed not only to secure his own fief but to defend the whole of Normandy.

Marshal was part of the army sent to secure Eu. By June he was at Lillibonne Castle; a former possession of the Count of Boulogne. Funds arrived from the exchequer to pay for his troops but the improvement of the fortifications in his own lordships was paid from his purse. Lyons fell. In July, Eleanor of Aquitaine found herself under siege at the hands of her grandson in Mirebeau. John, who was at Le Mans, marched through the night capturing Arthur and the Lusignan commanders. The Poitevin Revolt was crushed but the French remained and William de Roches, John's seneschal in Anjou, abandoned him when he saw how badly the king treated his captives.

Roger of Wendover claimed that John's subsequent failure to take advantage of the victory at Mirebeau was because of the influence of his wife, Isabella of Angoulême. The chronicler stated that the king preferred to spend time bedding her rather than protecting his realm from the continuing incursions of the French. Nor were matters helped when Arthur's imprisonment became more severe and he was transferred from Falaise, in the custody of William de Braose, to Rouen. He vanished from history in April 1203.

By August Richard I's great castle at Gaillard perched on the Rock of Les Andelys overlooking the River Seine was under siege. Taking it would be a challenge but John made no real attempt to relieve the castle even though it was only twenty-five miles from Rouen. Instead, the king gave orders to attack Brittany in an effort to draw Philip's army away. John was not the commander that his father or brother were. The morale of Normandy's barons plummeted. It might still have been conceivable for John to arrive at an accord with Philip. Otherwise, they risked losing everything. It was whispered that John could not honour the terms of any agreement with the French because he could not produce Arthur of Brittany when Philip II pressed for him to do so.

Gaillard fell in March 1204. In May, Marshal and Robert de Beaumont, 4th Earl of Leicester tried to negotiate a truce that would preserve the duchy and their estates with it.[9] Privately, William arranged to give the castles at Orbec and Longueville into French hands. If the earl paid homage to Philip as a vassal by the end of the following year for the lordships, his possessions would be returned to him. In return for the delay in annexing his fief, Marshal paid Philip, who was his friend since his days as a tournament knight in the service of the Young King, five hundred marks. Marshal and Isabel were gambling on the earl's vaunted loyalty to the Plantagenets as well as John's continuing favour to ensure that their possessions in Normandy remained intact.

Normandy fell to the French by the end of August and Philip occupied Anjou and Poitou. All that remained of John's empire was his mother's duchy of Aquitaine. She died on 1 April 1204 and the alliances that she nurtured threatened to unravel. All that remained was to retreat. Marshal was with John on 4 December 1204 when the king arrived at Barfleur. The following day the earl was on board the vessel that carried John back to England.

William remained at court that Christmas. By 24 December, the king was at Marlborough and on Christmas Day he was at Tewkesbury. Isabel travelled from Striguil for the celebrations that required four thousand plates and five hundred cups.[10] Late in December Marshal, whose missions usually ended in success rather than failure travelled with Isabel to Pembroke. The earl and his men captured Cilgerran Castle from the Welsh which had been granted to him by the king in 1202 if he could hold it. The fortification once belonged to Isabel's grandfather, Gilbert de Clare. The *Brut Chronicle* noted both the speed by which William won the castle and the impressive size of his army. It perhaps went some way to soothe him for the losses of the last year. The

Marshals were also newly in possession of Goodrich Castle which was either the last of Aoife's dower or was granted to them by the king as compensation for the damages in Normandy.

The gifts were a sign of the king's continued favour of Marshal. The previous year he granted, for a price, the lordship of Limerick and Munster to another of his favourites – William de Braose, 4th Lord of Bramber. Like Marshal, de Braose was a Marcher baron, favoured by Richard I, who supported John's claim to the throne. It was he who captured Arthur at Mirebeau and was said to know what happened to the boy at Rouen during Easter 1203. The family's main residence was at Abergavenny; the ties of service to the Plantagenet monarchy that existed between the two men and the geographical location made it inevitable that Isabel and de Braose's wife, Maud, knew one another. She was about twenty years older than Isabel and described as 'tall and beautiful, wise and vigorous'.[11] Gerald of Wales who could usually be relied upon for his misanthropic views described her as both a virtuous woman and an industrious wife.

Marshal accepted the castles and estates offered to him by the king but had no intention of forfeiting his Norman lordships. He and Isabel decided what needed to be done to preserve their interests. Success would be reliant on John's understanding and acceptance of what William intended. In April 1205, the Earl went to France with instructions to negotiate with Philip II. Before he departed, Marshal asked for permission to pay homage to the king for his Norman lands. It was a calculated risk but John gave his assent and issued letters informing Philip that Marshal was authorised to do homage for his estates in Normandy.[12] The oath William swore to Philip in exchange for his lordships went further than the king expected, or at least that was what he claimed as relations between the two men soured. Marshal offered, on his return to England as he had on at least one other occasion in his life, to take part in a trial by combat to defend his honour. Despite the earl approaching his sixtieth year, no one was eager to test his sword or his word. The king became more rather than less angry.

Marshal's agreement with Philip meant that he effectively served two masters. He was one of a small number of men, who included among their number Robert de Beaumont, 4th Earl of Leicester, who paid homage to King Philip of France. Neither man could fight on John's behalf in Normandy against the French because of the loyalty that they now owed to the French king. The Earl of Leicester avoided further censure by dying in October 1205.

The death of Robert de Beaumont meant that Marshal was the most significant landowner in the country at the head of an increasingly powerful kinship network. He and Isabel arranged their eldest son's marriage to Alice de Béthune, the daughter of Marshal's friend Baldwin de Béthune, Count of Aumale *jure uxoris* in 1203. Aumale was seized by the French in 1196 but Béthune controlled extensive Yorkshire holdings including the lordships of Skipton and Holderness. Baldwin, old friend and part of the Marshal family, was one of the barons who tried to smooth a path between the earl and the king in 1205.

The king was now alarmed that he had created both an overmighty and treacherous subject. At Michaelmas, John revoked estates in Sussex from William's control that were part of his inheritance from his elder brother. The king also demanded that Isabel and Marshal hand over William the Younger, now aged 15-years, as a hostage for Marshal's good faith. It was a reminder that despite Isabel's wealth and the respect in which the earl was held that the power remained with the king. Refusal to comply with John's demands was tantamount to treachery.

It was true that while William the Younger was a hostage, the experience at court was also an essential part of his education as an aristocrat with as much power as he would one day wield as an earl of Pembroke. With a place in the king's household, serving as a squire he was better placed to understand politics than his father, who began life as a lowly knight, had ever been. The situation in which hostages found themselves being kept might have been more akin to ward, foster child or guest rather than prisoner depending on the circumstances in which the arrangement was made. It was an indicator, however, that the king no longer trusted Marshal.

The earl remained at court until the spring of 1206. When the king crossed the Channel to Poitou where he intended to conduct a campaign against the French, Marshal left his eldest son and returned to the Marches with Isabel. Neither the earl nor his countess returned to court that Autumn when John arrived back in England. Royal favour had shone upon the earl since his marriage to Isabel in 1189 but the couple were about to discover what it was like to be ostracised by a Plantagenet.

The *Histoire* makes little mention of Isabel until 1207. Perhaps, during Marshal's time at Chepstow in 1206 she had the opportunity to discuss Leinster and the gradual erosion of her rights there. The earl sent his nephew John Marshal there in 1204 to take over as its seneschal. It is thought likely that John, who was a seasoned campaigner, was placed as the earl's agent there in the face of increasing hostility shown by Meiler FitzHenry, the king's justiciar in Ireland. By the end of 1206, they agreed that they needed to assume management of the fief for themselves. It was also convenient to put some distance between the king and their family while Marshal was out of favour.

Chapter 13

Leinster

In the autumn of 1206, Isabel finalised arrangements for her eldest daughter's wedding which took place the following year before the start of Lent. Maud was 13-years-old and adult enough to marry her espoused husband Hugh Bigod, the eldest son of Ida de Tosny and Roger Bigod, 2nd Earl of Norfolk. Marshal and his wife were fulfilling their obligations in securing Maud's future before they went to Ireland. The *Histoire* described Maud who was a favourite of her father and the marriage that was arranged for her:

> To whom God had shown great favour in granting her the gifts of wisdom, generosity, beauty, nobility of heart, graciousness, and all the good qualities that a noble lady should possess. Her worthy father who loved her dearly, married her off to the best and most handsome party he knew to Sir Hugh Bigod.[1]

It is inconceivable that Marshal made the arrangements without consulting Isabel. Maud took up residence in Framlingham where she completed her education and learned how to manage the estates that she would one day run for her husband.

The Bigod family were distantly related to the de Clares. Hugh's mother, Ida de Tosny, was a royal ward who became Henry II's mistress before her marriage to Bigod. She gave the king a son, William Longspée who became the 3rd Earl of Salisbury by his marriage to Ela the daughter of William FitzPatrick. He maintained a good relationship with his Bigod half-siblings and was related to William Marshal through his wife, Ela. Longspée held several important offices throughout the reigns of both his half-brothers and was well-known to Isabel and her husband. Maud's new sister-in-law, Alice Bigod who was the same age as Maud, was the bride of Aubrey de Vere, 2nd Earl of Oxford.[2] Familial alliances created through strategic marriages added to the political power that Marshal wielded as a landowner even if he was out of favour with the king and would help to keep Maud safe.

Isabel returned with her husband and family to Leinster in either late February or March 1207 after Marshal received the king's licence to travel as did key members of his *mesnie*, including John d'Earley and Henry Hose.[3] Although John granted authorisation for Marshal to go to Leinster, like Henry II before him he had second thoughts and sent a messenger to Striguil revoking his permission. William discussed the matter with his countess and the most trusted members of their household. Together they resolved that they would take the risk and make the journey. When news of their departure reached the court, John, his anger banked, reclaimed control of Gloucester and its castle, the Forest of Dean and the castle of St Briavels as well as Ceredigion Castle. The losses weakened the earl's control of the Marches and Wales but did not damage the lordships of Pembroke or Netherwent.

At about the same time, the earl and countess received news that the king wished to levy a tax on his subjects to raise funds to regain his lost empire. In February, at Oxford, John demanded a tax based on the value of every man's belongings as well as his income. It was levied at one shilling per mark. A mark was worth slightly more than thirteen shillings[4] so the tax came to be known as the Thirteenth. It was not a popular tax, especially as the king appointed officials to raise the funds. Everyone was required to swear to the value of their movable goods and their land so that sheriffs could collect the correct amount. In York, John's half-brother Archbishop Geoffrey threatened to excommunicate any man who tried to collect the tax within his diocese. The king demanded that the archbishop come to court to answer for his actions and seized Geoffrey's estates having mocked his appeal for redress. The archbishop went into exile where he complained to the pope.

In April 1207, John, still angered by Marshal's oath to the French and the manner of his departure to Ireland, demanded that the earl and countess give another son, Richard, as a second hostage for Marshal's future loyalty. Isabel is known to have demurred at the prospect. The boy's role at court could be dressed up as a continuation of the education that a nobleman required but in reality, both her eldest sons were in danger. If Marshal did anything that John, who was increasingly suspicious of all his barons, regarded as treason, one or both his sons would pay with their lives. On this occasion Marshal disagreed with his wife. He explained that he had nothing to fear for his sons because his loyalty was to the Crown.

By taking Marshal's two eldest sons the king was reinforcing his dominance over the earl. For Isabel it was a time of fear. She knew all too well that one of her mother's brothers was blinded while he was a hostage and another killed. And there were rumours about what happened to John's prisoners when he was driven by spite, jealousy or drunkenness. The king's own nephew, Arthur of Brittany, was never seen again after he was taken into John's custody in 1203. Rather than reinforcing the social system, hostage taking could go badly wrong where the hostage taker felt that promises made by the hostage giver were not honoured.

The countess was not alone in being forced to provide hostages. Across the realm barons and knights far less powerful than William were required to give family members as surety for the payment of fines as well as good behaviour. It helps to explain why clause forty-nine of the Magna Carta references the release of 'all hostages and charters delivered to us by Englishmen as securities for peace or faithful service'.[5]

The king was already embroiled in a dispute with the papacy before Geoffrey's intervention over the seizure of his property. The crisis began in 1205 when Hubert Walter, the Archbishop of Canterbury died. The monks at Canterbury tried to elect one of their number as his replacement but John disputed the result. He was determined that either John de Gray, Bishop of Norwich be appointed or that the diocese be kept vacant for as long as possible so that he could make use of the See's income for himself. In Rome, Pope Innocent III quashed the election results and rejected the king's candidate. Instead, he presented his own candidate; the reformer Stephen Langton. John's determination to claim the Crown's traditional rights in episcopal election and subsequent refusal to accept Langton was part of a long running dispute that dated back to the reign of King Stephen. The more that John resisted, the more decided Pope Innocent became that the erstwhile monarch should be punished. Roger of Wendover described John's fury: irascible on occasion the king was increasingly capricious.

In Ireland, Marshal faced several challenges if he was to safeguard Isabel's inheritance. They had been absentee overlords since William married Isabel in 1189. There was an urgent need to re-establish authority in Leinster. Isabel and her family moved to Kilkenny where Geoffrey FitzRobert, who was Isabel's brother-in-law, gave the town's inhabitants their first recorded privileges in 1199. Now, Marshal, having discussed the matter with Isabel issued a charter recognising the burgesses rights. As well as encouraging commerce, it helped promote good-will to the Marshals and encouraged more people to take up residence there.

Some of Ireland's barons, the epitome of medieval warlords, believed themselves to be more battle-hardened than Marshal who they chose to regard as a mere tournament knight. The king's justiciar, Meiler FitzHenry in particular, resented the possibility of his power and territorial ambitions being curbed by a man who was his overlord by right of his wife rather than by his sword. Isabel, the daughter of Strongbow and Aoife of Leinster, was required to act every inch a countess in her encounters with FitzHenry and the de Lacy family who controlled neighbouring Meath and Ulster. Marshal needed to win magnates who regarded Ireland as their home to his side and in part it was achieved by Isabel who comported herself like an Irish princess and hosted feasts in the great hall at Kilkenny that masked political manoeuvring with a veneer of social bonhomie. Aoife's daughter needed to learn about the complicated familial relationships and kinship networks that existed, who was married to or descended, like her, from native Irish heiresses and who might provide useful alliances.

The earl and his wife expedited some of the challenges by coming to an effective working arrangement with the Church in Ireland including the Anglo-Norman Bishop of Ossory, Hugh de Rous. The original Irish settlement at Kilkenny was under the authority of the bishop but the town that grew up around the castle was built further downstream. Isabel and William wanted to expand the township but to do that they needed land that was held by the Church. A deed dating from 1207 shows that Isabel agreed to the exchange of property that was part of her patrimony at Aghadoe in exchange for land at Kilkenny.[6] Transcripts from the *White Book of the Diocese of Ossory* refer to two charters relating to property in the diocese and name both Marshal and his countess in the terms of the agreement reflecting her active involvement in the administration of Leinster.[7] The *Chartae Hiberniae* contain two charters dating from this period in the town's history. The first, which was granted soon after Isabel's arrival identifies both the countess and her husband.[8] Kilkenny, known as Hightown, or Englishtown, to differentiate it from the original Irish centre of Kilkenny expanded with settlers from England and Wales under the earl and countess's patronage. The re-building of St Canice's Cathedral by de Rous had been underway since 1202. Isabel's presence led to both investment and expansion in the town. The siting of an Augustinian priory on the other side of the river along with its own suburbs demonstrated the effectiveness of the earl and countess's plantation policies.

It quickly became clear that Isabel and William had not escaped King John by crossing the Irish Sea. The king's scheming was damaging the loyalty of the magnates who held land there as well as weakening their own position within Ireland. The tensions between Marshal and the king combined with the effects of the earl's prolonged absence from Irish affairs was personified, in 1207, by Meiler FitzHenry, the grandson of King Henry I by his mistress Nest of Wales. FitzHenry was part of the first wave of Geraldines to arrive in Ireland in 1169 alongside his uncle Robert FitzStephen. In 1172 King Henry II had assigned the knight, who had a reputation for bravery bordering on foolhardiness, to the retinue of Hugh de Lacy. FitzHenry's standing in Ireland grew with the years along with the number of estates he acquired. After Strongbow's death in 1176 he continued to accrue power under the command of his kinsman Raymond le Gros before transferring his service to John who was Lord of Ireland. John made FitzHenry his justiciar in Ireland in 1198 and reappointed him to the position within two years as well as rewarding him with grants of land.

FitzHenry resented Marshal as an interloper and dismissed him as a real political power in the region. The justiciar's contempt was manifested by the seizure of Offaly in Kildare. He claimed it by right of a grant made by King John in 1207 despite the fact it was part of Marshal's fief. FitzHenry's attempts to annex the territory for himself was only possible because the king ignored Isabel's birth right. John's ploy of playing FitzHenry off against Marshal, who he was determined to punish, was an inspired choice. It was no consolation to Isabel that John's justiciar also seized Fercall in Meath which was under the lordship of the de Lacy family. The king employed a similar policy elsewhere in Ireland by pitting William de Braose, Lord of Limerick, against the long-established Geraldine clan. Sowing discord between his barons in Ireland so that they were riven by faction meant that John could control them more effectively. On this occasion, the king's tactics offered the additional benefit of hamstringing Marshal, who like his father-in-law before him, was perceived as holding too much power, should he choose to assert it, for John's liking.

The earl, who was determined to regain possession of Offaly and Dunamase Castle which the justiciar also misappropriated, summoned FitzHenry to appear before a feudal court in Kilkenny. William was not exceeding his power. He was the feudal overlord of Leinster, the land in question was part of the fief, and Meiler was Marshal's vassal. FitzHenry refused to recognise Marshal's rights. He argued that he was not a feudal tenant but the king's representative fulfilling a royal command. This supposition was a direct assault on the established patterns of feudal lordship in Ireland which were more akin to the freedoms enjoyed in the Marches of Wales than elsewhere in the kingdom of England because of the way in which the lordships had been carved from the land by the first Cambro-Normans to arrive in Ireland. In challenging FitzMeiler, Marshal came to be seen as a counterbalance to the king and his justiciar. But, in John's mind it confirmed that the Earl of Pembroke was a man who challenged royal authority to his own advantage. The king could see none of William's precious loyalty and honour in the way the earl responded to him.

FitzHenry's appropriation of other men's estates permitted the earl and his countess to build alliances more quickly than they might have done otherwise. In addition, some of the disgruntled barons or their kin were among Isabel's neighbours in the Welsh Marches. For instance, at the beginning of November 1204, William de Braose was ordered by the king to hand the city of Limerick into FitzHenry's custody. Like Marshal, de Braose was something of a latecomer to Ireland and in all probability FitzHenry resented his presence just as he begrudged Marshal's claims to Leinster. During the winter of 1206 John's justiciar took the whole of Limerick by force. De Braose, enduring his own fall from royal favour, was still in England when the assault happened. His son-in-law, Walter de Lacy, Lord of Meath, was resident in Ireland and he responded by attacking FitzHenry. De Lacy was joined in the campaign against the justiciar by his younger brother Hugh, 1st Earl of Ulster. The earldom granted in 1205 reflected the de Lacy family's long service to the Crown in Ireland, and Hugh's support for the Plantagenet monarchy against John de Courcy who conquered Ulster in 1177 without royal permission. The earldom may also have been given as a counterbalance to Marshal's own comital status.[9]

In 1207, the de Lacys were quick to recognise the benefits of working with Marshal against the king's schemes to seize lands and change the terms by which they were held. Marshal wished to strengthen his own position in Leinster; Walter and Hugh wanted to regain their own estates from the clutches of FitzHenry and they all recognised that the justiciar was the tool by which John intended to extend his hold over Ireland at the expense of its barony. They sent a letter to the king demanding that Meiler be made to comply with the order to attend Marshal's court hearing so that Offaly could be returned to its rightful owner. Among the men who commissioned the epistle was Philip de Prendergast, the son of Maurice de Prendergast who sailed to Ireland with Strongbow. He was part of Marshal's *mesnie* in Ireland as well as being a part of Isabel's own extended family. He was married to Maud de Quincy, the daughter of Isabel's half-sister Basilia from her first marriage to Robert de Quincy.

John's response to the supplication from Ireland was a furious rebuke penned on 25 May 1207. He categorically denied Marshal's right to establish a feudal court without royal assent. He claimed that it was contrary to Irish custom. To him it was yet another example of Marshal's attempts to place himself above royal control. He insisted that Offaly was not something for discussion. So far as the king was concerned the case was closed. In future the barons of Ireland would do well to consider royal rights before their own.

The king's prerogative, feudal rights and the autonomy not only of his barons but also of the Church was much on his mind that summer. On 17 June 1207 the Pope insisted that Stephen Langton be installed as archbishop. John remained stubborn in his refusal to allow the archbishop entry to his realm. Soon afterwards all the bishops of England and Wales received a 'monition and exhortation'[10] to support Langton. Failure to see the archbishop installed would have dire consequences for John's realm. It was followed by a similar notice to England's magnates. Sooner or later, the Earl of Pembroke's own papal correspondence arrived in Kilkenny where he was alerted to the growing dispute. Isabel and Marshal knew what to expect if John continued to resist papal demands. In Leon an interdict laid on the realm in 1198 lasted until 1204. Excommunication of a monarch meant that all his people, from the poorest peasant to the mightiest magnate, suffered the consequences. There would be no Masses, no marriages and no burial in consecrated ground. The immortal souls of all John's subjects in England would be imperilled.

Chapter 14

Lady of Leinster

In September 1207 the king recalled Marshal to England and also summoned FitzHenry to resolve the continuing dispute between the earl and the justiciar over tenure of Offaly. The Irish barons who signed the petition to the king in May were also called back to England for a meeting in October with John at Woodstock.

Isabel and Marshal decided that she would remain in Leinster while William returned to England. The resolution might have related to her pregnancy but she travelled widely throughout her married life and at different stages of motherhood. It is more plausible that she remained to assert her rights as Diarmait MacMurchada's granddaughter and Strongbow de Clare's only surviving legitimate heir. Marshal left his *mesnie* with Isabel, choosing to take only Henry Hose back to England with him. He assured Isabel that men who were loyal to the Marshal family in Ireland would be present at court.

Before William's departure, the earl and countess held a council meeting. John d'Earley and Jordan de Sauquerville, or Sackville, were appointed to act as Isabel's bailiffs. D'Earley was responsible for the southern half of Leinster. He would be supported by Marshal's cousin Stephen d'Evereux who was also related to the Lacy family. De Sauquerville, who held lands in Ulster under the feudal lordship of its earl, was responsible for the rest of the fief. His position in Marshal's *mesnie* was derived from the lands he held in Normandy and in Buckinghamshire. They would be reinforced in their task by Geoffrey FitzRobert, Baron of Kells who had his own links to the Geraldines through the kinship networks of his new wife Eve de Bermingham.

Isabel and d'Earley were of the opinion that the Marshals should take hostages as surety of good faith. This included men like Isabel's nephew-in-law, Philip of Prendergast, who was also returning to England but William refused. He preferred, he said, to trust the honour of the men who owed him allegiance as their feudal overlord. Instead, he and Isabel put on a show designed to remind everyone gathered at a meeting held in the great hall of Kilkenny Castle of the loyalty that they owed to the granddaughter of Diarmait MacMurchada:

Lords! See the countess, whom I here present to you; your lady by birth, the daughter of the earl who freely enfeoffed you all when he conquered this land. She remains amongst you, pregnant. Until God permits me to return, I pray you to keep her well and faithfully, for she is your lady, and I have nothing but through her.[1]

The earl and countess understood that Isabel's Hiberno-Norman ancestry was the key to securing their place in Ireland. It was apparent to all their vassals gathered at Kilkenny that Isabel intended to administer her Irish estates and defend them from her husband's enemies.

The boat carrying Marshal, his nephew John Marshal and Henry Hose arrived back in Wales on 29 September. The king was in Winchester where Queen Isabella gave birth, on 1 October, to a son they named Henry. It was an occasion for celebration. The kingdom had its heir. God, it seemed, was finally favouring King John.

The king's strategy for Ireland and for the earl, which soon became evident, was to weaken Marshal's support among the barony in Leinster by buying them off. He offered grants of land to Marshal's nephew John and to Philip de Prendergast as well as several other magnates. Isabel's nephew by marriage, Prendergast, already held land in Wexford from Marshal but the forty knights' fees[2] that the king gave him near Cork elevated his position beyond anything that William or Isabel could offer. John Marshal was confirmed as the king's marshal in Ireland. It has been suggested that John Marshal, who delayed his acceptance of the new title by a week, discussed the matter with his uncle before accepting.[3] John was awarded various Irish manors but he preferred to execute his office through deputies rather than going in person to Ireland afterwards.[4] By focusing on Isabel and Marshal's kinsmen, the king was able isolate the earl at Woodstock with practised ease. Of the men who returned to England with William only Henry Hose remained loyal.

Men who had sided with Marshal in May were quick to take the estates that the king offered them under terms that increased John's authority in Ireland. Adam de Hereford, Richard Latimer, David de Rupe and Richard de Cogan were among the men who received grants of land in Ireland witnessed by FitzHenry, John Marshal and Prendergast. King John ensured that there was a body of men who were more sympathetic to him because they owed their advancement to the Crown.

Marshal's treatment was nothing compared to Isabel's experiences in Ireland. Meiler, knowing that the earl was summoned to England, arranged for his men to lead a campaign against Leinster a week after his own departure. New Ross was attacked and more than twenty men killed. Granges were looted and burned. It was the start of a season of fire and death. The *Annála Rioghachta Éireann* more commonly known as *The Annals of the Four Masters* or just the *Four Masters*, compiled during the seventeenth century from earlier Irish accounts recorded the outcome of the dispute:

> A great war broke out among the English of Leinster; i.e. between Meyler, Geoffrey Mares, and William Mareschal. Leinster and Munster suffered severely from them.[5]

The Annals of Clonmacnoise focused more closely on the strife that arose between the justiciar and Hugh de Lacy. Of Isabel there is no word, even though in Marshal's absence, it was she who was in command of the situation. It was the Lady of Leinster that the earl and countess's tenants turned to for shelter and protection and it was Isabel who fulfilled her feudal obligations as their overlord. It was Isabel who held councils of war with Marshal's *mesnie* and it was Isabel who refused to be cowed throughout the long winter that followed. While they waited, Isabel and the men who advised her concluded that it was essential to build closer ties with de Lacy in Ulster if they were to have enough men to outmanoeuvre FitzHenry. Isabel sent de Sauquerville to negotiate with the earl who was his feudal overlord on her behalf.

In January 1208, King John wrote to John d'Earley, Stephen d'Evreux and Jordan de Sauquerville demanding their presence within fifteen days of receiving the order. He gave the letter to Thomas Bloet, the brother of Marshal's knight Ralph. Three of Bloet's brothers served John. Their preferment arose from John's good relationship with their mutual half-brother, Morgan. The king also gave Meiler FitzHenry and the men who received grants from him permission to return to Ireland. John and his justiciar calculated that without her husband or his most trusted deputies at her side that Isabel's resistance would fold like a house of cards.

It must have been a turbulent winter crossing for Bloet, FitzHenry and Prendergast who had been given permission to return to Ireland during the storms that kept most vessels tied to their moorings. Marshal, given the cold shoulder by courtiers who saw which way the wind blew, could only bide his time knowing that the three men summonsed by the king had a difficult decision to make. If they did not obey the king's order, their lands in England and Wales would be forfeit but if they came to court his own position in Ireland would be further destabilised and Isabel left isolated. Marshal could not risk leaving court to re-join his family. Their sons, William and Richard, were still John's hostages. It was his heirs who would pay the price for

Marshal's perceived treason. The king placed a man known for his loyalty to the Plantagenet monarchy in an impossible position.

In Ireland, FitzHenry must have delighted in sharing the information that two of Isabel's extended family, John Marshal and Philip de Prendergast, had betrayed the earl and that the rest of the men who travelled to Woodstock the previous autumn had distanced themselves from their former ally. The justiciar also ensured that John's orders for d'Earley, d'Evereux and de Sauquerville to depart from Ireland were given to them immediately after his own arrival.

John d'Earley was Marshal's ward before he became his squire or knight. The earl, having taken responsibility for John, taught his charge the values of loyalty and chivalry. The *Histoire* contrasts the perfidy of the men who went to Woodstock with the devotion of Marshal's trusted *mesnie*. D'Earley refused to abandon Isabel because of the bonds of loyalty he owed the Lady of Leinster. D'Evereux and de Sauquerville agreed. All three men remained at their posts. Loss of wealth was preferable to loss of honour.

FitzHenry marched on Kilkenny and laid siege to the countess. Isabel was equal to the challenge. She demonstrated, like many other medieval women who defended their homes during times of war, that she knew how to keep a cool head. 'She had a man let down over the battlements to go and tell John d' Earley that it was the very truth that she was besieged in Kilkenny.'[6] FitzHenry had badly underestimated both of them. Isabel had no intention of yielding her home to the justiciar. During his absence in England, she placed the castle and its inhabitants on a war footing. The justiciar was about to discover that the blood of Irish warriors and Norman freebooters ran in the countess's veins.

Throughout the winter months Marshal was kept in the darkness about what was happening in Ireland to his wife, family and his estates. The dreadful weather prevented safe passage of the Irish Sea in either direction. At court he remained isolated but was at least able to see his elder sons on occasion. Few men wished to be seen in the company of a man the king was intent on ruining and John delighted in tormenting the earl. He told Marshal when his officers confiscated the estates of d'Evereux and d'Earley. Even the king knew that the knight was as close to Marshal as one of his own sons. Laughing, on another occasion, while resident in Guildford, he announced that Isabel was under siege at Kilkenny. He added that both d'Earley was mortally wounded and that d'Evreux and another member of Marshal's *mesnie*, Ralph FitzPagan, were dead. Isabel and her younger children were, John indicated, vulnerable without their protectors. The king poked at the weak spot in the earl's defences hoping to provoke him into an overt act of treason. Marshal did not fall into the snares that John laid for him. His response was both measured and calm, reminding the king that the knights he named were his own men as well as the earl's.[7]

In February, John demanded that Marshal, who was sheriff of Sussex, surrender Chichester Castle which had been in his possession since 1195. He also issued orders that no Welsh mariner was to cross to Ireland 'as they love their lives and chattels'.[8] By March, the king and his court were at Bristol. Marshal followed after them although his presence was unwelcome.

When news finally did begin to filter across the water, the king had little to celebrate. Isabel and her commanders successfully counter-attacked FitzHenry in alliance with Hugh de Lacy, Earl of Ulster. The king's justiciar in Ireland had failed to attain his victory over Leinster's countess. Instead, Isabel gave orders for his possessions to be seized. He and Philip de Prendergast were captured and forced to submit, on their knees, to the enraged countess in the hall at Kilkenny.

The granddaughter of the last king of Leinster was less tolerant than her husband when it came to men who broke their oaths and assaulted her property. She took their sons as hostages as guarantees for their future good behaviour and vented her anger on the men who came to terms with the king at Woodstock. Their sons were also in her custody. If there were no sons to be pledged Isabel demanded younger brothers. She did not accept more distant relations because she understood all too well how much leverage could be bought to bear on men and women whose immediate family lived with their lives in the balance. Isabel intended to impose her will on her fief whether her husband was there or not.

When Marshal appeared before the king on 5 March 1208, he knew that Leinster was safe. Isabel sent a messenger to her husband as soon as it was safe to travel. The earl was enough of a diplomat to pretend ignorance of FitzHenry's defeat. Instead, he allowed John to give him the good news that his countess was in good health and delivered of another son, named Ansel, or Anselm, after one of William's brothers. The king chose to ignore his own intrigues with FitzHenry as though they never happened and resumed good relations with the earl. On 7 March, the king sent a letter to his justiciar:

William earl Mareschal came to us unbidden, and in a disposition to comply to our will; and from Bristol we purpose proceeding towards the council which weare to hold at Winchester (on the 12 march); and although we wished that the said Earl would go and visit his lands until the day of the council, yet he would not quit our side, but intends to accompany us step by step to the council, disposed and ready, as he says to execute our will.[9]

John issued orders stating that FitzHenry was to make reparations for the damage inflicted on Leinster and promote no further conflict. By the 20 March, the king came to terms with Marshal. A messenger was sent commanding the justiciar to return Offaly to its rightful owner. It helped that William gave a pledge to pay 300 marks for the land which was rightfully part of Isabel's inheritance.[10]

Marshal recognised that FitzHenry was a scapegoat but that unless John was assured on his position in Ireland that there would be other men willing to take his place. The king would continue in his attempts to undermine barons, like himself, who were largely autonomous. Besides, victory would mean very little if John reclaimed all of his and Isabel's estates in England and Wales. Like Strongbow before him, William surrendered some of the liberties that he enjoyed in Leinster to preserve the whole of his lordship.

The king permitted Marshal to return to Ireland where he was reunited with his family and his *mesnie*. Now in his sixties, he had secured his Irish estates from the Crown and intended to turn them into a flourishing enterprise. Isabel was still intent on punishing the men who owed fealty to them but whose treachery nearly cost them Leinster. The earl, who had been a hostage in 1152 during his own childhood and very nearly hanged because of his father's failure to comply with the demands of King Stephen, returned most of his wife's hostages to their homes having accepted renewed oaths of homage from their fathers and elder brothers.

There were exceptions. Meiler's son stayed in Isabel's custody as did Philip de Prendergast's son, Gerald, even though Prendergast begged for Marshal's mercy and was reconciled with the earl with a kiss of peace that could only be described as cold. The *Histoire* recorded Isabel's irritation with her husband's moderate approach and her desire for vengeance, noting, 'for they had done her many wrong[s] and hurt and their crimes were many'.[11] She did not appreciate being besieged in her own castle. The biographer went on to add, 'I can assure you, that had he listened to her, the earl would have exacted a savage revenge upon them'.[12] Instead, Gerald was sent to England where he remained until 1215.[13]

If Isabel's troubles were over, King John's were not. The spring of 1208 brought other messengers besides those from Ireland. Pope Innocent III placed England under interdict on 23 March 1208. This meant that not only did church bells fall silent but that many of the religious services provided by the clergy were withdrawn from the whole of his realm. That Easter there were no Masses celebrated. Gerald of Wales wrote about both the lack of divine services and the way in which the king stole clerical possessions during the years when clerical vacancies were not filled. The churches closed their doors and the clergy sought clarification about what was permitted and what was not. Some priests held services in their churchyards, in other areas the clergy carried on as though there was no interdict in place, while in others the rituals by which men and women lived their lives halted. There were no Masses, marriage services[14] or burials in church yards.

Only baptism and the sacrament for the dying were permitted. Baptism required the use of holy oil, or chrism, but priests were not allowed to bless more oil when their supplies ran out. It became inevitable that unless the clergy interpreted the Interdict with a degree of flexibility that the immortal souls of unbaptised infants would be jeopardised. Christian burial did not resume until July 1214 despite the fact that priests still visited the sick, heard their confessions and absolved them from their sins. For John's subjects it meant life and death, with the fear that burial in consecrated ground might mean that they would never get to Heaven.

In Ireland, where the Interdict did not run, Isabel could only pray for the souls of her two eldest sons at the court of King John, for her daughter Maud learning how to be a countess in Norfolk, and for her tenants in the Marches. It looked unlikely that she would return to England from Leinster for the foreseeable future.

Chapter 15

An Irish Retirement

Following the pattern of their lordships in Normandy and the Marches, William and Isabel tended to the security of their Irish domain using Marshal's preferred continental principles of castle building. As well as being defensive the fortifications offered a jumping off point for further prizes in Ireland just as Marshal's castles in the Marches provided potential bases for the annexation of territory in Wales. FitzRobert, Marshal's seneschal, built a castle at Ferns, Diarmait MacMurchada's political powerbase, in 1200. Now, under the earl's supervision, Carlow, Callan, Kilkenny and Old Ross were fortified or remodelled.

At the same time, Isabel and William continued their campaign of monastic patronage in Leinster as well as establishing a network of townships and markets. Isabel oversaw continued investment in Kilkenny and its market. The town expanded on a regular grid pattern with twenty feet wide burgage plots that fronted onto the street and which abided by the charter granted to the town by the earl and countess in 1207. It was shaping up to be a model town designed to draw in settlers, merchants and to make a long-term profit for the Marshals. In 1269 an Inquisition taken at Kilkenny investigated to whom the income from the market rightfully belonged. Bishop Hugh granted Marshal and Isabel the land on which the market was held in return for an annual rent of an ounce of gold. Marshal and his heirs were in receipt of 'a toll out of the vill from 9 o'clock on Friday till 9 o'clock on Saturday.[1]

The economic development of Leinster focused on the *caput* at Kilkenny and the port at New Ross which now flourished to the extent that it diverted trade from the king's port at Waterford.[2] Having experienced the difficulties of winter crossings, the earl and his countess also founded a borough and a port at Clonmines in Bannow Bay. It did not lend itself to commerce but it offered safe anchorage during winter as well as providing the monks at Tintern Parva with a trading route.[3] More enduring than Clonmines, the Marshals also commissioned the four-storey lighthouse on the Hook Peninsula to guide vessels safely into the harbour at New Ross. The fire that lit the tower at night was tended by the monks from Rinn Dubháin.

In about 1211, Marshal granted land to the Augustinians of Kilkenny so that they could build a new priory. The canons were charged with caring for the poor and infirm. Together, he and Isabel endowed the priory with lands, fisheries and an annual pension.[4] Not only were they fulfilling their spiritual obligations but they were ensuring the new town of Kilkenny was provided with a recognisable framework for poor relief.

Marshal's consultation with his countess on matters relating to the development of Leinster are apparent through the number of charters that reference her advice and agreement. In Dublin, with access to her own resources, Isabel grateful to God for all she possessed and eager to secure the salvation of her family, confirmed an earlier grant made to the Cathedral Priory but made a new condition that half the tithes from the land should be kept to say masses for the souls of her father Richard, her husband, herself and her children while the other half of the tithes were to be devoted to the 'maintenance of the priory's linen.'[5] Isabel was a patroness with an eye for good housekeeping as well as expressing her piety in an accepted form. It is interesting to note that she emphasised her Norman ancestry, rather than her Irish claims to Leinster through Aoife who was not named on this occasion. Long established Cambro-Norman-Irish families were reminded that she was Strongbow's daughter and that Marshal's *jure uxoris* claims to Ireland were of better standing than their own.

It was during the period between 1208 and 1210 that Isabel gave birth to her last child, Joan who joined Ansel in the nursery at Kilkenny. Their sisters Eva born in 1203, Sibyl born in about 1201 and Isabel born in 1200 continued to be educated under the countess's watchful eyes. Like their mother, they grew up speaking Irish. Isabel's sons Walter and Gilbert were too old to be educated by women. Walter joined his father's household to continue his education as a knight but Gilbert's talents lay elsewhere. Isabel's chaplain recognised the boy's potential as a scholar. The countess's life as the mother of young children was coming to a natural end. She and Marshal began to consider who might make appropriate husbands for their four daughters and how to divide their estates among their sons without damaging William the Younger's inheritance.

The politics of Ireland were also changing. FitzHenry, the last of Strongbow's freebooters, was removed from power and replaced as justiciar by John de Grey, Bishop of Norwich. Marshal knew him from his service to John and from their unsuccessful mission in 1203 to make terms with Philip II for the preservation of Normandy. De Grey was with Marshal and the king when they boarded the boat at Barfleur signalling the king's loss of his father's empire. The bishop's task in Ireland was to extend John's authority in Ireland. The barons still possessed far too much autonomy for his liking. De Grey was just as capable as FitzHenry in a fight but he recognised that there were other ways of bringing about the changes that the king desired. In 1210 orders were issued that coins in Ireland should in future be minted to the same standards as the money in England.

It was also evident to other magnates, besides Marshal, that the king wanted to impose the kind of control on Ireland that he possessed elsewhere in his realm. Recognising the inevitable, Walter de Lacy chose to accept new terms for Meath at the same time that Marshal came to terms with John for Leinster.[6] John's determination to extend the authority of the Crown into Ireland was reflected by the imposition of military service in the form of 100 knights in the field for Leinster and 50 for Meath.[7] William de Braose who held the lordship of Limerick was less clear-sighted about the consequences of defying the king.

In Leinster itself, the grants of land that Marshal and Isabel made to Marshal's *mesnie* gave them more influence in their fief while the men who opposed the earl faced increasing isolation. One man, David de la Roche, was even publicly snubbed by an ally of Marshal at a council meeting in Gloucester because of his failure to serve his feudal overlord.[8]

The relationship between de Braose and the king deteriorated steadily from 1202 onwards. John grew more suspicious as de Braose fell behind in his payments for the honour of Limerick. Even so, the exact nature of John's growing antipathy towards de Braose is unclear. The baron, like Marshal, had smoothed the king's way to the throne and, like Marshal, was initially a royal favourite. In 1207, at the same time as he plotted against Isabel and William, John moved against de Braose. Marshal must have been witness to the king's pettiness during his enforced stay in England although he later claimed to have no knowledge of any dissent between the king and his friend.

In 1208, the king demanded that de Braose give his son William as hostage as security against payment of his debts. De Braose's wife, Maud, a formidable woman, was outspoken in her refusal. According to Roger of Wendover, 'with the sauciness of a woman'[9] she told the king's messenger 'I will not deliver my son to your lord, King John, for he foully murdered his nephew Arthur, who he should have cared for honourably'.[10] It is plausible that she did know the truth behind 12-year-old Arthur's disappearance. De Braose captured the boy in 1202 at the Siege of Mirebeau and was at Rouen the following Easter when Arthur is thought to have been killed. It is possible that the description of John's drunken murder of his nephew contained within the *Margam Abbey Chronicle*, a near contemporary account, was a rendering of a story told by a member of the de Braose family. Realising that the manner of Maud's refusal was disastrous for the entire family, de Braose returned his castles in the Welsh Marches to the Crown in the hope that it would placate John before fleeing to Ireland with his wife and two of their sons.

It did not escape the king's notice that they were 'there harboured by Earl William Marshal and Walter and Hugh de Lacy'.[11] It was true that Isabel and her husband provided their friends with a safe haven at Wicklow for nearly three weeks while they were enroute to Trim Castle in Meath where they stayed with their daughter Margaret and her husband Walter de Lacy, Lord of Meath. According to the *Histoire*, Marshal declared of his guests that he knew nothing about treachery or their fugitive status.[12] The lords of Ireland closed ranks around de Braose who spent 1209 under the protection of the de Lacys before agreeing with de Grey, in 1210, to make his peace with the king who was at Pembroke Castle gathering an army to sail to Ireland. De Braose offered 40,000 marks to John in return for forgiveness but by then the king was determined to embark on a personal expedition to Ireland.

Marshal thought it expedient to go to Pembroke to submit himself to the king's will when it became clear that John intended to bring an army to Ireland that summer. John still harboured suspicions against the earl who found it expedient, once again, to offer to undergo trial by combat. Aside from the fact that no one could be found willing to take to the field of battle against Isabel's husband, there was also the problem of finding someone to oversee the trial. Prior to the Interdict it was a role often filled by the clergy but since Innocent's decree it was another of the responsibilities that they declined to fulfil.

King John arrived at Crook, near Waterford, on 20 June 1210. The next day he was at New Ross and by the 23 June Isabel, dressed in her most expensive robes, greeted him at Kilkenny. The countess was expected to feed and house the king, his court and his entire army at her own expense. It was a heavy burden for Isabel, her servants and for her tenants but it was a challenge to which she rose. The royal stay at Pembroke was already the occasion of an unlooked-for drain on the Marshals' finances. It did not help that John's stated intention was to punish everyone who harboured William and Maud de Braose.[13]

The king stayed in Ireland for nine weeks in the summer of 1210. The *Barnwell Chronicle* recounted that it was John's purpose to punish the Earl of Ulster who owed his elevation to the king as well as pursuing the de Braoses. Walter de Lacy, Lord of Meath, recognising that John meant business sent his tenants to submit to the king when he departed Leinster for Dublin. It was to no avail. John intended to exercise his feudal rights as Meath's overlord. He confiscated Walter's lordship and seized all his castles. Walter's brother, Hugh, who was more closely associated with conspiracies against the king elsewhere in his realm, fled with the de Braoses to Scotland where Maud and her son William were captured and handed to John.

Having exercised royal authority over the lords of Limerick, Meath and Ulster as well as having seized castles, hostages and rebels, the king turned his attention once more to Leinster during his visit to Dublin where he intended to set up an administrative centre. He began, according to Roger of Wendover, by exacting an agreement that in future 'the laws and customs of England were extended to Ireland.'[14] The king intended to crush the autonomy of his Irish magnates and to extort funds for another attempt to regain his continental territories.

Next, he summoned Marshal to answer to a charge of treason for harbouring the de Braoses. Marshal and Isabel maintained the stance that they were unaware that the king was on anything other than good terms with the couple who were old friends of William's. Marshal, who was now in his sixties, added that he would defend himself in any way that the court chose. Inevitably, none of the barons present in Dublin felt the need to test their sword arm against Marshal's military prowess. John chose to accept the earl's account but confiscated Dunamase Castle as a pledge for Marshal's future conduct. Isabel's sons, William the Younger and Richard, were still hostages in the king's custody but now he demanded even more hostages of the earl.

Marshal's trusted knights, John d'Earley, Jordan de Sauquerville and Geoffrey FitzRobert, were required to submit themselves to the king. The three were Irish landowners, an important part of the Marshals' administrative network and had taken to the field against Meiler FitzHenry when Isabel was under siege at Kilkenny. History does not record the countess's emotions when she said her farewells to the men who served her so loyally during her husband's absence. D'Earley was sent to Nottingham Castle where he was subject to ill-treatment for a short while before being permitted to return to court, de Sauquerville to Gloucester and FitzRobert to Hereford where he died in captivity.

The news about the de Braoses, when it arrived back in Leinster, was not good. At first, they were imprisoned in Bristol Castle. It was agreed that if de Braose paid 40,000 marks that his wife and son would be freed but when the baron was unable to raise the first instalment of the ransom, William was declared to be an outlaw. Maud and William were moved to closer confinement in Corfe Castle, or possibly Windsor,[15] where they both starved to death. A story was told that Maud's body was found collapsed over that of her son. William's cheek still carried the teeth marks that showed that his mother, driven insane by hunger, turned to cannibalism in order to stay alive a little longer herself. De Braose escaped to France but died the following year in Paris. If John's intention was to intimidate his barons in England and Ireland he had succeeded. For Isabel who knew Maud and William de Braose, whose own family was suspected by the king, and whose sons were under his control, it must have been even more frightening.

In England political quick sands pooled around John's feet. In 1212, the pope issued a papal bull reinforcing John's excommunication from the Catholic Church. More significantly it absolved John's subjects from their oaths of loyalty to him. In Winchester, Prince Henry was placed under heavy protection in case disgruntled barons decided to put John's heir on the throne in place of his father.

Llywelyn ap Iorwerth, Prince of Gwynedd, saw an opportunity in the increasing discord in England to write to Philip II of France to make an alliance against King John who was Llywelyn's father-in-law since his marriage to the king's illegitimate daughter, Joan, in about 1205. The alliance may have been assisted by the agency of Maud de Braose's second son, Giles, who was the Bishop of Hereford. His ecclesiastical rank was due to his father's favour with the king in 1200 but now, in exile and determined upon vengeance, he was a thorn in the king's side. Llywelyn's own intention was to push back the Marcher lords from Wales and to establish his own identity in continental Europe as a prince of Wales. Llywelyn's desire stemmed, in part, from a victorious campaign led by John into Wales the previous year and a programme of royal castle building. In 1212 the Welsh prince, like England's magnates, was absolved by papal bull from any oaths or agreements he might formerly have made with John. The Marches were a front line once again as the king planned a campaign to subdue his son-in-law.

On 16 August, John was at Nottingham, where he had already hanged twenty-eight Welsh hostages, when rumours of a northern plot led by Eustace de Vesci, Lord of Alnwick and Robert FitzWalter, Lord of Little Dunmow, a distant kinsman of Isabel's, reached his ears. Both men fled into exile but the king called off his war with the Welsh. Instead, he set about stabilising the position in which he found himself. The *Barnwell Chronicle* recorded the financial concessions and his promises to tackle abuses of Forest Law.[16]

Marshal wrote, with the rest of Ireland's landowners, to John affirming their own loyalty defusing the king's suspicions about Leinster. The earl offered to emerge from retirement if the king wished for his support in England or on the Marches. John responded positively to the hand of friendship. Isabel heard the contents of the royal correspondence with interest. In it, the king talked about William the Younger, who remained at court as a royal hostage:

You should provide better for your boy, who is with me and lacks horses or apparel. I will furnish him with the necessaries, if the Earl pleases and deliver him to John d'Earley.[17]

The same letter reminded Marshal not to remove his son from the realm without royal licence. It also denied a rumour that John intended to take William the Younger with him on campaign to Poitou later in the year. The implied threat of William's position remained in John's letter but Isabel's eldest son was translated from prisoner almost to the position of ward. The last time she saw William before he went to court, he was a boy. Now he was a young man of 22-years. It is impossible to know how many times the countess slipped a gift or a note for either of her elder sons into the hands of a messenger before he left Ireland for England, how often she sent new clothing, or how hopeful she was that their long parting was finally coming to an end.

The king proved true to his word and gave William into the keeping of John d'Earley who was appointed Sheriff of Devon in 1211. The king's new found favour was further reflected in d'Earley's promotion as Marshal of the Royal Household. Isabel's second son, Richard, was moved into the care of Thomas de Sandford, another of Marshal's knights recalled to England as a hostage for the earl in 1210.

Chapter 16

Troubled Times

In the Spring of 1213, Marshal was recalled by King John to England so that he could fulfil his function in the Marches to put down Welsh aggression orchestrated by Llywelyn and help to defend the realm from the French who were preparing to invade England. For Isabel it meant a return to Pembroke and Striguil. Her sons were at last safe from John's hangmen but her husband's loyalty to the Crown placed him at the forefront of events.

At least Isabel arrived in a realm at the end of its long Interdict. By May, John recognised that he needed to bring the conflict with the papacy to an end. He agreed to accept Stephen Langton and the other bishops who had gone into exile as well as the lords who fled the country the previous year. On 15 May 1213, Marshal, who may have had a hand in persuading him, witnessed John's resignation of his crown into the hands of Pandulf, the papal legate in England. The king formally submitted to papal authority and gave England to the pope who returned it to the king as a papal fief. By submitting to Innocent III, John hoped to improve his increasingly tenuous hold upon his throne. On 20 July, John was received back into the Church turning from an outcast into a favoured son of the church.

At about the same time the king wrote from Winchester to his justiciar in Ireland, ordering that protection should be provided by the justiciar for the lands and belongings of the Earl of Pembroke who was retained in the king's service in England.[1] Isabel and her children were already in residence in the Marches where the countess took up the threads of old friendships and saw for herself the changes of the last seven years.

Marshal's power began to accrue as he rose in royal esteem. John gave him the port and castle of Haverfordwest in October 1213 in exchange for a fee. The earl was quick to grant a charter to the burgesses of Haverfordwest confirming the rights and privileges extended to them by both King Henry I and King Henry II. Ceredigion Castle was restored to him. He was also granted the Gower and Carmarthen. The *Histoire* stated that William 'forgot the king's cruel conduct towards him'[2] but does not record Isabel's views on the matter.

John spent much of 1214 in France. He left the administration of England in the hands of his justiciar, Peter des Roches, Bishop of Winchester who was also guardian to the king's heir, Prince Henry. Marshal's oath of allegiance to the French king meant that he could not serve John. Any relief Isabel may have felt was balanced by the scutage of three marks per knight's fee that her husband was required to pay for his failure to appear in the king's army in France. Feudal taxation was levied on ten other occasions in John's reign but this was the highest ever demanded.

On 27 July 1214, John's army was defeated at Bouvines and his half-brother, William Longspée, 3rd Earl of Salisbury was made a prisoner of the French. The king was forced to agree to a five-year truce, returning to England in October. He was at Westminster at the end of the month but his defeat weakened his control over his realm. The barons who surrounded him muttered their grievances to one another.

Isabel was most likely to have spent the Christmas season in Worcester in 1214 where Marshal was once more an essential part of John's court. Evidence for the earl's presence comes from his witnessing of three charters. It was an opportunity for Isabel to meet with Maud who was now a mother herself. It was another reason for Isabel to resent the king. She was not able, in 1209, to be by her eldest daughter's side when she gave birth to a son named Roger, after his handsome father, and it is unlikely that the countess was present for the birth of her second grandson, Hugh, who was born in 1212. From Maud, Isabel discovered, if she did not already know, that the 2nd Earl of Norfolk who was frequently with the king on royal business sided with the aggrieved barons as did Maud's own husband.

Isabel could only envy the cohesiveness of the Bigod family. Her own son, William the Younger was on the verge of rejecting John's kingship. His antipathy could have had its roots in his years spent as a hostage as a guarantor for his father's loyalty. It is equally possible that the decision that he would side with the rebels was reached after a family conference. Families made similar choices in England's other civil wars to ensure that their lands and titles remained safe no matter what the outcome of the conflict. For Isabel it meant that her family was as divided as the realm.

On the 26 December 1214 the king gave orders for the court to move to London travelling first to Tewkesbury before progressing south through Gloucestershire to Guiting where New Year was celebrated. Despite the feasting, singing and general merriment there was a growing undercurrent of tension. When the king arrived in London on 7 January 1215, he lodged at the New Temple headquarters of the Knights Templar where Marshal's friend Aymeric de St Maur was the Grand Master. The following day, a dozen barons hostile to John met with him to air their grievances. The king's former suspicions about his tenants-in-chief including the ever-loyal Marshal, his cruelty towards some of them, their families and his prisoners, and his abuse of the feudal system of fines and amercements in part used to raise funds to fight in France were like chickens coming home to roost. John's barons, on whom the burden of his demands and vices had fallen, demanded reform based on King Henry I's coronation charter.

John replied that he would give his magnates an answer at Easter. The *Croyland Chronicle* noted that the king refused to address their complaints or to confirm their rights at the first angry meeting. He issued a letter of safe conduct guaranteeing the welfare of the barons until Easter when he required their presence at Northampton. The letter stipulated that there was enough time for the men who lived furthest away from there to return in safety to their homes. His words were witnessed and vouchsafed by churchmen and magnates loyal to the Crown. Among their number was William Marshal and Isabel's kinsman the Earl of Arundel. The king took his court out of London and headed west after the exchange. He had no intention of attending the meeting or permitting his barons to check his royal authority.

History does not document the conversations that took place between Isabel and Marshal in the aftermath of the meeting. As winter turned into spring it was the Archbishop of Canterbury who claimed a neutral Church position and the earl, widely respected by his peers, and acting on the king's behalf who met and negotiated with the barons. John, doubtful of the outcome, took the precaution of taking a vow to go on a crusade like his brother before him. In doing so he gained the protection of the Church. The Pope sent a letter on 19 March to John's magnates sorrowful for the disagreements which had arisen but instructing them to be loyal to their feudal overlord. He also wrote to John suggesting that moderation and reform were essential. By then the king was garrisoning his castles with mercenaries from Poitou.

As well as the backing of the Church, John set about assuring himself of the loyalty of men like William Marshal. The earl was granted custody of the vacant bishopric of St David's in Pembrokeshire. The Earl of Arundel received a property in the London Jewry. The Templars accepted land in Northamptonshire and Buckinghamshire. The king also arranged for his half-brother, Longspée, to be exchanged for an important prisoner of his own, Robert of Dreux who was Philip II's cousin. When the earl arrived in England there were rumours that his wife, Ela of Salisbury, had been seduced by the king. The unsubstantiated titbit found its way into the *Barlings Chronicle*[3] and the writings of the French chronicler, William le Breton.[4]

Men who were angry with the king emerged into the open. Isabel's distant cousin, Robert FitzWalter, took to describing himself as the 'Marshal of the Army of God'.[5] The Earl of Norfolk, Maud Marshal's father-in-law, became one of the king's prominent critics. Roger of Wendover recorded that instead of submitting to John, the barons gathered an army at Brackley in Northamptonshire before marching on Northampton where they expected to meet him that Easter. It was a time of increasing panic and military preparation. The king was not fully aware of the extent of the opposition he faced but had no intention of answering his barons in person. Instead, royal castles across the country were placed on a war footing, commissions of array dispatched and money for the payment of troops borrowed from the Templars.

Stephen Langton and William Marshal met with the increasingly hostile barons in Brackley at the end of April. It soon became clear that if the king refused to give the barons satisfaction that they would take up arms. Amongst the familiar faces siding with FitzWalter were his and Isabel's kinsmen Gilbert de Clare and his father Richard, 3rd Earl of Hertford as well as the Bigods. The barons issued their ultimatum in the form of the so-called Unknown Charter covering aspects of forest law, military service, justice and inheritance law. Marshal and the Archbishop of Canterbury received the list of demands and returned to London where the king lost his temper.

Isabel might have been interested to note that the barons were infuriated by the excessive fees charged by the Crown for heirs to enter into their inheritances and that widows should be allowed to remarry according to the wishes of their families rather than the king who was known to auction off prospective brides to the highest bidder irrelevant of age. The Charter went on to demand that widows should be permitted to continue to live in her marital home for forty days after her bereavement until such time as she was granted her rightful dower. The barons concluded by observing that the king ruled by the 'common counsel of the barons of the whole kingdom of England'.[6]

By 5 May the rebel barons renounced their oaths of homage to the Crown and laid siege to the royal castle at Northampton soon after. Marshal was sent with letters to Newark with orders to secure the castle there for the Crown. Isabel had already retreated, in all likelihood to Striguil or Pembroke, which was also on a war footing.

It was up to the countess in her husband's absence to defend the South Marches from the king's enemies. The Welsh forged an alliance with the de Braoses and began their campaign at the beginning of May according to the Welsh chronicles. Giles de Braose, Bishop of Hereford and his brother Reginald took Abergavenny, Skenfrith, White Castle and Grosmont. They also attacked Radnor, Hay and Brecon. Llewyllyn ap Iorwerth launched an attack against Shrewsbury, capturing the borough and the town's castle with little or no difficulty. John's victimisation of the de Broases meant that he was the first king to face the wrath of an alliance of all the leading Welsh princes and a powerful group of Marcher barons.[7] With the Welsh occupying Shrewsbury, Isabel was on the front line of a war that men loyal to John were losing.

Isabel, a castellan again, oversaw the management of supplies, while men who owed their feudal duty to Marshal did their best to fend off the Welsh who overran the northern parts of the Gower, Pembrokeshire and Carmarthen in June and July that year. The town and castle at Kidwelly went up in flames and Cilgerran took a battering. Marshal was likely to have been present for the latter part of the campaign but that spring and during the early part of the summer he was about the king's business elsewhere.

On the morning of Sunday 17 May the barons captured London and more men flocked to join the insurgents. Negotiations recommenced. On 30 May, Marshal and other men loyal to the king were sent to deliberate with the barons at Staines which was midway between London and the king's residence in Windsor.

King John signed the resulting agreement Magna Carta on 15 June 1215. Ralph de Coggeshall recorded that the barons trusted him so little that they arrived at Runnymede fully armed. On the 19 June messengers carried letters to sheriffs through England announcing the news. During the month that followed John issued a series of orders that redressed acts of injustice and which complied with the clauses of Magna Carta but the king, who objected to the controls which the charter placed on the Crown, had no intention of abiding by his oath in the longer term.

John applied to Innocent III to have the oath he took when he agreed to Magna Carta revoked. The pope agreed and voided the document. By the end of the summer England was at war with itself once again. The rebels sent representatives to France to ask for Philip Augustus to send his son Louis to England. They offered the crown to Louis as an inducement; he was married to Henry II and Eleanor of Aquitaine's granddaughter, Blanche of Castile. It seemed unlikely that the French would turn down the opportunity to acquire the throne of England for themselves.

In Ireland, Marshal's bailiffs collected weapons to be sent to England for the defence of the 'the King's and the Earl's land'.[8] John sent orders from Dover that the earl should have use of two of the royal galleys to transport the armaments. In Kent, King John laid siege to Rochester and seized it but by the end of 1215 John was forced to split his army in half. The king, accompanied by Marshal would go north while John's half-brother William Longspée would remain in the south with the other half of the royal army. Roger of Wendover recorded the destruction wrought by the soldiers as they marched north to Nottingham where John spent Christmas. At home, however, Isabel and her husband were increasingly isolated by their support for the king.

In the spring of 1216, King John sent Marshal to negotiate with Philip of France to try and persuade him to decline the rebels' request. The earl continued to be Philip's vassal for the lands at Longueville. Isabel might have assumed the reigns of command in the Marches during her husband's absence or the couple might have decided that it would be an opportunity for Isabel to go to Longueville to visit their son Richard who oversaw Marshal interests in Normandy. Alternatively, she might have remained by the earl's side. If this was the case, it was Isabel's task to smooth the way for William during informal social occasions. It was a role she was well used to after years attending court with her husband during the reigns of King Richard I and his brother John. Marshal may also have found that the information she gleaned from the wives and daughters of the French nobility was a useful addition to his bargaining. It was the last time the earl left England and the negotiations were a failure.

On 22 May 1216, Louis landed at Sandwich in Kent with an army. By the summer King Alexander II of Scotland invaded from the north on the pretext of siding with the barons. John moved to Corfe while his heir was sent to Devizes. Of the leading barons only the earls of Chester, Derby and Warwick stood alongside the king aside from Marshal. Armies manoeuvred across the realm like pieces on a living chess board. Louis took Winchester and with it the submissions of the Earl of Arundel and even John's hither-too loyal half-brother William Longspée. John's chief forester, Hugh de Neville, also deserted the king. Rumours circulated that John had lain with the wives of both men. London fell into the hands of the French. It must have felt to Isabel as though her husband was fighting for a lost cause.

Chapter 17

The Regent's Wife

On 12 October 1216, King John's baggage train, which was somewhere in the region of a mile long, became bogged down in the Wellstream Estuary which is part of The Wash that separates Norfolk and Lincolnshire. As the tide turned the royal regalia and all of John's personal belongings were lost. Roger of Wendover's account suggests that the king only narrowly escaped death himself when he turned back to try and help. Among the items lost to quick sands and water was what remained of the king's war chest. He died at Newark a week later on 18 October from the bloody flux, as dysentery was then known. There were rumours that he may have been poisoned. The *Annals of Clonmacnoise* reported that the source of the poison was 'a cup of ale wherein there was a toad pricked with a broach'.[1] The same tale was told in the thirteenth century *Brut Chronicle*.[2]

As the last of Henry II's sons lay on his deathbed, he appointed thirteen executors and begged that the government of the country be given into the hands of William Marshal to rule on behalf of John's 9-year-old son 'for he will never hold the land save through him'.[3] The dying king recognised the wrong he had done the earl and asked for his forgiveness. He was more likely to receive it from Marshal than from Isabel who may not have forgotten the king's attempts to ruin them or the many cruelties visited upon her family.

When the news reached Marshal, he was at Gloucester. He rode to Worcester leaving Isabel behind, assuming she was with him, to meet the funeral cortege and arranged for Thomas de Sandford to fetch John's son, Henry, from Devizes Castle and to meet with him at Malmesbury. The boy knew and liked Marshal. The sight of the earl so overwhelmed Henry that he burst into tears and, according to the *Histoire*, surrendered all authority into the hands of Isabel's husband.[4] John's queen, Isabel of Angoulême, remained at Corfe with her younger children where they were safe so it was only the king's household that Isabel was required to provide shelter and food for when William fetched the new king to Gloucester. Even though he was only a child, Isabel knelt before Henry when she greeted him.

The coronation that followed, at Gloucester Abbey, was a hurried affair but, significantly, Guala Bicchieri, the papal legate played an active part in the ceremony which included homage to the pope for both England and

Ireland. Marshal could not afford to let Louis gain an advantage by having himself crowned England's king but it meant there was not enough time to replace John's lost crown. Instead, one of Isabella of Angoulême's gold circlets was used. Nor was the Archbishop of Canterbury present. Stephen Langton was not even in England at the time of John's death. Instead, the crowning was completed by the Bishop of Winchester. Even worse, most of England's barons, who had been fighting against John, were elsewhere. Other men, including Isabel's powerful neighbour, Ranulf, 6th Earl of Chester, arrived after the coronation because of the haste with which it occurred. Isabel may well have had to smooth the ruffled feathers of her kinsman and his retinue who missed the ceremony by just one day.

Isabel also had other things to worry about other than the sensitivities of Marshal's peers, the feeding arrangements for a court and an army or even the tiredness and grief of one small boy. As the coronation feast got under way a messenger arrived. Goodrich Castle was under attack, either by the Welsh or the de Braoses. The care of Isabel's estates and tenants was a priority to the countess but on this occasion, Marshal is more likely to have been alarmed by the fact that Goodrich was less than twenty miles from Gloucester.

Isabel was not present at the council meeting that decided what her and Marshal's future was to hold in the coming months and years. Minority governments were unheard of in England. One of the reasons that Marshal preferred to back John's claim to the throne after Richard I's death in 1199 was because he was an adult. The earl argued that he was too old to be regent. According to the *Histoire* he added ten years to his age and offered to assist Ranalf if he was elected regent.[5] Isabel knew that her husband would not wish to be seen as over ambitious or eager for power in case Henry III's fragile regime shattered before it was even established. The Earl of Chester played his part arguing that Marshal was both valiant and wise and that it was he who should be the regent because it was only Isabel's husband who held the respect and trust of all the barons. Guala closed the argument by offering William remission for all his sins if he would assume the responsibility.[6]

While Marshal, who was seventy or thereabouts, was to be regent, Peter des Roches, Bishop of Winchester continued in his guardianship of Henry. Des Roches had been one of John's confidants and had a shrewd political mind. It meant that Isabel did not have to worry for long about maintaining a royal household. Hubert de Burgh, besieged at Dover, continued in his office as justiciar but his situation meant that, for the time being at least, Marshal's influence would be dominant. The new king and his government moved to Bristol soon after the coronation. A council meeting was arranged for 11 November. Letters instructing barons and bishops to attend the assembly and to pay homage to their new king were issued.

The French did not simply retire across the Narrow Seas with the death of King John nor did the rebellious barons immediately lay down their arms. Marshal had to win back the realm for Henry. The French controlled the southeast of England, the northern barons were still in revolt, Alexander II of Scotland held Carlisle, and in Wales Llywelyn Ap Iorwerth continued to expand both his influence and control over the region. Marshal knew that he could not stay in the Marches to fight the Welsh if he was to rid the realm of the king's enemies. Nor could he take Henry III with him on campaign if he was to succeed in saving the boy's kingdom. Instead, the king was sent to the safety provided by Corfe Castle. It was a home for the royal family from 1215 onwards and beside being a mighty stronghold, it offered Henry continuity as well as the companionship of his younger siblings.

The future of Isabel and her family was tied to the Plantagenet cause more than it had ever been before. Marshal had always been loyal but during John's time on the throne his loyalty sometimes turned in the direction of pragmatism. It fell to Isabel to raid the coffers of the lordships of Netherwent, Pembroke and Leinster to raise the funds that were necessary for her husband to keep Henry on the throne. The king had little or no gold. Leinster offered both a safe haven should one be needed as well as its resources. Marshal was heard to announce, having sworn his oath of loyalty to Henry, that he would carry the boy, on his back if needs be, to Ireland, where the barons had not risen in revolt against the king's father.[7]

Marshal began to mend the divisions by sending letters to many of the rebels offering them restitution if they would return to the new king's side. Less than a month after John's death, on 12 November, he reissued, under his own seal and that the of papal legate, Magna Carta with some amendments making it more palatable to the royalists. The timing of its release turned it into a coronation charter of the kind that barons were familiar with since the time of King Henry I. It also clarified some of the original clauses to avoid future dispute. It was a reminder to the barons who invited Louis to England that he had made no commitment to their charter.

There were also other reasons to stand by King Henry III. Louis could not give all the barons the lands and rights that they desired. For each man he rewarded, another was deprived of his ambitions, and was therefore more likely to return to the king's side in the hope that Marshal might be more forthcoming. As tenants-in-chief resumed their fealty to the Crown, it fell to Isabel, as Marshal's wife, to smooth the way by offering hospitality to the men who attended her husband. She had known many of them for most of her life. The Earl of Salisbury was one of the first men to offer their allegiance to the king as was her own son, William the Younger.

Soon after they were reconciled with their eldest son, William the Younger took his men and besieged Marlborough Castle. William the Younger hoped, originally, to regain it for the Marshal family from Prince Louis as a reward for supporting the French. But when Louis captured it in July 1216 rather than giving it to William, who had a familial claim to it, the dauphin handed it into the keeping of Robert of Dreux. William's dissatisfaction at this outcome led, in part, to his withdrawal from the ranks of the rebels before the death of King John at Newark. Father and son were united by the intention that Marlborough should return in Marshal hands. When it fell, the earl, in his capacity of regent granted Marlborough and Ludgershall which King John had turned into a magnificent residence and hunting park, to William the Younger. Neither of them regarded it as nepotism.

In February 1217 the papacy issued a monition to the rebels to return to their rightful allegiance to the king. Among the men receiving the papal command were the earls of Clare and of Norfolk.[8] For the time being Isabel and her daughter Maud remained in opposite camps as the fighting continued. The cinque ports of Winchelsea and Rye were prised from French hands.

At the same time, Ranulf of Chester laid siege to Montsorrel Castle in Leicestershire. Its ownership, along with other properties, were among the grievances that caused Saer de Quincy, Earl of Winchester to join the rebels in 1215. De Quincy showed no inclination to be reconciled with the Plantagenet monarchy after John's death. Louis and his French forces in the south of the country, were unable to take Dover Castle which lay under siege. The dauphin divided his army. De Quincy and FitzWalter led half the army north to raise the siege on Montsorrel while the other half remained in Dover. Ranulf withdrew before the barons arrived but their army turned east to Lincoln where Nichola de la Hay held out for the royalist cause. Lincoln Castle's hereditary constable had no intention of yielding to the French.

When Marshal, who was at Northampton, learned that the French force was divided he saw a chance to defeat the rebels. The king was fetched in the company of the papal legate to Nottingham. On 20 May, Marshal advanced upon Lincoln with the intention of raising the siege there. With him were Ranulf Earl of Chester, William the Younger and other men who Isabel must have prayed for until she heard of their safe deliverance. It is unknown whether the countess was with the king at Nottingham or whether she was elsewhere.

Thomas, Count of Perche, who commanded the forces loyal to Louis at Lincoln, refused to give battle to Marshal's army, preferring to remain inside the town walls. All they had to do was wait. Fortunately, Peter des Roches, the battling Bishop of Winchester, discovered a blocked gateway in the western part of the town wall which might be opened with the aid of a battering ram.

Its location was conveniently close to the north end of the castle. Ranulf of Chester began the battle by attacking the north gate of the town while another force was sent to find its way through the west gate which had been blocked since 1215.

Quite what Isabel made of the story of her 70-year-old husband being so caught up in the moment that he would have charged into combat without his helmet if his squire had not intervened is perhaps best not contemplated.[9] Marshal, it seems, still preferred to lead from the front and having won a decisive victory, galloped from Lincoln to Nottingham where King Henry awaited news.

Isabel's cousin Gilbert de Clare, the eldest son of Richard, 3rd Earl of Hertford was among the men captured after the battle. He was transported to Gloucester where he remained until he and other rebels submitted to the king that autumn.[10] The senior line of the de Clare family was both rich and powerful and Gilbert, who was the 3rd Earl of Hertford's heir, was unmarried. Because of their kinship, and as rules introduced by the Fourth Lateran Council tightened, papal dispensation would be required, but Isabel and Marshal recognised Gilbert's potential as a husband for their daughter Isabel who was in her seventeenth year.

It had been impossible for Isabel and Marshal to negotiate matches for their daughters during their exile in Leinster or during the last years of King John's reign when they were in opposition to the majority of their peers. Now that the tide of the war was turned in Henry III's favour this was a chance to make a match that would turn Isabel's second daughter into a countess and make the power of the Marshal affinity in the Marches an unassailable one.

Fortune's wheel turned upwards in favour of the Marshals in Ireland as well, thanks to William's new found influence. King Henry's justiciar in Ireland was instructed that the service which Meiler FitzHenry owed for Offaly was in future to be paid to Marshal rather than the Crown. Isabel's own grievances against John were finding redress. There were other rewards for the regent, his family and his *mesnie* that strengthened the earl's power base in Ireland, Wales and in the Marches. No doubt Isabel rejoiced at the news. She would also have been delighted to learn that vessels would, in future, be allowed to ply between the royal port of Waterford and their own harbours in Leinster upon the payment of an appropriate fee.

It is unclear whether Isabel remained in the Marches to oversee the running of their estates or whether she accompanied William to Oxford during the second week of August for a council meeting. Her husband showed no sign of slowing down despite his advancing years. He travelled extensively and exerted himself on Henry III's behalf to reconcile the English barons and to secure the realm. On 24 August he was at Sandwich to witness a French fleet carrying reinforcements being destroyed by Dover's castellan, Hubert de Burgh. By the middle of the following month Louis resigned all claim to Henry III's throne and returned to France in exchange for 10,000 marks. It was a huge amount of money that represented a quarter of the Crown's annual revenue.[11]

The regency council's next task was to restore royal authority. Marshal and the papal legate, Guala, reissued Magna Carta on November 6 1217 but removed the clauses relating to controlling the Crown, because the king was a minor and under the control of his regency council. They also took out sections pertaining to forest laws. The redacted clauses formed part of a new agreement: the so-called Forest Charter. The documents extended a promise of good faith to the realm's tenants-in-chief. Henry III's council determined that all the king's barons were to enjoy the protection of Magna Carta; even those men who rebelled against their king. It helped that the reissue of Magna Carta in 1216 and 1217 was authenticated by the personal seal of the Earl of Pembroke.

Marshal's policy of reconciliation was personified by his daughter Isabel's marriage to Gilbert de Clare which took place on 9 October 1217 at Tewkesbury Abbey. Gilbert was twenty years older than Isabel but as her mother could tell her, the age-difference was not a deterrent to happiness. Fortune's wheel continued on its upward trajectory for Isabel's daughter. King John's former wife, Isabel of Gloucester died on 14 October. She was married three times but had no children. Her sister, Amicia of Gloucester, inherited Isabel's estates and titles. Amicia was unhappily married to Gilbert's father, Richard de Clare, who became Earl of Gloucester *jure uxoris*. By the end of the year the new earl was dead and Gilbert, who was 37-years of age inherited the earldom of Gloucester by right of his mother. He also inherited the honour of Clare from his father. The earldom of Gloucester included the lordships of Glamorgan and Gwynllwg from his mother and the other half of the Giffard inheritance by right of his father's descent from Rohese Giffard. The alliance was to the advantage of both the de Clares and the Marshals but Isabel, Countess of Pembroke must have been very satisfied by the outcome. Two of her daughters were married into comital families and would run estates of the kind that she herself managed.

For more than eighteen months Isabel was effectively England's first lady because Marshal was England's regent. In 1217, Isabel kept Christmas in Northampton. Alexander II of Scotland, who had previously seized Carlisle was present as well. In return for confirming him as Earl of Huntingdon, Alexander returned Carlisle to English hands. There was also supposed to be an agreement with the Welsh that Christmas but despite the safe conduct that had been offered, the Welsh did not come to court.

Chapter 18

The Marriage Market

O nce the Christmas festivities were over, Marshal, with Isabel at his side, threw himself back into the business of government. In January they were at Westminster, by the middle of February they were at Exeter and in Sherborne by 20 February, 1218. By the end of the month William and Isabel were at Sturminster in Dorset which was one of Marshal's manors. Isabel and Marshal granted his manor an annual three-day fair while he was there as well as giving the same right to another of their manors at Speen in Buckinghamshire.[1] It was an exhausting record of winter travel on difficult roads.

He and Isabel were at Worcester on 11 March. It was essential to come to terms with Llywelyn Ap Iowerth who had exploited the Barons War as well as the fall of the de Braoses for his own ends. The recent marriage of Isabel's daughter to Gilbert de Clare reinforced an alliance that helped to re-establish the network of border defence that failed when the barons rebelled in 1215. Gilbert's father, Richard de Clare, 3rd Earl of Hertford was prominent among the barons who opposed the king. Other Marchers who held territory of strategic importance to the security of the borders who sided with the barons included the earls of Hereford and Winchester as well as the Earl of Gloucester, Geoffrey de Mandeville, who assumed the title *jure uxoris* when he married Isabel of Gloucester in 1214. Geoffrey was part of the FitzPeter family who were conspicuous in their opposition of the king.

The root of Llywelyn's success, aside from the chaos in England, was based on the connections he made with the de Braose family. In 1212, Giles de Braose, Bishop of Hereford aided Llywelyn in his bid to make an alliance with Philip II and in 1214, having been permitted to return to England, Giles threw in his lot with the prince when he was unable to wrest his father's extensive estates from the Crown on behalf of his nephews, the sons of his elder brother, William. It was the bishop who helped Llewelyn to attack Wigmore Castle in the Middle Marches of Herefordshire, an estate belonging to the Mortimer family, who unlike most of their immediate neighbours continued their loyalty to the Crown. Giles was reconciled to the king when he gained custody of much of his family's former lands, including the barony of Bergavenny, but he died unexpectedly in 1215. His brother Reginald de Braose continued to support the rebels. Llywelyn cemented the alliance by arranging for de Braose to marry one of his daughters, Gwladus Ddu.[2]

That winter, which was a mild one, Llywelyn's army advanced south through Deheubarth gathering more men as it went. In three weeks, the prince took seven castles including Carmarthen and Ceredigion. In the south of Wales, the lordships of Pembroke and Haverfordwest remained in Marshal's capable hands even when they were raided and some of his tenants taken hostage. The following year Llywelyn overran Powys when its prince entered into an alliance with King John.

In 1217, Marshal, who was an old friend of Reginald's father and who had sheltered him in Ireland, persuaded de Braose to come to terms with Henry III's regency council. Reginald's grant gave him livery of familial honours including Bergavenny, Bramber in Sussex, Totnes and Barnstaple at the expense of his nephew, John de Braose whose father, William, was starved to death in Corfe. Llywelyn responded to the news of de Braose's defection with an attack on the Gower which he had previously retained from Llywelyn and the seizure of Swansea Castle,[3] a wooden fortification, which was razed to the ground.

In March 1218, at Worcester, Llywelyn agreed terms with Marshal and Guala, the papal legate. While he recognised Henry III's overlordship he was able to keep custody of both Carmarthen and Ceredigion castles. He promised that he would do his best to surrender to Guala all the estates and castles in South Wales that were annexed from their Anglo-Norman occupiers so that the papal legate might return them to the families who owned them before they were seized. Isabel, on hearing this, was resigned to the loss of Cilgerran for the foreseeable future knowing that it was unlikely to be returned.[4]

Henry III's regency government recognised that until land disputes could be settled there was little chance for long term reconciliation between the barons. Hostilities were likely to resume on a regional basis, especially as the Crown controlled very few key castles thanks to King John's policy of granting them to his foreign mercenaries. The idea of Welsh intermarriage as a way of settling the territorial dispute brewing in the Gower appealed to both Llywelyn and Marshal. In 1219, John de Braose, the rightful heir to his grandfather's estates and titles, married Marared, another daughter of the prince's. Her dowry was the Lordship of Gower and its *caput* at Swansea.[5] It tied the Marshal family closer to the Welsh prince through John de Braose's extended family network. His mother, Maud de Clare, was the daughter of Roger de Clare, 3rd Earl of Hertford.[6] It was to be hoped that the extending knots of kinship would prevent a renewal in the region's conflicts.

The marriage alliances that Isabel and Marshal negotiated for their own daughters extended powerful social and political networks and created a dominant affinity in the first half of the thirteenth century. By 1218, Isabel's second daughter, Isabel, was already a countess and her elder daughter Maud was married to the heir of Roger Bigod, Earl of Norfolk. Two of Isabel's other daughters, Sibyl and Eva, were of an age to be married and Reginald de Braose, Lord of Bergavenny's eldest son, William, was a similar age to Eva. He would succeed his father to Bergavenny, Builth and other lordships that were key to the security of the Marches.

Isabel raised her daughters to know that they would marry a man selected for them by their father and that it was their duty to be obedient to his wishes. Marshal is unlikely to have made the arrangements without consulting Isabel first and the *Histoire* makes it clear that William was not a man who would marry his daughters where he thought they would be unhappy. It is not known when negotiations for a match between Eva and William de Braose began but she was married before her father's death and the eldest of her four daughters was born in 1222.

The only alternative to marriage for Isabel's remaining daughters was to take the veil. It is an indicator of the family's wealth that none of the countess's offspring were destined for a convent. Traditionally, where a family had several sons to provide for, and daughters to dower, at least one of the daughters would find herself given to God as a means of preserving the family estate. In 1218, Sibyl was 16-years old and Eva 15. Even Joan, aged 8-years, was of an age when a betrothal might be arranged.

At about the same time that Isabel and Marshal opened negotiations with the Lord of Bergavenny, they were approached by William de Ferrers, 4th Earl of Derby. His loyalty to King John was never questioned and he reaped extensive rewards in Derbyshire including the office of bailiff of the Peak Forest as well as holding Peak Castle at Castleton. In 1216, at the start of Marshal's regency, he had been with the royal army at Lincoln. In 1218, the earl decided to emulate his father and joined the Fifth Crusade. His intention was to join other crusaders traveling overseas that autumn. Before he departed, de Ferrers wished to ensure his family's future. His heir, named William, was presented to Marshal and Isabel as a prospective son-in-law. Aside from the promise of a third earldom, it was not a brilliant match. William, who was in his mid-twenties was crippled by ill-health, described as gout that had afflicted him since childhood. When he travelled it was always by litter.[7] The lands associated with the earldom of Derby included three counties in the Midlands besides Derbyshire. The union would strengthen the Marshal family's position in the Marches. Conversation must also have revealed that William de Ferrers understood and emulated Isabel and Marshal's own policy of encouraging the growth of markets and towns. Marshal agreed to dower Sybil with the manor of Mildenhall in Wiltshire. The marriage took place before Marshal's death[8] and secured another thread of the growing Marshal affinity into place.

There was another marriage that weighed upon Isabel's mind. The only one of her sons to be married was William the Younger who married Alice de Béthune in September 1214.[9] The young couple had known one another since childhood. The alliance connected the Marshal clan to the Mandevilles and FitzHerberts through her half-sister, as well as William de Forz, 3rd Count of Aumale who was Alice's elder half-brother. Roger of Wendover, quoted later by Matthew Paris, described de Forz as a 'feudal anarchist'[10] because he changed sides four times during the Barons War. His challenge to Alice's share of her mother's inheritance came to an end shortly after her marriage to William when she died before the end of 1215.

Four years later, William, a warrior like his father and the heir to the earldom of Pembroke, needed another wife so that he could beget the next generation. The matter of ensuring the continuation of the Marshal dynasty was something that Isabel and Marshal did not undertake. Unlike the unions they promoted for their daughters, none of their sons was betrothed during William's regency. It is possible that that Isabel and William did not arrange marriages for their sons to ensure that their estates were not broken up. Or, the regent and his wife, amid the difficulties of an empty treasury, the need to reunite the barony under the Crown and the problems of fulfilling the terms agreed by the Charter of the Forest which included the deforestation of areas brought with Forest Law by both kings John and Richard, simply did not have the leisure time to identify suitable spouses for their sons. It meant that Isabel did not have an understudy to continue the work as chatelaine to the earldom which William the Younger would one day inherit.

Chapter 19

One Final Kiss

Marshal fell ill at the beginning of February 1219. He journeyed from Westminster to the Tower of London with Isabel where they consulted with doctors and hoped that his condition might improve. William the Younger and his father's most trusted knights joined Isabel in their vigil while Marshal continued to govern on Henry III's behalf. By March it was clear that William was dying. He and Isabel moved by river on 21 March, to Marshal's manor at Caversham near Reading. The royal court was accommodated by the nearby abbey at Reading.

Henry III arrived at Marshal's beside on 8, or 9 April so that the earl could explain to the young king that it was impossible for him to continue in his service. Peter des Roches, Bishop of Winchester was also present. He hoped to succeed to Marshal's position as regent. He was already responsible for Henry's day-to-day care. However, William had no intention of permitting so much power to lay in the bishop's hands. Finding another regent who was as respected as the earl would be a difficult task. Des Roches and the justiciar, Hubert de Burgh were jealous of one another's authority and the Earl of Chester had joined the Fifth Crusade. Instead, the earl gave the king and his realm into the keeping of the new papal legate, Pandulf. Marshal believed that only the papal legate might hold the balance of power. The following day William the Younger publicly entrusted the king into Pandulf Verraccio and the Pope's keeping to prevent des Roches circumventing Marshal's wishes.

Isabel and William the Younger were joined by all of Isabel's children except for Richard who was in France at the court of Philip II. John d'Earley was also present. Marshal discussed the terms of his will with his family and the most trusted members of his household. Isabel would retain her own inheritance as her dower for the rest of her life: Striguil, Leinster, Netherwent and her half of the honour of Giffard. William the Younger would inherit his father's lands until the countess's own death. Isabel and William's Norman fief at Longueville became Richard's. William the Younger would not offer his feudal service to the kings of France but the Norman estates would remain in the Marshal family through Isabel's second son. Walter received Sturminster and Gilbert was also granted some land.

Only Ansel received nothing. William added that he loved his youngest son but his future would be that of a knight who, like his father before him, would have to win his own fame and fortune. It was John D'Earley who protested at the unfairness of the decision, demanding that at least the boy should have enough land to equip him with the means to shoe his horse. In the end, Marshal granted Ansel land worth £140 a year.[1]

William the Younger was the direct heir of the Marshal estates that his father inherited after his elder brother John's death in 1194 as well as the domains which were given to his father before his marriage to Isabel. He also remained in control of the castles at Marlborough and Ludgershall. The regency council were sufficiently alarmed by this to offer him the hand of Henry III's young sister Eleanor even before William's father was dead. At the time that they made the proposal the king's sister was not yet 5-years of age. In return for the royal match the council wanted the return of the two Wiltshire castles. One of the concerns the regency council had was that too many of the Crown's formers castles were in the possession of John's former castellans which had the effect of weakening the royal position.

Isabel's four elder daughters received nothing because the estates they were granted as part of their dowers reflected what their inheritance might otherwise have been. Marshal recognised that had he lived longer he and Isabel would have arranged a good marriage for their youngest daughter, Joan who was in her tenth year at the most in 1219. She was to receive land worth £30 a year as well as 200 marks in cash. When the will was finally drawn up, Isabel attached her seal to it alongside William's and that of their eldest son. Even at the end of his life, Marshal took no decisions and made no grants without consulting his countess first.

Marshal sent John D'Earley to Striguil to defend it against a Welsh incursion by Llywelyn but he was ordered not to tarry. He was to collect two pieces of cloth from Stephen d'Evereux and return immediately.[2] The material which was to be the earl's burial shroud were purchased in the summer of 1183 when Marshal went to the Holy Land on behalf of his recently dead overlord, Henry, the Young King. Henry II's son swore to go on pilgrimage but died of dysentery before being able to fulfil his vow. Marshal went in his stead, taking with him Henry's cloak to place upon the altar of the Holy Sepulchre. The *Histoire* recorded that Marshal spent three years there before returning to Normandy with the silk. Now, thirty years later, the intended purpose of the cloths was to be fulfilled:

When I am dead, cover me with them, and cover and surround the bier in which I am carried. And there is another instruction I wish to give you: if there is snow and bad weather, go and buy lengths of burel, I don't mind which, attractive or otherwise, and cover the silk with them, so that it be not damaged or dirtied by the damp weather. And after I am buried, give the cloth there, to the brothers, and they will do with it as they wish.[3]

It has been argued that the silks were symbolic of a vow that Marshal took during his time in the Holy Land. As well as the silks, there was also a Templar mantle which the earl commissioned the year before that only his almoner knew about. After settling his worldly affairs, Marshal summoned his old friend Aymeric de St Maur who was the Templar Master in England.

Having announced his decision to be buried as a Templar, Marshal asked one last thing of Isabel, 'fair lady, kiss me now, for you will never be able to do it again'.[4] It was an embrace that ended in tears for both of them. Isabel had to be helped from the room by her daughters. Wherever the earl was throughout their married life the *Histoire* recorded that his countess was not usually far away but the vows taken on his death bed meant that Isabel would not lie beside her husband until the Day of Judgement and would not care for him during his final days. Instead, William the Younger and the most trusted members of Marsal's *mesnie* tended the dying earl.

Isabel's thirty-year marriage ended with William's death on 14 May 1219. He died absolved of his sins, with his gaze fixed upon the cross in his room and surrounded by his countess who was permitted to attend him in his final hours, his family and friends. His body was prepared for burial and the journey that would precede it. His body was sewn up in a bull's hide packed with salt before being placed in a coffin.[5]

Soon afterwards he was carried to Reading Abbey and placed in the chapel that he and the countess founded there. After a Mass was said the coffin and funeral procession made its way to Staines and then Westminster Abbey. The Church taught that the countess should accept her bereavement as divine will. Her husband was a good man and she would have believed that once Marshal passed the ordeal of Purgatory he would be welcomed in Heaven.

William Marshal, 1st Earl of Pembroke was laid to rest in the Temple Church, London. The service was conducted by Stephen Langton, Archbishop of Canterbury and was attended by the realm's greatest magnates. Langton described Marshal as 'the best knight who ever lived'.[6] Afterwards, as Marshal wished, William the Younger and the earl's executors distributed alms to the poor in the form of food, robes and shoes.[7]

Chapter 20

A Matriarch Takes Up the Reins

Isabel sent letters shortly after Marshal's death to England's justiciar, Hubert de Burgh, who she described as 'her dear lord and friend'[1] requesting the writs of seisin (possession) for her land in England and Ireland. She was no longer hidden in the legal shadow of her husband. There was no delay in the matter of proving Marshal's will. Completing the necessary inquisitions post-mortem to determine by what right lands in the different counties of England and Ireland were held, writs of seisin demonstrating possession and delivery of Isabel's family estates into her hands were quicky established and issued on the 18 June.

Widows, like the countess, were more visible in the historical record because of evidence provided in the routine administration of their estates and, like Bertrada, the dowager countess of Chester, who died in 1227, as witnesses to their sons' charters.[2]

The justiciar in Ireland, Geoffrey de Marisco,[3] was less convinced of Isabel's lawful possession of her estates and attempted to appropriate part of Isabel's Irish fief. Marisco had received grants from King John in Limerick and was married to Geoffrey FitzRobert's widow, Eva de Bermingham in whose right he held lands in Offaly.[4] His relationship with the regency council was marked by their distrust of his misuse of funds and failure to account for Irish revenues. On this occasion he underestimated the countess's determination and the extent to which she had the respect of the ruling elite. On 19 June a mandate was sent from Westminster to the Irish justiciar confirming that Isabel was to have 'seisin of all the lands, castle, and vills which are of her inheritance in Ireland, and which the Earl held'.[5]

The countess might have been grief stricken but Isabel understood both the feudal and administrative necessities of holding what was hers both by right of birth and Marshal's last testament. She travelled to France to do homage to King Philip II for her lands there. Her papers include the record of the agreement she made with the king and the deliverance of her estates into her keeping and the keeping of her children. The keepers of her Norman castles were required to deliver them into the custody of the king at his command if required. In addition to her lands, Isabel's sons William and Richard received licence to come and go across the Channel with a retinue of five knights and their servants on the understanding that they would do no harm to the king.[6]

William the Younger's mother-in-law, Hawise of Aumale, who was described by Richard of Devizes as 'a woman who was almost a man, lacking nothing virile except the virile organs'[7] was forced into marriage by the Crown each time she was widowed because of the wealth and estates which she represented until she promised to pay King John a fine of 5,000 marks after the death of her fourth husband. Isabel did not have to consider the option of paying a fine to ensure she was not distrained to marry. In theory, clauses 7 and 8 of Magna Carta protected a widow's marriage portion, inheritance and dower rights and also agreed that no widow could be compelled to make a new marriage provided she promised to gain her feudal overlord's consent if she did decide to remarry.[8]

Instead, Isabel turned her attention to Joan's future. The girl was betrothed soon after her father's death to Warin de Munchensy, Lord of Swanscombe,[9] a man who was both powerful and of 'suitable birth'.[10] A dispensation was required before the wedding could take place when Joan was old enough to marry. Warin's mother was one of Isabel's cousins. Aveline de Clare was a daughter of Roger, 3rd Earl of Hertford. Isabel's new son-in-law was one of the men who suffered under the rule of King John and took up arms against him. He was captured at the Battle of Lincoln on 20 May 1217. Under William Marshal's regency, Munchensy was reconciled to the Plantagenet Crown. It is possible that Isabel and William discussed the Lord of Swanscombe's potential as a husband for their youngest daughter before Marshal's death. The union was another which served to reconcile opposing factions as well as providing Joan with a husband who would be able to provide for his young bride. The familial link may also suggest that Countess Isabel looked among her extended kinship networks to identify a potential husband with the necessary bloodlines and status that would ensure that Joan did not have to marry below her rank as the daughter of an earl.

Isabel also began to assert her presence as a landowner in her own right by acknowledging grants previously made from her estates in William's name, as at Bec-Hellouin:

> Notification that under God's inspiration and for the souls of herself and her husband, Earl William Marshal, she has conceded the acknowledgement of the abbey's right which her husband made concerning the church of St Mary of Orbec,[11] Calvados, which her ancestors granted to the abbey, and concedes the same for the abbey's own use claiming nothing by right from the church or whatever belongs to it for herself or her heirs.[12]

Surviving charters show that not only did she confirm Marshal's grants but that on occasion she extended them. Reading Abbey received a new water meadow in addition to the clearings that Marshal granted the abbey at Caversham and Henley-on-Thames. These grants were part of the responsibility that every medieval widow had towards her husband's soul. The gifts that she made in the months following William's death were made to commemorate the earl and to ensure, by Masses and prayer, a swift passage through Purgatory to Heaven. Once she fulfilled her obligations to the monastic foundations that were made during William's lifetime, she set about making further grants in her own right. It was common throughout the medieval period for female benefaction and personal piety to be evidenced during widowhood.

In May 1220, Isabel received the news that her daughter Isabella, Countess of Gloucester had given birth to a daughter named after her paternal grandmother, Amice of Gloucester.[13] The Marshal and de Clare families, it seemed, were thriving. Richard was born in 1222, followed by a second daughter in 1226 named after Isabel herself and two more sons.[14]

The Countess of Pembroke might reasonably have expected to enjoy her dower rights for many years following her husband's death and to see her family continue to expand. It was not to be. She became suddenly ill in the winter of 1220. William, 2nd Earl of Pembroke, rushed to Striguil to be with her. She was about 48-years old. Life expectancy on average in the medieval period was late forties.[15] However, the life span of a noteworthy number of individuals was significantly longer. The low life expectancy indicated by the average includes high infant mortality rates as well as deaths that occurred during childbirth or on the battlefield. Isabel survived the vulnerable stages of her life as a child and woman of childbearing age and given her social status, might have expected to live a relatively long life, like her husband and the redoubtable Eleanor of Aquitaine who died when she was 82-years old.

It is unclear what ailment Isabel suffered from although it is almost certain that her symptoms would have been ascribed to an imbalance of the four humours. Even healthy people underwent bloodletting several times a year in order to maintain a balance to their humours as a preventative to illness. Roger Bacon, writing in the middle of the thirteenth century, collected cures for various ailments in his *Opus Majus*. Book VI of the text covers old age. According to him, the cooked flesh of dragons, prepared in the same way as snake meat, was a cure for the ailments of old age[16] although he gave no indication where a dragon might be located. Old age was associated with an excess of black bile, which was colder and thicker than blood, and which was believed to be cold and dry. Bile was viewed as the opposite humour to blood.

Heat carried by the blood was thought to encourage action; cold the opposite. Galen described black bile as being like mud in the blood.

The influence of the humours changed with the seasons and with life. Inspired by Galen's theories, it was commonly believed throughout the medieval period that as people aged their flesh dried and their humours cooled until they died. Unsurprisingly perhaps, black bile was associated with the winter months. This was accompanied by an excess of melancholy. Other symptoms included light-headedness, tremors and stiffness. Arthritis and rheumatism were ascribed to an abundance of black bile. Isabel, a widow in her first year of widowhood, may easily have been depressed and given her age she is also likely to have suffered from some of the aches and pains associated with ageing. It was believed that the kidneys and spleen produced black bile and that the best way of reducing it was through purging, either by laxative such as figs or raisins or by means of an emetic. Bathing was also something that might have been advised as a gentler way of drawing in heat and unblocking humours.

Peppers, ginger, cloves and red wine were thought to have warming properties to counterbalance the surplus bile and encourage blood to flow. Given their wealth, the Marshal family could have afforded to purchase cumin which was also believed to be a warming and pain-relieving herbal remedy. Chicken broth, warm, hydrating and rich in nutrients, was a good way of stimulating blood flow and advised as part of a diet for the elderly or infirm. Medieval medicine believed wine, which looked like blood, was a restorative. People thought that it helped provide the heat necessary for strength, so painkilling drugs were administered in wine. If Isabel was in any pain or discomfort there was little that her household could do for her other than provide drowsiness inducing drinks. Camomile was used as a mild sedative. Willow bark, for fevers and lower back pain, contained salicylic acid and could be chewed. It was a common ingredient in the medieval medicine cabinet. Isabel might even, in earlier years, have used it to help with pain during childbirth. Opium and henbane were also used as painkillers. In the wrong dose they were both lethal.

While she was still able, Isabel may have asked to be buried beside her mother in Tintern, and bequeathed goods or money to the monks there so that they would celebrate masses for her. It was her right as the *suo jure* Countess of Striguil to be buried there. Like William before her, a good death included repayment of any debts, the giving of personal gifts to family, friends and loyal retainers and resignation to God's will. When it became clear that Isabel was on her deathbed, a priest was summoned. He visited her chamber often that winter as her illness progressed. Confession was believed to free the soul from sin and aided a speedy physical recovery. The Fourth Lateran Council of 1215 required all Christians to make regular confession and declared that physical sickness was sometimes the result of spiritual sickness.

Isabel, conscious that this might be her last illness, perhaps looked back over her life to make amends for her past sins. Her first concern was the well-being of her soul as it continued on its journey after her death. Confession during the last moments of anyone's life was essential. It did not matter that Isabel lived a life of piety, attended mass regularly, prayed often, gave alms, and supported the Church. Now was the countess's last chance to prepare to face God. She could not know that she was going to Heaven unless she repented and was granted salvation.

The priest, having heard Isabel's confession, absolved her from her sins, anointed and blessed her with holy oil. The anointing, called extreme unction, was applied to Isabel's eyes, ears, nose, mouth, hands and feet. The act cut Isabel de Clare, Countess of Striguil and Pembroke's links and ties with the earthly world. She was somewhere between life and death. A last communion was also given to the dying woman. If she was unable to swallow the bread the priest assured her that faith was enough. A cross was placed in her hands or held in front of her to comfort her as she approached her final minutes. Its presence was also to drive away devils who lay in wait for the countess's soul.[17]

On 9 March 1221, the bell of Striguil Castle began to toll. It signalled the passing of William Marshal's countess and it summoned her household and family to prayer. Throughout the preceding winter Isabel's friends, family and tenants had prayed for their countess; masses were said in the churches of Chepstow, all interceding for her soul in life as they now did in death. It was believed that prayers would speed her through Purgatory, a place where souls went to be purified before being permitted to enter Heaven and eternal salvation. It was an idea that the Church accepted as doctrine and which encouraged intercessory prayers and Masses. Isabel's family may also have fasted and given alms as a way of speeding Isabel's soul on its journey.

The countess's body was washed and laid out before being wrapped in a shroud by her grieving women. Alternatively, Isabel may have been dressed in clothes appropriate for a woman of her rank. The body was then placed in a coffin or on a funeral bier. The body then lay in state while the funeral was arranged. Bodies were usual buried quickly after death. The funeral cortege set off from Chepstow to travel the $5^1/_2$ miles to Tintern Abbey where the monks prayed the office for the dead. There was a requiem mass before her body was buried in the most hallowed ground inside Tintern Abbey church near the altar. It was her privilege as kin of Walter de Clare and her right as a countess of Striguil.

Both Isabel and Aoife would have expected their tombs at Tintern to survive until they were awakened from the dead on the Day of Judgement. Statues of the Irish countess and her daughter in repose, dressed in their best clothes, were a reminder to the people who saw them to pray for the salvation of their souls. The monks who lived at Tintern were expected to offer an eternity of intercessions for the laity who lay within their hallowed spaces. The sculpture of William Marshal on his tomb depicts him in the prime of his life. If Isabel's tomb at Tintern included an effigy it would have depicted her as a young woman rather than in old age. Effigies of the twelfth and thirteenth centuries showed men and women as they hoped to be when they were resurrected rather than ravaged by illness, injury and time.

A month after Isabel died, in April 1221, William the Younger returned Marlborough and Ludgershall Castle to the Crown. He intended to make Henry III's sister his wife. Isabel's dower was now his. The loss of the two castles did not hold such significance as they once did. Hubert de Burgh, the justiciar and part of the regency council wanted the match, first proposed in 1219, between the earl and Eleanor to go ahead because it would help to ensure that William, a powerful political influence, supported de Burgh and the papal legate, Pandalf, in the developing power struggle between the justiciar and the Bishop of Winchester.

In 1223, William the Younger confirmed the charters of his predecessors. He also continued the de Clare and Marshal tradition of patronage at Tintern when he endowed the abbey with additional lands, woods and warrens. The monks were also granted hunting rights on land belonging to the Marshal family.[18] In return for arable land at Rogerstone the monks were committed to keeping a lamp burning on Isabel's tomb. She might have gone but she was not forgotten. Roger Bigod, Isabel's grandson, made his own endowment of the abbey with land at Accle and the advowson of the church in Halbergate in Norfolk.[19] In 1301 he confirmed the gifts of his ancestors when he financed the rebuilding of the church. The east window contained eight panels of stained glass depicting the earl's heraldic achievements. None of them could have imagined that the abbey would be dissolved in 1537; that its furniture and anything of value would be sold, the lead stripped from the roof of the church or that the site would be granted to Henry Somerset, 2nd Earl of Worcester. The tombs of Aoife and Isabel fell into ruin and finally disappeared beneath the carpet of grass that grew where tiles bearing the De Clare and Marshal arms once lay.

There is an intriguing possibility that Isabel's heart lies buried in New Ross. The churchyard at St Mary's contains a broken memorial stone engraved with the words *Isaebl Laegn* meaning Isabel of Leinster. There was only ever one Isabel of Leinster. In addition to the words the monument contains the eroded relief of a face wearing a barbette or hair net that is concurrent with the countess's lifetime. Beneath the face the mason added a foliated cross.[20] The stone may have been set up as a memorial or it might have marked the location where the countess asked for her heart to be buried. It was reasonably common practice at the time having become popular during the Crusades. King Richard I's body was buried at Fountrevraud Abbey but his heart was buried at Rouen. Most famous of all, Isabel's descendant Robert the Bruce's heart was taken on crusade to Grenada before finally being buried at Melrose Abbey. The practice was condemned in 1299 by Pope Boniface VIII.

Chapter 21

Isabel's Sons

On 23 April 1224, near where his father was buried in the Temple Church, William Marshal, 2nd Earl of Pembroke, married the king's 9-year-old sister, Eleanor. It strengthened the bonds between the royal family and Isabel's descendants as well as the long-standing alliance with Hubert de Burgh who proposed the union. It also meant that William would be approaching his fortieth year before he was likely to father an heir. The following month William was appointed justiciar in Ireland for life.

William's task in Ireland would be to combat Hugh de Lacy, 1st Earl of Ulster. Much had changed since Hugh rode to Isabel's aid at Kilkenny in 1208. He was forced from his earldom in 1210 by King John and when he returned three years later, he allied himself with the Irish against his own countrymen. In 1220, he made a pact with Llywelyn ap Iorwerth and the pair attacked Marshal's fief in the Marches. In 1223, he invaded Ulster, where William's cousin, John Marshal, administered the lordship on behalf of the king and razed Coleraine Castle before laying siege to Carrickfergus. By the end of June de Lacy was forced to surrender to William the Younger but there were pressures building elsewhere in Henry's realm.

At court there was increasing friction between Hubert de Burgh and his co-regent Peter des Roche, Bishop of Winchester which were magnified when Pandulf departed court in the autumn of 1221. The barons became increasingly fractious when de Burgh set about removing royal castles from private hands in order to bolster Henry III's authority. In 1224 Fawkes de Breaute refused to relinquish Bedford Castle and found himself under siege. When the castle fell, de Burgh ordered the garrison to be hanged.

In 1226, or thereabouts, William commissioned a history of his father's life and political career. Even in death, it seems that the earl, and to a lesser extent Isabel, continued to work for the benefit of their family. The work, a hagiography, was a reminder of what the king, his barons, and the realm as a whole, owed to Marshal and, by association, to his heir.

The mood of the council was not ameliorated by Hubert de Burgh's policy of encouraging Henry to reward his friends. The justiciar was an ambitious man. He was married, in 1221, to Margaret, a sister of King Alexander II of Scotland. Under the terms of the agreement made between King John and King Alexander at Norham in 1209, it was Henry III who should have been the groom, but Margaret had other sisters. It was whispered that de Burgh intended to make himself the king's brother-in-law. The match led in 1227 to de Burgh being created Earl of Kent. The heir to the earldom was Margaret of Scotland's only child, a girl also named Margaret but known as Megotta. In 1228, de Burgh's ambitions were on the cusp of fulfilment when he was appointed justiciar for life. His policy of self-enrichment and self-empowerment made him many enemies.

In France, events overtook de Burgh adding to his lack of popularity. La Rochelle remained unconquered by the French in 1204 but it fell in the summer of 1224 when Hubert failed to renew the truce with France. Even worse, despite warnings the previous autumn,[1] he neglected to adequately provision the defences there for a prolonged siege. It meant that Poitou was lost. Gascony, however, was recovered in 1225 though this required a general taxation of a fifteenth being levied on movable property. The king's younger brother Richard 1st Earl of Cornwall, who led the expedition, became something of a national hero leading to a strain between the two brothers and Henry's plans for a military campaign of his own in Poitou and Brittany.

William the Younger's relationship with Hubert deteriorated when the justiciar's power in the Marches was enhanced with the grant of Carmarthen to de Burgh in 1229 as a hereditary right.[2] He already held the so-called Three Castles of Whitecastle, Skenfrith and Grosmont and had built a new castle at Montgomery. William had regained Carmarthen from Llywelyn in 1223 along with Ceredigion and controlled both castles on behalf of the Crown. Now though, Hubert's dominance in the Marches was becoming a threat.

The balance of power in Wales and on the Marches continued to shift. Eva Marshal's husband, William de Braose was killed after a catastrophic error of judgement. De Braose was previously captured by Llywelyn Ap Iowerth in 1228. Part of the terms agreed for his release included the marriage of his eldest daughter by Eva Marshal, Isabel, to Llywelyn's own heir, Dafydd. Isabel, who was born in 1222, was to be dowered with Builth, an area of strategic importance to the command of the Wye Valley. De Braose took Isabel to Llewelyn's Easter court in 1230 where he resumed a liaison with Llywelyn's wife, Joan, and was discovered in a compromising position in her bed chamber. 'William de Braose was charged by Llywelyn, with adultery with his wife, and was hanged. And the woman was imprisoned for a long time.'[3]

At a stroke the Braose estates, which provided a sturdy bulwark along the Marches against the Welsh, were split and Hubert was able to extend his authority in South Wales. Eva was left a widow and her four daughters became co-heiresses. In the short term this proved beneficial to the 2nd Earl of Pembroke who was appointed by the king, without payment of a fine, as his nieces' guardian.

Llywelyn was quick to retrieve what he could from the diplomatic wreckage. He recognised that alliance with the most important families in the Marches helped to ensure his supremacy in Wales. If the marriage between Dafydd and Isabella went ahead he would be allied to both the de Braoses and to the Marshals. Besides which, Isabel was still at the Welsh court surrounded by the men who witnessed her father's execution. The prince wrote to Eva and to the Earl of Pembroke explaining that he had no choice but to execute de Braose based on the advice of his own nobles. Eva was not initially predisposed to be sympathetic. Her chaplain excommunicated Llywelyn[4] but by the end of the year the threat of war was lifted and the breach between the Marcher lords and the Welsh prince healed.

In 1230, Marshal and his brother-in-law, Gilbert de Clare, 4th Earl of Hertford and 5th Earl of Gloucester, mustered at Portsmouth at the start of Henry's campaign to retake Poitou and to fulfil the terms of an alliance with Peter Mauclerc, Duke of Brittany *jure uxoris* through his marriage to Alis who was recognised as the Duchess of Brittany after the presumed death of her half-brother Arthur in 1203 and imprisonment of her half-sister Eleanor, the so-called Fair Maid of Brittany at Corfe Castle. On the other side of the Narrow Seas, Richard Marshal answered King Louis IX's summons to perform service for his lordship of Longueville and because his wife, Gervasia of Dinan's family supported French interests.[5]

De Clare died in Brittany on 25 October 1230 from the sickness which afflicted King Henry III's army there. His body was returned to Tewkesbury Abbey, which chronicled the funeral, and he was buried in front of the high altar fifteen days after his death by the abbots of Tewkesbury and Tintern.[6] To William the Younger's fury, Gilbert's heir Richard de Clare, aged 8-years, was for the price of 7,000 marks placed in the care of the justiciar. It meant that de Burgh gained control of all of the new earl's properties and that the justiciar superseded the Earl of Pembroke as the predominant power in the Marches.

William signalled his change of political affiliation when he arranged for his widowed sister Isabel to marry Richard of Cornwall without royal consent. Although she was nine years older than her new husband, she remained a woman of beauty. Rather than being a bulwark of the Crown the earls of Pembroke would in future be regarded as part of a dissident faction.

The earl was in Ireland in the spring of 1231 when he died unexpectedly on 5 April. He was succeeded by his brother Richard who reunited Isabel and Marshal's fiefs in England and Ireland with their Norman territory. Hubert and the king were alarmed by the new earl's status as a vassal of the French king. Richard blamed the justiciar for the confiscation of his fiefs even though the king promised William in 1229 that he would allow his younger brother to succeed him in the event of William's death without heirs.[7] It was only the intervention of the Bishop of Winchester, back in England from the Sixth Crusade after an absence of more than three years, that led to Richard's licensing as the 3rd Earl of Pembroke.

Inevitably, Llywelyn ap Iorwerth took advantage of the situation to attack Marcher held regions. Henry's plans to mount a campaign in Wales were met by a lacklustre response from his magnates. In June, the king met with the Bishop of London to consider the possibility of excommunicating the prince.[8] By then, rumours circulated the court that Richard of Cornwall had formed an alliance with his new brother-in-law to assist Richard Marshal invade England. In August, Richard was licensed to enter his estates but the old Marshal loyalties to the Crown were no more.

William's 16-year-old wife, Eleanor Plantagenet, became an extremely wealthy widow. In addition to her jointure rights, she was also entitled to a third of her husband's estates as her dower. King Henry III instructed the earl's executors to ensure that her dower rights were secured. A dower was the lifetime interest in a property acquired by a widow from her deceased husband's estate. Magna Carta fixed the amount as a third of the estates that a man held in fee during his life time. The only exceptions to this ruling were if the agreement made before the wedding stipulated a smaller amount or if the husband deeded his estates to trustees prior to the wedding. On occasion a parcel of land transferred from a woman's family was held by the couple as a shared interest, a jointure, during the couple's life time and was used as all or part of the dower.

In return for an annual payment of £400, Eleanor resigned her dower rights in Ireland and Wales ensuing that the Marshal fiefs remained largely intact.[9] Achieving an agreement about what properties she was to hold as part of her dower rights proved problematic. Richard, now 3rd Earl of Pembroke, was reluctant to see his inheritance fragmented and was also exercising his power by objecting to the king's proposed marriage to Marjorie of Scotland, who was a younger sister of Hubert de Burgh.

In August 1232, de Burgh fell from power and was imprisoned at Devizes. He was replaced by Peter de Roches and a clique of royal favourites from Poitou including Henry III's half-brothers from his mother Isabella of Angoulême's second marriage to Hugh X of Lusignan. The Countess of Striguil's grandson, Richard de Clare was placed in the custody of Peter des Roche and the de Clare territories in Glamorgan and Carmarthen retained by Peter de Rivaux, who aside from being a Poitevin courtier, was also closely related to Roches.

Despite the change of guardianship, Margaret of Scotland orchestrated a marriage between Richard de Clare and her daughter Megotta. The betrothal between the two children went ahead without the king's approval, or des Roche's knowledge, to ensure that the de Clare estates remained in de Burgh's hands. The two children were a similar age and raised in the same household where they were said to have developed a deep bond for one another. When King Henry III found out he demanded that the marriage should be annulled. Megotta died in 1237 having been separated from the young man she thought of as her husband. Soon afterwards, Richard de Clare was married on the orders of the king to the Earl of Lincoln's daughter Matilda de Lacy demonstrating that it was not just females who might be regarded as representative of lands and titles; or as pawns on the medieval marriage board.

By August 1233, there was growing tension between the extended Marshal clan and Henry III's government. The king's own brother Richard of Cornwall who was married to Isabel Marshal in 1231, without royal consent, thought that it should be him who held the guardianship of his young step-son rather than des Roches. Richard Marshal remained under suspicion because he refused to serve Henry III on foreign soil. He still held his fiefs in Normandy as a vassal of the French throne. Like his brother-in-law he was increasingly hostile to the king's foreign favourites, especially as it seemed that they were clamouring for reward at the expense of families who served Henry throughout his minority. Des Roches appointed his own adherents to key positions and used Poitouvin mercenaries to fulfil his will in the name of the king. Men became fearful for their lands and, when Henry III began to demand hostages, for the safety of their families.

Among the men to suffer was Gilbert Basset, Lord of Wycombe, castellan of St Briavels Castle and governor of the Forest of Dean. He was part of the Marshal affinity and tied to the earl through marriage to Isabel de Ferrers, a daughter of Sybil Marshal. Some of his property was confiscated and his nephew, Richard Siward, held hostage for Basset's future conduct.

Chester's chronicler recorded that war broke out in South Wales between Richard Marshal and the king when Richard received word of a plot to seize him in August 1233. Isabel's patrimony was in danger of being forfeited to the Crown because Richard turned traitor. The *Margam Chronicle* blamed the start of the war on the foreign born court faction allied with des Roches, who came from Touraine.[10] Richard was temporarily marginalised at the start of the so-called Marshal War when des Roches bought off the nobility who pocketed the bribes but proved loath to take on William Marshal's son in his home territory. Usk fell to the king's army.

Isabel's son mustered his men, the support of his extended kinship network and allied himself with Llywelyn ab Iowerth who was also part of the complicated web of political and social ties that laced the border together. Richard even went so far as to sack Shrewsbury. He rescued Hubert de Burgh from Devizes Castle and met with him at Striguil before ambushing Henry and his men at Grosmont on 11 November 1233. By February 1234 the king was forced to dismiss des Roches and make a truce with Richard. The shadows of the Second Barons War were beginning to collect around the throne.

Assured, for the time being, of his lands in England and Wales, Richard journeyed to Ireland to secure his fief there. The king's justiciar, Maurice FitzGerald, had attacked Leinster in alliance with the de Lacys. On 1 April 1234, Richard was wounded during fighting near Kildare and seemed likely to make a full recovery. But then he developed sepsis and was dead by the middle of the month. His death resolved the immediate problem of Marshal loyalty and permitted the Archbishop of Canterbury to plead with the king that Isabel's third son Gilbert should inherit the earldom and its associated fiefs. It left Leinster vulnerable to men who wanted the Marshal estates for themselves but Richard's victory over the king in England and his alliance with de Burgh meant that the stalemate in Ireland resulting from Richard's death did not turn into a disaster for the Marshal family or their supporters when Gilbert became earl.

Gilbert Marshal was reconciled with the king on 30 May 1234 at Gloucester and licensed to enter his estates as the 4th earl of Pembroke. Having repudiated his status as a clerk in minor orders, he was knighted by Henry III on 11 June. The following year, conscious of a need for a legitimate heir, Gilbert married Marjorie of Scotland at Berwick-upon-Tweed, the youngest sister of Margaret de Burgh, Countess of Kent, once intended as a bride for Henry himself.

The Marshals' Norman estates did not fall into Gilbert's hand with the same ease. Louis IX of France refused to recognise Gilbert's rights. When Isabel and Marshal disposed of their lands to Richard in 1219, they did not consider that their two eldest sons would not have heirs of their own. There was also the problem of Eleanor Plantagenet's dower which had fallen into arrears.[11] However, Henry recognised that he needed the support of the new earl. He granted Gilbert the honour of Pevensey in 1234, which had been in the hands of the earl's great grandfather Gilbert de Clare until his rebellion against King Stephen in 1147, in lieu of his Norman losses and continued to demonstrate generosity to the earl throughout his life.

The king also consolidated Gilbert's possession in the Marches, granting the earl custody of his nephew's de Clare lands in 1235. It was only after the death of Llewelyn ap Iowerth in 1240 that the earl was able to regain control of Ceredigion Castle in a campaign led by his brother Walter. At the same time, Gilbert negotiated a treaty with Maelgwn Fychan, the son and grandson of Welsh princes who had fought against the 1st Earl of Pembroke after his marriage to Isabel in 1189. Under the terms of the treaty, Gilbert married his illegitimate daughter, another Isabel, to Maelgwn's son Rhys. Both men became vassals of Gilbert for the land in Ceredigion with which Gilbert dowered his daughter.

By the following year the fourth earl was dead. He was killed on a tournament field at Ware on 27 June 1241 when his horse threw him and dragged him along the ground. The tournament was unlicensed and Gilbert had not received the same training that his brothers did. The king was furious. Walter Marshal, who had been part of his elder brother's retinue fled to Wales after Gilbert's burial alongside his father and eldest brother. He was licenced to enter his brother's estates but only after the king upbraided him for his older brother's failings.

Like Gilbert before him, Walter's parents had not envisaged that he would inherit any lands other than what his father bequeathed him in 1219 and no marriage was arranged for him. He married Margaret de Quincy, the niece of Ranulf, 6th Earl of Chester and a descendent of King Henry I, joined the king on campaign in Gascony in 1242, protected the southern Marches against the threat posed by Llywelyn Ap Iowerth's son Dafydd and negotiated terms with Maurice FitzGerald in 1244, bringing an end to a ten-year feud with the Geraldines which originated with the death of William the Younger. Walter spent the summer of 1245 in Leinster but became ill on his return to the Marches. He died on 27 November 1245 at Goodrich Castle.

Isabel's youngest son, Ansel succeeded to the Marshal titles and fiefs but he died just eleven days after Walter without appearing at court to pay homage to the king or pay the fine that would have permitted him to enter his estates as an earl of Pembroke. Both men were buried in Tintern, as was their right, as Lords of Striguil near to their mother and grandmother. The legacy that William and Isabel worked to consolidate and extend throughout their lives was destined to pass into the hands of other families. By then, the Crown had forgotten what it owed to the 1st Earl of Pembroke or his countess.

Chapter 22

Too Many Heiresses

Fortune's wheel turned against the Marshal dynasty within a generation of its founding. Isabel and William's inheritance was to be divided equally amongst their five daughters and their descendants regardless of gender. Prior to 1135, Maud Marshal, Isabel's eldest daughter, might have held all her parents' estates in her own right if she was powerful enough to quash the claims of the rest of her family but a ruling made at the end of Henry I's reign sought to avoid violence within families by including younger sisters as co-heiresses in an estate where there were no more male heirs.

An inquisition post-mortem was held to ensure that Walter Marshal's estates were divided as they should be. The aim of an inquisition was to find out exactly what income and rights were due to the Crown and how the land should be parcelled out between widows with dower rights and the heirs to the property. There was an enquiry in each county where Walter held land, directed by a royal official called an escheator. Each escheator took control of Marshal estates in the county for which he was responsible, summoned a jury of local gentry, sought answers relating to size, tenure and value of the lands as well as identifying the heirs with a claim to the estates in that particular county. Any division of the estates needed to take into consideration the order in which heirs were born, land tenure, and the difficulties of dividing lands in a region subject to violent incursion. The resulting partition was recorded in the charter rolls.[1]

The dower rights of William Marshal the Younger's widow Eleanor, Walter's widow Margaret, and Ansel's widow Matilda de Bohun needed to be settled before the coheirs received their share from the residue of the inheritance that remained. Despite having taken a vow of chastity soon after William the Younger's death, Eleanor married Simon de Montfort and the couple claimed a third of all her first husband's estates after Ansel's death as her dower. Their assertion was unsuccessful even though the annual payment of £400 was a poor deal.

Margaret of Scotland, Walter's widow, received five English manors including Hamstead Marshall and Caversham. Matilda de Bohun[2] was the least fortunate of the Marshal widows. Ansel was only a fifth son when he died rather than an earl of Pembroke because he had not given his oath of fealty or paid the necessary fines to enter into the inheritance. Her marriage to Ansel was facilitated by Gilbert and Walter Marshal while she was still a child as a means of strengthening their political affiliations along the Marches with the increasingly influential de Bohun family. Ansel's widow received £60 each year from his Leinster estates but not the dower rights of a countess. She continued to be known as Matilda Marshal for the rest of her short life although she married for a second time to Roger de Quincy, 2nd Earl of Winchester.

Isabel's eldest daughter, Maud, was already a wealthy woman in 1245 because she was a widow twice over with dower rights accrued from both unions. Hugh Bigod was 3rd Earl of Norfolk for only a short time before dying in February 1225. Less than a year after Hugh's death, in October 1225, Maud married William de Warenne 5th Earl of Surrey who was the son of Henry II's illegitimate half-brother Hamelin Plantagenet as well as being a neighbour of the Bigods in Norfolk. Like her mother before her, Maud was a valuable prize, but, unlike Isabel at the time of her widowhood, her son had not yet attained his majority. It's likely that Maud's second marriage was made either for the countess's protection or, that the earl purchased the marriage to hold her dower lands indicating that the promises made by Magna Carta were ignored.

After the death of her second husband in 1242 followed by the last of her brothers at the end of December 1245, Maud 'was undoubtedly the most powerful and wealthy woman in England'.[3] She already held land in East Anglia and Yorkshire as well as the castellanship of Conisbrough Castle. After the death of her youngest brother, she received a fifth of the Marshal inheritance and the titles to the earldom Netherwent as well as the hereditary role as Marshal of England which she used throughout the rest of her life. In 1248 Maud transferred the castle at Chepstow to her eldest son prior to her death and wrote to King Henry III 'requesting the king to accept Roger's homage for it.'[4] Roger Bigod, 5th Earl of Norfolk inherited vast estates and turned Striguil, which was his main dwelling, into a palatial residence.[5]

Maud was the only one of the countess's children still alive in 1245 to benefit from the break-up of her parents' estates and titles. Her sister Isabel was too important to be left unmarried for long after the death of Gilbert de Clare in 1230. Isabel's second husband, Richard of Cornwall, was King Henry III's brother. Part of the reason he wanted to marry Isabel within months of her widowhood was because of her dower rights to the land in South Wales which abutted his own. There was also the matter of Richard de Clare's wardship to be taken into consideration. The de Clare line was assured by the birth of three sons: Richard, William and Gilbert born the year before his father's death as well as three daughters: Agnes, Amice, and Isabel. The union between

Isabel and Richard strengthened Cornwall's ties to the powerful Marshal and de Clare affinities but did not find favour with King Henry III who did not grant custody of Richard or his valuable domains to his new stepfather. Magna Carta might have granted widows more rights when it came to remarriage but baronial women like Isabel still required royal consent before taking a second husband. The king had also been in the process of negotiating a more advantageous match for his brother[6] who could be seen as wasting a wedding alliance given that his sister, Eleanor, was already married to William Marshal the Younger. King Henry also recognised that if he were to die without an heir himself, that Richard would ascend the throne with Isabel at his side.

Isabel bore her new husband three children, two of whom died during infancy, before she fell pregnant for a fourth time. She died at Berkhamsted on 17 January 1240 from complications. According to Matthew Paris she died from 'yellow jaundice'[7] a symptom of liver disease. Modern medicine recognises that some liver disease is unique to pregnancy. Although she asked to be buried at Tewkesbury, Richard interred her remains at Beaulieu. Her heart was removed before her interment and taken to Tewkesbury where it was buried with Gilbert.

Richard de Clare, 5th Earl of Hertford and 6th Earl of Gloucester was heir not only to his father's estates but to one fifth of the Marshal inheritance through his mother, Isabel Marshal. Richard, received Usk, as well as a large share of Leinster including Kilkenny. In 1253, like his grandfather before him, the earl would find it expedient to avoid conflict with a king by crossing to Ireland to attend to his affairs there. Isabel's patrimony remained in the de Clare family until the 8th earl of Gloucester, another Gilbert de Clare, was killed at the Battle of Bannockburn in 1314 leaving three sisters as co-heiresses. The estates, and their associated wealth and political power, changed hands again with the marriages of Eleanor, Margaret and Elizabeth to favourites of King Edward II.

For Isabel's three daughters (Agnes, Amice and Isabel) there was little left to inherit once their brother received his share of his parents' estates. For Isabel de Clare born in 1220 there was only a minimal dowry of a single manor in Sussex and the promise of admittance into the powerful de Clare affinity. Her husband was Robert Bruce, Lord of Annandale. Her own grandchild would be crowned King of Scotland in 1306 leading to the Scottish Wars of Independence.

Kildare and its castle were granted to Sibyl Marshal's heirs. She gave William de Ferrers, 5th Earl of Derby no male heirs prior to her death sometime before 1238. De Ferrers made advantageous marriages for Sybil's seven daughters but the arrival in 1239 of a male heir by his second wife meant that they were not co-heiresses to the earldom of Derby. Sybil's eldest daughter Agnes married William de Vesci, son of Eustace de Vesci in about 1244. William de Vesci supported Simon de Montfort during the Second Barons War and suffered as a consequence. It took a decade following the royalist victory at Evesham in 1265 for him and his elder brother John to be rehabilitated at court. Agnes's eldest son, William, inherited some of his great grandmother's Irish estates. In 1290, following the death of the Maid of Norway, William became a competitor for the Scottish crown through his paternal grandmother Margaret who was an illegitimate daughter of William the Lion.

Family and neighbours were of political and social service to one another. The marriages of Sybil's daughters reflect the way that patterns of landholding and familial networks were interlinked. Her daughter Isabel married first into the Basset family and secondly to the Lord of Dunster who was a de Bohun, affirming regional alliances in the Marches and West of England. Sybil and Joan were also married into the increasingly influential de Bohun family, Agatha married into the Mortimer family and Eleanor, who would marry four times, was still married to William de Vaux in 1246. The de Vauxs were vassals of the Bigod family.[8] The affinities that evolved would become increasingly important to medieval politics with the passage of time.

Eva Marshal died soon after Ansel at the beginning of 1246. She did not remarry after de Braose's execution in 1230. She remained close to her brothers. William the Younger became guardian to her younger daughters. Like Maud, Eva's presence is better recorded in the records than her own mother's and several of her sisters because of the sixteen-year period in which she held the de Braose lands and administered them as well as her own dower which included Hay Castle. Her loyalty to the earls of Pembroke resulted in the confiscation of her estates during Richard Marshal's rebellion. It was also Eva who paid feudal dues including, in 1242, a fine for the right to decide who her youngest daughter, Eleanor, would marry. In 1246 her proximity to, and close association with, her brothers ensured that her daughters and their descendants benefited more than some of the other claimants to the Marshal domains. The eldest, Isabella was married to Dafydd ap Llywellyn and in 1447 Maud married Roger Mortimer, 1st Baron Mortimer of Wigmore. Eva was united with Sir William de Cantelupe and Eleanor, whose marriage occurred in 1242 affiliated the Marshal and de Braose families with the de Bohuns.

The honour of Bergavenny transferred through marriage into the hands of the Cantilupe family as did Cilgerran. The Mortimers of Wigmore acquired Radnor and St Clears adding to already extensive Mortimer estates. Thanks to their holdings in the centre of the Marches and the south-west of Wales the family evolved as significant political players. It helped that Maud's husband

Roger Mortimer was a companion of the future King Edward I. Eleanor de Braose inherited Haverfordwest from her mother as well as the lordship of Brecon and the castle at Hay from her father. The amalgamation of land changed the balance of power in the Marches to increase the influence of the Bohun family although they were never as powerful as the earls of Gloucester who held Glamorgan. The alliances created by a series of weddings across two generations changed the political structure of the Marches.

Joan Marshal, Isabel's youngest daughter who died in 1234, left only one child, Joan de Munchensy. She gained Wexford as well as estates associated with Pembroke.[9] The earldom of Pembroke was granted to William Marshal in 1199 by King John rather than through his marriage to Isabel ten years previously. It fell to the youngest of Isabel and William's daughters because of the order in which it became part of the family's domains. The inheritance meant that Joan 'inherited one of the largest and wealthiest estates in England'.[10] After Joan de Munchensy became an heiress in 1247, King Henry III married her to his own half-brother, William de Valance; an unpopular foreign favourite. Joan's life was punctuated with property disputes that she pursued, sometimes at the expense of her coheirs. Part of Joan's portion of the Marshal included Goodrich Castle. It was during Joan's tenure that Goodrich was reshaped and, in 1296 when William died, it became one of her principal residences.

Joan's seal, *'S'Johanne dñe d'Penbroc uxor' W'd Valencia'*,[11] like her grandmother's, reflects her authority and her pride in her matrilineal heritage. The exercise of power was a complicated business but it endured through Isabel, her daughters and her granddaughters' *suo jure* rights. Church and State may have attempted to render medieval women invisible but it is impossible to dismiss the authority of William Marshal's countess, her administrative capabilities, her hold over her family's affairs or the legacy she bequeathed her daughters and the families they married into.

Who's Who

Angevin Dynasty

Henry II	King of England, 1154-1189, married to **Eleanor, Duchess of Aquitaine.**
Henry the Young King	(1155-1183) Eldest surviving son of King Henry II and Eleanor of Aquitaine. Crowned as king in 1170, alongside his father. He was married to Margaret of France.
Richard I 'the Lionheart'	(1157-1199) King of England, 1189-1199. Second surviving son of King Henry II and Eleanor of Aquitaine. He died at Chalus, in the Limousin region of France, from an infected wound.
Geoffrey Duke of Brittany	(1158-1186) Third surviving son of Henry II and Eleanor of Aquitaine. Married Constance, Duchess of Brittany. His heir **Arthur of Brittany** was born in 1193 after his father's death and was a claimant to Richard I's realm in 1199.
John I	(1166-1216) King of England, 1199-1216. He married **Isabella of Angoulême** in 1200 triggering the loss of the Angevin Empire. Isabella gave John five children: Henry III, Richard of Cornwall, Joan, Isabella and Eleanor. He fathered numerous illegitimate children including a son Morgan, on his mistress Nest Bloet, and a daughter **Joan**, by an unknown woman, who he married to Llywelyn ap Iowerth in 1204.
Geoffrey	**Archbishop of York** (d.1212). Illegitimate son of Henry II.
Henry III	(1207-1272) King of England, 1216-1272.
Richard of Cornwall	(1209-1272) Younger son of King John. He married Isabel Marshal, the widow of Gilbert de Clare, 5th Earl of Gloucester by whom he had four children who died in infancy.

Eleanor of England	Countess of Pembroke and Leicester (1215-1275). The youngest daughter of King John and Isabella of Angoulême, promised in marriage to William Marshal the Younger in 1219. After William's death she took a vow of chastity but married Simon de Montfort, 6th Earl of Leicester in 1238.

The Capetians

Louis VII	(1120 –1180) King of the Franks 1137-1180. First husband of Eleanor of Aquitaine by whom he had two daughters. In addition to an heir, Philip, by his second wife Constance of Castile, he fathered Margaret and Alais of France.
Philip II	Also known as Philip Augustus. King of France, 1180-1223.
Louis VIII	(1187-1226) King of France 1223-1226. He invaded England, at the invitation of the barons in May 1216.

The Irish

The names in brackets are the English spellings of the Irish names used in the text.

Domnall Mac Gilla Pátraic	(Domnal MacGillapatrick) King of Osraige (d.1185). Long term antagonism between Osraige and Leinster led to Domnall making an alliance with Ruaidri Ua Conchobair.
Muirchertach Mac Lochlainn	High King of Ireland from 1156 until his death in 1166.
Conchobar Mac Murchada	(Connor MacMurrough) Son of Diarmait, executed in 1170.
Diarmait Mac Murchada	(Dermot MacMurrough) King of Leinster (1110-1171). He promised his daughter, Aoife, and his kingdom to Strongbow in return for successfully restoring Diarmait's own rule in Leinster.
Domhnall Caomhánach Mac Murchada	(Donal Kavangh) (d.1175). The eldest illegitimate son of Diarmait Mac Murchada.

Énna Mac Murchada	(Enna MacMurrough) Son of Diarmait, blinded in 1168.
Aoife ni Murchada	(Eve MacMurrough) Princess of Leinster (c.1145–1188). The daughter of the last king of Leinster Diarmait Mac Murchada and his second wife Mór Ni Tuathail. She married Strongbow de Clare. Her only surviving child was Isabel de Clare.
Domnall Mór Ua Briain	(Donal 'the Great' O Brian) King of Thomond. Married to Aoife's half-sister Órlaith.
Conchobar Ua Conchobair	Ruaidri's eldest son. Military commander opposing Cambro-Norman annexation of Ireland.
Ruaidri Ua Conchobair	(Rory O'Connor), King of Connacht (d.1198). The High King of Ireland who invaded Leinster in 1166 and exiled Diarmait. In 1175, he signed the Treaty of Windsor with King Henry II.
Derbforgaill	(Derval or Devorgilla), (d.1193). A daughter of the King of Meath. She was married to Tigernán Ua Ruaire. In 1152, she was abducted, possibly at her own request, by Diarmait Mac Murchada which triggered the feud that toppled him from his throne.
Tigernán Ua Ruaire	(Tiernan O'Rourke) King of Breifne (d.1172). In 1152, his wife, Derbforgaill, was abducted by Diarmait Mac Murchada. He formed an alliance with Ruaidri Ua Conchobair in 1166 and drove Diarmait from his kingdom of Leinster. In 1171, he took part in the unsuccessful siege of Dublin and submitted to King Henry II the same year. He attempted to kill Hugh de Lacy and Maurice Fitzgerald but he died instead.
Lorcán Ua Tuathail,	(Lawrence O Toole) Archbishop of Dublin (1128-1180). Aoife's maternal uncle.

The Welsh

Morgan ap Caradog	Lord of Afan, (d.1208) who rose in rebellion against his Norman overlords in Glamorgan in 1183.
Owain ap Gruffydd	(Owain Gwynedd, Owain Fawr or Owain the Great) King of Gwynedd from 1137 (c.1100-1170). Owain took advantage of the Anarchy to extend the borders of his kingdom.

Rhys ap Gruffydd	**King of Deheubarth** from 1155 (d.1197).
Llywelyn Ap Iorwerth	**King of Gwynedd** (c.1173-1240). Recognised as a Prince of Wales by King Philip II of France. He married King John's illegitimate daughter, Joan, in 1205.
Dafydd ap Llywelyn	**Prince of Wales** (1212-1246). Married to Isabel de Braose, the eldest daughter of Eva Marshal and William de Braose, Lord of Bergavenny.

The de Clares

Megotta de Burgh	(d.1237). Married to Richard de Clare, 6th Earl of Gloucester by her mother, Margaret of Scotland, and without the permission of Henry III, to secure Richard's estates during his minority. The union was subsequently annulled.
Aline de Clare	Illegitimate daughter of Strongbow, married to William FitzMaurice.
Basilia de Clare	(d.1201). Daughter of Gilbert de Clare and Isabel de Beaumont. Sister of Strongbow, married to Raymond le Gros.
Basilia de Clare	Illegitimate daughter of Strongbow, married to Robert de Quincy, Constable of Leinster. She was the mother of Maud de Quincy. History is unclear whether de Quincy's wife was Strongbow's daughter or his sister.
Gilbert de Clare	(c.1173-1185). Son of Aoife of Leinster and Richard 'Strongbow' de Clare who died before attaining his majority.
Gilbert de Clare	**1st Earl of Hertford** (d.1152). Eldest son of Richard FitzGilbert and Adeliza, a sister of Ranulf de Gernon, 4th earl of Chester. He was a hostage as surety for de Gernon's continued loyalty to King Stephen. In 1147, following the confiscation of his castles he joined with Ranulf in rebellion. He was succeeded by his brother, Roger de Clare.
Gilbert de Clare	**1st Earl of Pembroke** (c.1100-1148). A younger son of Richard FitzGilbert and Rohese Giffard, who initially inherited nothing. The deaths of his uncle Roger and Walter without heirs, and the favour of King Stephen,

bought him land in Normandy as well as the lordship at Netherwent. He was married, before 1130, to Isabel de Beaumont who gave her husband two children: Basilia and Richard, better known as Strongbow.

Gilbert de Clare **4th Earl of Hertford and 5th Earl of Gloucester (1180-1230).** Eldest son and heir of his father, the 3rd Earl of Hertford, and his mother, Amice, 4th Countess of Gloucester. He sided with the barons during the First Barons War. He married Isabel Marshal in October 1217.

Richard de Clare **3rd Earl of Hertford (d.1217).** Eldest son of Roger de Clare, 2nd Earl of Hertford who sided with the barons against King John. He was one of the twenty-five sureties for the Magna Carta. He was married to Amice of Gloucester.

Richard de Clare **5th Earl of Hertford and 6th Earl of Gloucester (1222-1262).** The eldest son of Gilbert de Clare and Isabel Marshal. His first marriage was made as a child to Megotta de Burgh but the union, which did not meet with Henry III's approval, was annulled. He was married in 1238 to Maud de Lacy, daughter of the 1st Earl of Lincoln.

Richard de Clare **'Strongbow' Lord of Netherwent (1130-1176).** Son of Gilbert, 1st Earl of Pembroke and Isabel de Beaumont. King Stephen recognised him as Earl of Pembroke but King Henry II refused to recognise his rights to the earldom because of his family's associations with King Stephen during the Anarchy. He married Aoife of Leinster in August 1170 and secured Leinster for himself by *jure uxoris*. He married his illegitimate children, Aline and Basilia, to secure alliances in Ireland. His heir, Gilbert, died before attaining his majority. His legitimate daughter Isabel de Clare became sole heiress to all his estates.

Roger de Clare **2nd Earl of Hertford (1116-1173).** Succeeded his brother Gilbert as Earl of Hertford and secured a grant from King Henry II to seize and hold territory in South Wales.

Walter de Clare	**Lord of Netherwent** (d.c.1137/1138). A younger son of Richard FitzGilbert and Rohese Giffard. He was granted the lordship of Netherwent in the Wye Valley which included Striguil Castle by King Henry I before 1119. He founded the Cistercian abbey at Tintern in 1131. He died without any children.
Gilbert FitzRichard	**2nd Lord of Tonbridge and Clare** (d.c.1117). Succeeded to his father's possessions in England in 1088. In 1110, King Henry I gave the lordship of Ceredigion to Gilbert if he could hold it.
Richard FitzGilbert	**1st Lord of Tonbridge and Clare** (d.c.1090). Married to Rohese Giffard.
Richard FitzGilbert	**3rd Lord of Tonbridge and Clare (d. 15 April 1136).** He inherited all his father's lands in England and Wales. It is thought that he was created Earl of Hertford either by King Henry I or King Stephen but there is no written record to confirm the elevation to comital status of the senior line of the de Clare family during Richard's lifetime. He was ambushed and killed by Iorwerth ab Owain in 1136 as he travelled from Hereford in the direction of Ceredigion.
Robert FitzRichard	**Lord of Little Dunmow** (d.1136). A younger son of Richard FitzGilbert and Rohese Giffard. He was granted the barony of Little Dunmow in Essex and constableship of Baynard's Castle in London by King Henry I. His son Walter FitzRobert inherited the barony.
Robert FitzWalter	**Lord of Little Dunmow** (d.1235). Grandson of Robert FitzRichard. One of the leaders of the barons opposing King John during the First Barons War.
The FitzGeralds	Descended from Nest of Wales, the daughter of Rhys ap Tewdr, King of Deheubarth and her husband Gerald of Windsor. The Geraldines also comprised Nest's offspring from her second husband, Stephen, Constable of Ceredigion Castle and a child, Henry, by King Henry I.
David FitzGerald	**Bishop of St David's** in Pembrokeshire (d.1176). His own son **Miles (or Milo) FitzDavid** joined his uncles in Ireland.

Maurice FitzGerald	Lord of Llanstephan (d.1176). Recruited, in 1169, by his half-brother Robert FitzStephen to join the expedition to Leinster.
Meiler FitzHenry	(d.1220) His father, Henry FitzHenry, was an illegitimate son of King Henry I. He accompanied his uncle, Robert FitzStephen, to Ireland in 1169.
Gerald FitzMaurice	1st Lord of Offaly (d.1204). Was the ancestor of the FitzMaurice Earls of Kildare.
Robert FitzStephen	Nest's son by Stephen. Arrived in Leinster on 1 May 1169.
Raymond 'le Gros' FitzWilliam	An early Cambro-Norman invader of Ireland under the command of Earl Richard Strongbow. In 1174, he married Strongbow's sister Basilia.
Gerald of Wales	A grandson of Nest's who became a royal clerk and chaplain, travelling with King Henry II and King John. He wrote an account of his journey to Ireland, the *Topographia Hibernia* and then a history, *Expugnatio Hibernica*. The Marshals and their extended family networks
Alice de Béthune	(c.1198–c.1215) Sole heiress of Baldwin de Béthune (d.1212). Married to William Marshal the Younger in 1214. Her mother was Hawise, *suo jure* Countess of Aumale.
Hugh Bigod	3rd Earl of Norfolk (c.1182–1225). First husband of Isabel de Clare's eldest daughter Maud Marshal. His father Roger Bigod, 2nd Earl of Norfolk opposed the king during the First Barons War.
Roger Bigod	4th Earl of Norfolk (c.1209-1270). Eldest son of Maud Marshal and Hugh Bigod. He married Isabella of Scotland in 1225 but had no legitimate heirs of his own. He was succeeded by his nephew Roger Bigod, 5th Earl of Norfolk.
William de Braose	Lord of Bergavenny (d.1230). Married to Eva Marshal. He was captured in 1228 by Llywelyn ap Iorwerth but ransomed and a marriage alliance made between his daughter Isabel de Braose and Llywelyn's legitimate son Dafydd. De Braose was hanged after he was found in adultery with Llywelyn's wife, Joan, Lady of Wales.

John d'Earley	(1172-1230) John became William Marshal's ward when he was about 14-years old. He remained close to the earl throughout the rest of Marshal's life and was married to Marshal's niece, Sybil, who was the illegitimate daughter of the earl's elder brother John. He was an executor of Marshal's will.
Ansel Marshal	(d.1245) The youngest of Isabel de Clare's five sons who died shortly after his brother Walter without being licenced to enter the earldom of Pembroke.
Eva Marshal	(1203-1246) Eighth child of Isabel de Clare and William Marshal. She was married to William de Braose by whom she had four daughters: Isabel married to Dafydd ap Llywelyn; Maud whose husband was Roger Mortimer, 1st Baron Wigmore; Eva married to William de Cantelupe; and Eleanor who was mother to Humphrey de Bohun, 3rd Earl of Hereford.
Isabel Marshal	**Countess of Hertford and Gloucester (1200-1240).** Daughter of Isabel de Clare married to Gilbert de Clare, 4th Earl of Hertford and secondly to Richard, 1st Earl of Cornwall. By her first husband she had five children: Amicia, Richard, Isabella, William and Gilbert.
Gilbert Marshal	**4th Earl of Pembroke, (c.1194-1241).** The third son of Isabel de Clare and William Marshal to succeed to the earldom of Pembroke. He married Marjorie of Scotland, sister of Alexander II, in 1235. He was killed when he fell from his horse during a tournament.
Joan Marshal	(c.1210-1234) Youngest daughter of Isabel de Clare and William Marshal married to Warin de Munchensy, Lord of Swanscombe.
John Marshal	(d.1194) William Marshal's elder brother who inherited their father's estates. He was King John's castellan at Marlborough. He left no legitimate heir.
John Marshal	William Marshal's nephew who entered the earl's *mesnie* in 1194. He was an illegitimate son of John Marshal. His own eldest son, another John, was appointed Marshal of Ireland by King Henry III in 1236.

Maud Marshal	**Countess of Norfolk and Surrey** (c.1192–1248). Eldest daughter of Isabel de Clare and William Marshal. She was married first to Hugh Bigod, 3rd Earl of Norfolk, and secondly to William de Warenne, 5th Earl of Surrey.
Richard Marshal	**3rd Earl of Pembroke** (1191 -1234). Second son of Isabel de Clare. His parents sent him to France where he held his parents' estates in Normandy at Longueville and Orbec. He succeeded to the earldom of Pembroke in 1231. In 1233 he became involved with a dispute with King Henry III which became known as the Marshal Wars. He was married to Gervaisia of Dinan but left no legitimate heirs.
Sibyl Marshal	(c.1201-before 1247) Daughter of Isabel de Clare and William Marshal married to William de Ferrers, 5th Earl of Derby. She gave her husband seven daughters: Agnes married to William de Vesci, the eldest son of the Lord of Alnwick; Isabel married to Gilbert Basset; Maud who married three times; Sibyl; Joan; Agatha; and Eleanor who was married to William de Vaux and secondly to Roger de Quincy, 2nd Earl of Winchester.
Walter Marshal	**5th Earl of Pembroke** (1199-1245). Fourth son of Isabel de Clare to inherit the earldom of Pembroke having served in the *mesnies* of his brothers Richard and Gilbert. Walter married Margaret de Quincy in 1242 but the marriage was childless.
William Marshal	**1st Earl of Pembroke** (c.1146-1219). Husband of Isabel de Clare, loyal servant of the Angevin Crown and regent of Henry III.
William Marshal	**'the Younger' 2nd Earl of Pembroke** (1190-1231). Isabel de Clare's eldest son who took for his second wife, Eleanor, a sister of King Henry III.
Joan de Munchensy	**Lady of Swanscombe and Countess of Pembroke** (d. 1307). Only surviving child of Joan Marshal who was married to Henry III's half-brother, William de Valence.
William de Warenne	**5th Earl of Surrey** (d.1240). Second husband of Isabel de Clare's eldest daughter Maud Marshal. His father Hamelin was an illegitimate son of King Henry II.

Significant others

Guala Bicchieri Papal Legate in England from 1216 to 1218.

Ranalf de Blondeville **6th Earl of Chester** (1170-1232). Co-regent during the minority of Henry III and supporter of William Marshal.

Maud de Braose **Lady of Bramber** (d.1210). Wife of William de Braose, 4th Lord of Bramber. She was arrested and starved to death with her eldest son, William.

William de Braose **4th Lord of Bramber** (d.1211). Powerful Marcher lord and favourite of King John whose fall from favour was pre-empted by Maud de Braose's refusal to yield their son as a hostage to the crown.

Hubert de Burgh **1st Earl of Kent,** (d.1243). Justiciar, regent and royal favourite until he was removed from office in 1232.

Walter de Coutances **Archbishop of Rouen** (d.1207). Servant of Richard I sent to England to secure peace between Prince John and the justiciar, William Longchamp

William FitzAldelm Appointed as governor of Leinster following the death of Strongbow in 1176.

Geoffrey FitzRobert Seneschal of Leinster (d.1211).

Ranulf de Gernons **4th Earl of Chester** (d.1153). A powerful lord whose strategy during the Anarchy was to support the side that would further his own interests most effectively.

Ranulf de Glanville (d.1190) Chief Justiciar of England during the reign of King Henry II and custodian of Isabel de Clare.

Hugh de Lacy **Lord of Meath** (d.1186). A marcher baron and favourite of Henry II who travelled to Ireland with the king in 1171. He was murdered in 1186.

Hugh de Lacy **1st Earl of Ulster** (d.c.1242). Younger son of the Lord of Meath, created earl in 1205 by King John.

Walter de Lacy **Lord of Meath** (d.1241). He married a daughter of William de Braose and his wife Maud in 1200. The following year his father-in-law granted him overlordship of Limerick. In 1210 he provided sanctuary to William and Maud and was forced into exile by King John.

Stephen Langton **Archbishop of Canterbury** (d.1228).

William Longchamp	Bishop of Ely and Chief Justiciar in England (d.1197).
William Longspée	**3rd Earl of Salisbury** Half-brother of Hugh Bigod, 3rd Earl of Norfolk through their shared mother Ida de Tosny. An illegitimate son of King Henry II, Longspée remained loyal to his half-brother John throughout the First Barons War.
Hervey de Montmorency	(d.1185) He arrived in Leinster in 1169 with Robert FitzStephen. His time in Ireland was often spent in competition with Raymond le Gros who replaced him as Strongbow's military commander after 1174. Following Strongbow's death, he returned to England, granted all his lands in Ireland to the Cistercians, and in 1179, or thereabouts, he became a monk at Christ Church, Canterbury.
Maurice de Prendergast	(d. 1174) One of the first Normans to arrive in Leinster.
Peter des Roches	**Bishop of Winchester** (d.1238). Regent and leader of faction opposing Hubert de Burgh.
Pandulf Verraccio	Papal legate in England appointed in 1218 who acted as regent for King Henry III.
Hubert de Walter	**Archbishop of Canterbury** and Chief Justiciar of England. (d. 1205).

Notes

All the authors referenced in the notes have their works listed in the bibliography at the end.

Introduction
1. Mantel, Reith Lecture 1, 2017, p.4.
2. By right of his wife.
3. Foucault regards power as something to be exercised within relationships and social networks. He does not regard individuals as inert; rather that power was something that passes through a person who can both submit to and exercise power. Foucault, Lecture 2, p.23-42.
4. McNamara, p.19.
5. Johns, p.3.
6. Bennett Connolly, p.53.
7. Ibid, p.55.

Chapter 1: The de Clare family establishes itself
1. Davis, p.114.
2. Orderic Vitalis, *Historia Ecclesiastica*, Vol. 3, p.340.
3. Bec is less than five miles from the castle at Brionne. Both Gilbert and his father Godfrey were patrons of the abbey.
4. Van Houts, p.70 in *The Works of Gilbert Crispin*, Sapir Abulafia and Evans, G.R., (eds) pp.68-71.
5. Cited in Morris, p.51.
6. Orderic Vitalis, *Historia Ecclesiastica*, Vol. 2, p.369.
7. According to William of Jumièges, following his defeat Guy was permitted to live under house arrest at Duke William's court.
8. Orderic Vitalis, *Historia Ecclesiastica*, Vol. 2. p.493.
9. Holt, p.192, nn 79.
10. Wace, p.232.
11. Davis, p.38.
12. Where he is likely to have been born.
13. *Anglo-Saxon Chronicle*, p.225.
14. Ibid.
15. Ibid, p.233.
16. Barlow: 2008, p.171.
17. *Anglo-Saxon Chronicle*, p.237.
18. William of Malmesbury, pp.345-346.

19. Lieberman, p.41.
20. Eadmer, *Historia Novorum*, ed. Rule, M., (Rolls Series LXXXI, 1884), pp.143, 185 cited in Altschul, p.20.
21. Turner: 2002, p.5.
22. *Gesta Stephani*, p.10-11; cited in Ward, p.274.
23. Hickey, p.64.
24. Ward, p.274.

Chapter 2: The Anarchy

1. *Gesta Stephani*, p.10.
2. Marsh, p.31.
3. *Anglo Saxon Chronicle*, p.268.
4. Venning, p.11.
5. Salzmann, p.3.
6. *Orderic Vitalis*, p.493.

Chapter 3: The earl and the King of Leinster

1. Gerald of Wales, p.206.
2. *Archealogogia Cambrensis*, p.191.
3. Holinshed, p.108.
4. Power, p.110-111.
5. Barlow: 1991, p.309.
6. Like Strongbow its former occupier, Roger, Lord of Berkeley and Dursley supported the losing side in the civil war and was diminished by the Angevin regime.
7. Jeayes, no 6, p.6.
8. Gerald of Wales, p.185.
9. The political situation in Ireland in the years before Dairmait's expulsion from Ireland are explored in detail in Kostick, pp.58-99.
10. Gerald of Wales, p.185.
11. Vincent, p.186.
12. Gerald of Wales, p.186.
13. Irish laws dating to the seventh century allowed a Brehon, or arbiter, to make legal decisions based on the rights and obligations laid out in Irish law books.
14. *The Song of Dermot and the Earl*, lines 340-345, p.28.
15. Gerald of Wales, p.226.
16. Ibid.
17. Ibid.
18. *Triads*, no 180, p25.
19. Rose, p.135.
20. Ibid, p.146.

Chapter 4: Winning Aoife

1. *Four Masters*, p.1183.
2. Gerald of Wales, p.189.

3. *Norden's Surveyor's Dialogue* quoted in Wright, p.285.
4. *Annals of Clonmacnoise*, p.207.
5. Gerald of Wales, p.205.
6. *Annals of Clonmacnoise*, p.207.
7. Ibid, p.212.
8. Gerald of Wales, p.214.
9. *Annals of Clonmacnoise*, p.208.
10. *Four Masters*, Vol. 2, p.1142.

Chapter 5: Pawns and players
1. Lomas, p.39.
2. Gerald of Wales, p.222.
3. Leland, p.77.
4. Roger of Wendover, i., p.235 and Roger of Howden, i, p.25.
5. Gerald of Wales, p.229.
6. Curtis, p.57.
7. Harris: pp.37-38.
8. Hamner, p.203.
9. McKerr, p.44.

Chapter 6: The Irish Countess
1. Gerald of Wales, p.259.
2. Ibid.
3. Duffy, p.93.
4. Gerald of Wales, pp.271-272.
5. Annals of Ulster, p.185.
6. Gerald of Wales, p.274.
7. Ibid, p.289.
8. *The Red Book of the Exchequer*, p.1319; Lomas, p.50; and Kenny, p.134.
9. Crouch: 2011, Chapter 3 discusses the earldom of Pembroke and compares Strongbow's dispossession with that of Simon of Senlis and the disputed honour of Huntingdon, Northampton in the context of an earldom as a personal dignity that was not erased by royal writ.
10. *The Great Roll of the Pipe for the twenty-third year of the reign of King Henry II A.D. 1176-1177 (Pipe Roll Society 26)*.
11. Kenny, p.134.
12. *The Great Pipe Roll*, (Pipe Roll Society, 37) p.xl.
13. Crouch: 2016, p.149.
14. MS. Lambeth 853, p.102, about 1430, written without breaks. Other MSS. are Trinity College, Cambridge, R.3, 19, and Ashmole 61, p.7 (printed in Queen Elizabeth's Academy).
15. A great granddaughter of Isabel de Clare and William Marshal through descent from their youngest daughter Joan Marshal. Evidence for her lineage is described in 'The Earls, Earldom, and Castles of Pembroke,' *Archeologia Cambrensis*, 1860 p.257.

16. Ibid, 293.
17. Hanawalt, p.20.
18. Duby, p.39.
19. Brown: 2017, p.126 cited in Hickey, p.82.

Chapter 7: A valuable prize
1. Crouch, David, 'The local influence of the earls of Warwick, 1088-1242: a study in decline and resourcefulness', *Midland History*, 21 (1996), pp.9-10 cited in Johns note 25, p.5.
2. Coss, p.23.
3. Turner:1994, p.91.
4. Ibid, p.59.
5. Crouch: 2002, p.81.

Chapter 8: A safe husband
1. Clark, p.27.
2. Van Houts, p.81.
3. Bhote, p.37.
4. *Histoire*, II. 9361-9371.
5. Cockeril, (66 acts).
6. Roger of Howden, Vol. 2, p.116.
7. Roger of Howden, https://sourcebooks.fordham.edu/source/hoveden1189a.asp.
8. Roger of Howden listed: Geoffrey FitzPeter or FitzPiers 1st Earl of Essex; William Bruyere or Bruer who was Henry II's Sheriff of Devon; Robert de Whitfield and Roger-RizRainfrey or FitzReinfrid, whose brother Walter de Coutance was the Bishop of Rouen. FitzRainfrey had been in royal service since 1173 and served the king's justice from 1176 onwards.

Chapter 9: Wife and chatelaine
1. *The Great Pipe Roll*, p.223.
2. Tanner. p.133.
3. Bedos-Rezak, p.64.
4. Ibid.
5. Turner, p.11.
6. Morgan, p.67.
7. Haskins, p.137.
8. Ideals, p.24.
9. Haskins, p.139.
10. Ibid, p.136.
11. Barkley, p.269.

Chapter 10: Motherhood
1. Munby, pp.43-44.
2. Joinville, p.45.
3. Warner, p.75.

4. Leyser, p.125.
5. Gilchrist, p.142.
6. Medicine, p.171.
7. Pipe Roll 2 Richard I, (Pipe Roll Society, 49), p.58 and Pipe Roll 6 Richard 1 (Pipe Roll Society, 43), p.239 quoted in Painter, p.83.

Chapter 11: Wife of a junior justiciar
1. Painter, p.87.
2. Ibid, p.229.
3. *Histoire*, 9828-9858.
4. https://elizabethchadwick.com/blog/the-irish-princess-finding-aoife/ citing Remfry, Paul Martin, Goodrich Castle; And the Families of Godric Mapson, Monmouth, Clare, Marshall, Montchesney, Valence, Despenser and Talbot (Castle Studies Research and Publishing, 2015).
5. Turner, p.12.
6. Howdon, Vol 2, p.266.
7. Cited in Painter, p.95.
8. John Marshal was its castellan.
9. Howdon, p.288.
10. *Histoire*, 9893-9904.
11. Painter, p.97.
12. Ibid, p.292.
13. Cockerill, p.326.
14. Crouch: 2002, pp.72-74.
15. Pollock, p.82.
16. *Rotuli Normanniæ*, Vol. I, p. 43.
17. *Histoire*, 11105-11264.
18. Crouch: 2002, p.82.

Chapter 12: Divided loyalties
1. Cockerill, p.370.
2. Blomefield, p.228.
3. Bartlett, p.158.
4. Chartularies of St Mary's 2: 307-308 cited in *The Acts and Letters*, nn 37 p.11.
5. Painter, p. 153.
6. Hogan, p.168.
7. Some sources, including the Dictionary of Irish Biography and Wikipedia state that Basilia was Raymond le Gros' widow rather than Strongbow's natural daughter. Debrett's Peerage, pp.1118-1119 suggests that following the death of le Gros in about 1189, that his widow married into the Montmorency family rather than FitzRobert. Clark, p.235 concludes that Raymond le Gros' wife was Strongbow's daughter rather than his sister but that she took FitzRobert as her second husband. The problem lays in the available documentary evidence.
8. Power: 2003, p.206.

9. Ralf de Coggeshall, pp.144-145, cited in Power nn. 38 p.207.
10. http://the-history-girls.blogspot.com/2015/12/king-johns-christmas-eve-by-elizabeth.html
11. *Anonymous of Bethune*, cited in Connolly, p.37.
12. Painter, p.139.

Chapter 13: Out of favour
1. Histoire, II, lines 18562-18570 cited in Mitchell, p.55.
2. Morris, p.3.
3. *Calendar of Documents Relating to Ireland*, 1206-1207, Feb 19, 313, p.46-47.
4. 13s 4d.
5. Bennett Connolly, p.220.
6. Bradley, p.21.
7. Berry, P.116.
8. *Chartae Hiberniae*, pp.33-34.
9. Veach, p.172.
10. *Calendar of Papal Registers*, 14 kal. Dec. St Peter's, (f.32).

Chapter 14: Lady of Leinster
1. *Histoire*, 13464-13550.
2. *Calendar of Documents, Relating to Ireland*: 1875, p.xxii.
3. Crouch: 2002, p.106.
4. Round, p.368.
5. O'Donovan, vol 3, p.155.
6. *Histoire*, 13824-13828.
7. Painter, p.158 notes that D'Earley and d'Evreux were tenants-in-chief in England, making them the king's men.
8. *Calendar of Documents Relating to Ireland*, 1207-1208, 20 Feb, no. 374, p.56.
9. Pipe Roll, p.124 quoted in Clark, p.32.
10. *Calendar of Documents Relating to Ireland*, March 21, 379, p.56.
11. *Histoire*, 14095-14100, cited in Tanner, p.49.
12. Ibid
13. Lomas, p.70.
14. This did not mean there were no marriages. It was legal to marry without a priest.

Chapter 15: An Irish Retirement
1. Calendar of Documents, 1269, 31 December, no. 861, p.140.
2. Painter, p.152.
3. Colfer, p.37.
4. *The Irish Penny Paper*, 30 March 1833, vol 1, no 13, p.97 (97-100).
5. *Acts and Letters*, No 103 Dublin, Cathedral Priory of the Holy Trinity (Christ Church), p.187.
6. *Calendar of Documents Relating to Ireland*, 1207-1208, March 19, no. 376, p56 and Close 9, John, m.7.

7. *Calendar of Documents Relating to Ireland*, 1208, March 28, no 381 and 1208, April 24, no 382, p.58.
8. Crouch: 2002, p.113.
9. Roger of Wendover, p.248.
10. Ibid.
11. *Calendar of Documents Relating to Ireland*, 1210, July 28, 408, p.66-67.
12. *Histoire*, 14199-14232 cited in Painter, p.162.
13. Brown, p.89, fn. 9.
14. Roger of Wendover, cited in Curtis, p.114.
15. Roger of Wendover, p.255.
16. Hallam, *Barnwell Chronicles*, p.298.
17. *Calendar of Documents Relating to Ireland*, 1212, October, 444, citing Close 14, John, m 4 dors pp.72-73. Cited in Painter p.173.

Chapter 16. Troubled times

1. *Calendar of Documents Relating to Ireland*, 1213, July 21, no.465, p.69.
2. Asbridge, p.322.
3. Bennett Conolly, p.78.
4. Marvin, p.45.
5. Asbridge, p.326.
6. Douglas et al, p.432 cited in Jones:2015, p.117.
7. Crouch: 2003, p.285.
8. *Calendar of Documents Relating to Ireland*, 1215, Sept. 8, no. 650, p.100.

Chapter 17: Regent's Wife

1. *Annals of Clonmacnoise*, p.229.
2. Was King John Murdered? (Available online). *History Extra*, 9 April 2021.
3. *Histoire*, 15153-15190.
4. Ibid, 15206-15286, cited in Painter, p.192.
5. Ibid, 15510.
6. Ibid, 14465-15561, cited in Painter, p.196 and Lewis, p.28.
7. Ibid, 15624-15696.
8. *Calendar of Papal Registers*, Regesta 9:1216-1218, 16 Kal. Feb. Lateran. (f.41d).
9. *Histoire*, 16629-16828.
10. Davis, p.121.
11. Jones, p.183.

Chapter 18: The marriage market

1. Painter, p.270.
2. Wilkinson, nn. 40, p.87.
3. Abertawe Castle.
4. Carpenter, pp.76-77.
5. Walker, p.94.
6. Burke, p.72.

7. Mathew Paris, vol 2, p.396 cited in Cox, p.127, Cokayne, p.66 and Turbott, p.199.
8. *Acts and Letters*, p.340.
9. Marsh, p.81.
10. Matthew Paris, p.33.

Chapter 19: One final kiss
1. *Histoire*, 18139-18148.
2. Ibid, 18171-18188.
3. Ibid, 18203-18260.
4. Ibid, 18359-18387.
5. Brooks, p.288.
6. Ibid, 19080; Kerr & Kerr, p.53.
7. Brooks, p.288.

Chapter 20: A matriarch takes up the reins
1. *Acts and Letters*, no.102 Burgh, Hubert de, p.186.
2. Johns, p.68.
3. Cited in Kenny, p.322.
4. Strongbow enfeoffed part of Offaly to Eva's father, Robert de Bermingham in Harris, p.19.
5. *Calendar of Documents Relating to Ireland*, 1219, June 19, no.880, p.131.
6. *Acts and Letters*, p.190.
7. Richard of Devizes, p.10.
8. Bennett Connolly, *The 1215 Magna Carta*, Appendix A, p.213.
9. Cokayne, p.513.
10. Cited in Wilkinson, p.34.
11. Orbec was a lordship associated with Isabel's ancestor Gilbert of Brionne.
12. *Acts and Letters*, no.101 Bec-Hellouin, Abbey of St Mary, p.185.
13. Weir: 2011, p. 69 and Bennett Connolly, p.104.
14. Davies p.viii and p.131.
15. Cummins, p.406.
16. *Opus Majus*, pp.624-625.
17. Daniel, p.36.
18. Dugdale, p.269.
19. Ibid
20. Leask, p.65-67.

Chapter 21: Isabel's sons
1. Carpenter: 1990, p.344.
2. Ibid: 2021, p.82.
3. *The Chronicle: 1215-34, Annales Cestrienses Chronicle of the Abbey of S. Werburg, At Chester*, pp.50-59.
4. Wilkinson, p.92.
5. Power, Daniel, 'The French Interests of the Marshal Earls', pp.220-221.

6. Tewkesbury Annals in *Annales monastici*, Vol 1, p.76.
7. CPR, 1225-1232, p.400.
8. Morris: 2005, p.69.
9. Baker, p.26.
10. Cited in Carpenter: 2020, p.138.
11. Baker, p.27

Chapter 22: Too many heiresses

1. *Calendar of Charter Rolls, 1226–1257*, p.142.
2. Dugdale, *Monasticon*, vol. VI, p.135.
3. Crouch: 2017, p.244.
4. *Acts and Letters*, no.276 Henry III, King of England, p.458.
5. Turner: 2002, p.15.
6. Altschul, p.32.
7. *Mathew Paris*, p.255.
8. *Battle Abbey Roll*, Vol 1., p. 294.
9. Wrottesley, *Coram Rege Roll, Easter Term*, 3.E.1., pp. 66-72.
10. Mitchel: 2016, p.2.
11. Ibid, p.57 and fig.1.

Bibliography

Primary Sources

Calendar of Charter rolls 1226-57, (1903).

The Great Roll of the Pipe for the twenty-third year of the reign of King Henry the Second, A.D. 1176-1177, Pipe Roll Society Publications, 26, (1905).

The Great Roll of the Pipe for the thirty-third year of the reign of King Henry the Second, A.D. 1186-1187, Pipe Roll Society Publications, 37, (1915).

The Song of Dermot and the Earl, available online at https://celt.ucc.ie/published/T250001-001/text002.html

Bliss, W.H., (ed.), 'Regesta 9:1216-1218' in *Calendar of Papal Registers*, (London: HMSO, 1893).

Browne, R., (trans.), *The Cure of Old Age and Preservation of Youth by Roger Bacon*, (London, 1683).

Burke, R. B., (trans.), *The Opus Majus of Roger Bacon*, Vol. 2, (New York, 1962).

Burton, Henry Richards Luard, (ed and trans), *Annales Monastici, Annales de Margan (A.D. 1066-1232) Annales de Theokesberia (A.D. 1066-1263) Annales de Burton (A.D. 1004-1263)*, Vol. 1, (1864).

Christie, Richard Copley, (ed.), *The Chronicle: 1215-34, Annales Cestrienses Chronicle of the Abbey of S. Werburg, At Chester*, (London, 1887).

Clark, Cecily, *The Thorney Liber Vitae*, (Woodbridge: Boydell Press, 2015).

Crouch, David, (ed.), *The Acts and Letters of the Marshal Family*, Camden Fifth Series, Vol. 47, (Cambridge: Cambridge University Press, 2015).

Dalby, Andrew, (ed. and trans.), Biblesworth, Walter de: *The Treatise of Walter of Bibbesworth*, (London: Prospect Books, 2012).

Douglas, D.C., et al. (eds), *English Historical Documents II 1042-1189*, 2nd edition, (London, 1981).

Evans, G.R. & Sapir Abulafia, Anna, (eds) *The Works of Gilbert Crispin, Abbot of Westminster, Auctores Britannici Medii Aevi*, (London: British Academy, 1986).

Forester, Thomas, (ed. and trans.), *Orderic Vitalus: The Ecclesiastical History of England and Normandy*, Vol. 2, (London: H.G. Bohn, 1853).

Forester, Thomas, (ed. and trans.), *The Historical Works of Geraldus Cambrensis, containing the Topography of Ireland, and the History of the Conquest of Ireland*, (London: H.G. Bohn, 1863).

Giles, John A. (ed.), *William of Malmesbury's Chronicle of the Kings of England*, (London: H.G. Bohn, 1847).

Giles, John, A. (ed.), *Roger of Wendover's Flowers of History*, Vol. 2, (London: H.G. Bohn, 1849).

Giles, John A., (ed. & trans.) *Matthew Paris's English History*, Vol. 2, (London: H.G. Bohn, 1852).

Hall, Hubert, (ed.), *The Red Book of the Exchequer*, Vol. 3, (Cambridge: Cambridge University Press, originally 1896, reprinted 2012).

Hallam, E. (ed.), *The Plantagenet Chronicles*, (London: Phoebe Phillips Editions, 1986).

Harris, Walter, (ed.), *Hibernica: or Some Ancient Pieces relating to Ireland, never hitherto made publick*, (Dublin: Edward Bate, 1747).

Hanmer, Meredith, *The Chronicle of Ireland*, Vol. 2, (Dublin: The Society of Stationers, reprinted by the Hibernia Press, 1809).

Holden, A.J., & Crouch, D (eds), Gregory, S. (trans.), *History of William Marshal*. 3 Vols, (London: Anglo-Norman Text Society, Occasional Series, 4-6 [2002-2007]).

Holinshed, Raphael, *The History of England, Books I-IV*, (London, 1588).

Howlett, R. (ed.), *William of Newburgh: Historia Rerum Anglicarum*, (London: Roll Series, 1884).

Hunter, Joseph, (ed.), *The great roll of the pipe for the first year of the reign of King Richard the First, 1189-1190*, (London: G.E. Eyre and A. Sprittiswoode, 1844).

Jeayes, Isaac, Herbert, (ed.), *Descriptive Catalogue of the Charters and Muniments in the Possession of Lord Fitzhardinge at Berkeley Castle*, (C.T. Jefferies and Sons, 1892).

Jones, T., (ed.), *Chronicle of the Princes: Brut Tywysogion or the Chronicle of the Princes*, (RS 17, 1860).

Le Prévost, Auguste, (ed.), *Orderic Vitalis: The Ecclesiastical History of England and Normandy*, Vol. 3, (Paris: Société de l'Histoire de France, 1838-1855).

Liebermann, F., *The Text of Henry I's Coronation Charter*, Transactions of the Royal Historical Society, New Series, Vol. 8, (1894), pp.21-48.

Luard, Henry Richards, (ed.), *Matthew Paris: Chronica Majora*, Vol. 3, (London: Rolls Series, 1872-1884).

Luard, Henry Richards, (ed.), *Matthew Paris: Flores Historiarum*, Issue 95, Vol. 3, (London: HMSO, 1890).

MacCarthy, B. (ed. and trans.), *Annala Uladh:1057-1131:1155-1378*, (London: HMSO, 1893).

Marvin, Julia, (ed. and trans.), *The Oldest Anglo-Norman Prose Brut Chronicle: An Edition and Translation*, (Woodbridge: Boydell Press, 2006).

Meyer, Kuno, *The Triads of Ireland*, (Dublin, Hodges, Figgis & Co, 1906).

Meyer, Paul, (ed.), *Histoire de Guillaume le Maréchal, Comte de Striguil et de Pembroke, régent d'Angleterre*, (Paris: Societé de l'Histoire de France [1891-1901]).

Michel, F., (ed.), *Anonymous of Béthune: Histoire des Ducs de Normandie et des Roi d'Angleterre*, (Paris: Societé de l'Histoire de France, 1840).

Murphy, Denis, (ed.) and Mageoghagan, Conell, (trans.), *The Annals of Clonmacnoise, Being Annals of Ireland from the Earliest Period to A.D. 1408*, (Dublin: Royal Society of Antiquaries in Ireland, 1896).

O Donnovan, John, (ed.), *Annals of the Kingdom of Ireland by the Four Masters*, 2nd ed., 7 Vols, (Dublin, 1856).

O'Meara, John, (ed.), *Gerald of Wales, The History and Topography of Ireland,* (London: Penguin, 1982).

Orpen, G.H., (ed.), *The song of Dermot and the Earl,* (1892).

Potter, K.R. & Davis, R.H.C., (eds), *Oxford Medieval Texts: Gesta Stephani,* (Oxford: Oxford University Press, 1976).

Riley, Henry T., (ed. and trans.), *Roger of Howden: The Annals of Roger de Hoveden: Comprising the history of England and other countries of Europe from AD 732 to AD 1201,* (London: H.G. Bohn, 1853).

Rule, M. (ed.), *Eadmer: Historia Novorum,* (Rolls Series 81, 1884).

Savage, Anne, (trans. and ed.), The Anglo-Saxon Chronicles, (Godalming: Past Times, 1995).

Stenton, D.M. (ed.), *The Great Roll of the Pipe for the sixth year of the reign of King Richard the First, Michaelmas 1194 (Pipe Roll 40),* Pipe Roll Society Publications, 43 (1928).

Stevenson, J., (ed), *Richard of Devizes, Chronicon de rebus gestis Ricardi I regis Angliæ,* (London: 1838).

Stevenson, J. (ed.), *Randulphi de Coggeshall Chronicon Anglicanum,* (RS, 1875).

Stubbs, W., (ed.), *Barnwell Chronicle: Memoriale Fratis Walteri de Coventria,* Vol. 2, (London: Longman, 1872).

Stubbs, William, (ed.), *Gervase of Canterbury: The Historical works of Gervase of Canterbury,* 2 Vols, (London: Longman, 1879).

Sweetman, Henry Savage, (ed.), *Calendar of Documents, Relating to Ireland: 1171-1251,* (London: HMSO, 1875).

Sweetman, Henry Savage, (ed.), *Calendar of Documents, Relating to Ireland: 1171-1307,* Vol. 1, (London: HMSO, 1877).

Sweetman, Henry Savage, (ed.), *Calendar of Documents, Relating to Ireland: 1252-1284,* (London: HMSO, 1877).

Taylor, Edgar, (ed. and trans.), Wace, Robert: *The Chronicle of the Norman Conquest from the Roman de Rou,* (London: William Pickering, 1837).

Wrottesley, G. (ed.), *Coram Rege Roll, Easter Term,* 3.E.1. "Plea Rolls for Staffordshire: 3 Edward I", in Staffordshire Historical Collections, Vol. 6, Part 1, (London: Staffordshire Record Society, 1885).

Secondary Sources

The Irish Penny Paper, 30 March 1833, Vol. 1, no 13, p.97 (97-100).

Anon, 'The Earls, Earldom and Castle of Pembroke,' *Archaeologia Cambrensis,* Vol. 6, third series, (London: Russell Smith, 1860).

Altschul, Michael, *A Baronial Family in Medieval England: The Clares 1217-1314,* (Baltimore: John Hopkins Press, 1965).

Asbridge, Thomas, *The Greatest Knight,* (London: Simon and Schuster, 2015).

Baker, Darren, *The Two Eleanors of Henry III: The lives of Eleanor of Provence and Eleanor de Montfort,* (Barnsley: Pen and Sword, 2019).

Barlow, Frank, *The Feudal Kingdom of England 1042-1216,* (London and New York: Longman, 1991).

Barlow, Frank, *William Rufus*, (New Haven and London: Yale University Press, 2008).

Barnard, Francis Pierrepoint, *Strongbow's Conquest of Ireland*, (London & New York: G.P. Putnam's Sons, 1888).

Bartlett, Robert, *England Under the Norman and Angevin Kings, 1075-1225*, (Oxford: Oxford University Press, 2002).

Bedos-Rezak, Brigitte Miriam, 'Women, Seals, and Power in Medieval France, 1150-1350', in Erler, Mary and Kowaleski, Maryanne, (eds.), *Women and Power in the Middle Ages*, (Athens: University of Georgia Press, 1988).

Berry, Henry Fitzpatrick, 'Ancient Charters in the *Liber Albus Ossoriensis*', *Proceedings of the Royal Irish Academy: Archaeology, Culture, History, Literature*, Vol. 27, (1908-1909) pp./115-125.

Bhote, Tehmina, *Mediaeval Feasts and Banquets: Food, Drink and Celebration in the Middle Ages*, Library of the Middle Ages, (New York: Rosen Publishing, 2004).

Blomefield, Francis, & Parkin, Charles, *An essay towards a topographical history of the county of Norfolk*, Vol. 10, (London: William Miller, 1809).

Bradley, John, *Irish Historic Towns Atlas, no. 10, Kilkenny*, (Dublin: Royal Irish Academy, 2000). (Availabile online at: www.ihta.ie), text, pp21-22.

Brooks, Richard, *The Knight Who Saved England: William Marshal and the French Invasion, 1217*, (Oxford: Osprey, 2014).

Brown, Daniel, *Hugh de Lacy First Earl of Ulster: Rising and Falling in Angevin Ireland*, (Boydell Press, 2016).

Brown, E., 'Philip the Fair and His Family: His Sons, Their Marriages and Their Wives'. *Medieval Prospography*, 32, (2017) pp.125-185.

Burke, Bernard, *Abeyant, Forfeited, and Extinct Peerages of the British Empire*, (London: Harrison, 1866).

Carpenter, David. A., *The Minority of Henry III*, (London: Methuen, 1990).

Carpenter, David, A., *Henry III, The Rise to Power and Personal Rule,1207-1258*, (New Haven & London: Yale University Press, 2020).

Clark, Cecily, *The Thorney Liber Vitae BL, MS Add. 40,000, fols 1-12v, Facsimile and Study*, (Woodbridge: Boydell Press, 2015).

Clark, George Thomas, *The Earls, Earldom, and Castle of Pembroke*, (Tenby: R. Mason, 1880).

Cleveland, Duchess of, *The Battle Abbey Roll with some Account of the Norman Lineages*, 3 Vols, (London: William Clowes, 1889).

Cockerill, Sara, *Eleanor of Aquitaine, Queen of France and England, Mother of Empires*, (Stroud, Amberley Press, 2019).

Cole, Teresa, *The Anarchy: The Darkest Days of Medieval England*, (Stroud: Amberley Publishing, 2019).

O Cronin, Daibhi, *Early Medieval Ireland, 400-1200*, (London: Longman, 1995).

Cokayne, George, Edward, *The Complete Peerage of England, Scotland, Ireland, Great Britain and the United Kingdom*, (London: St Catherine Press, 1998).

Connolly, Sharon Bennett, *Ladies of the Magna Carta*, (Barnsley: Pen and Sword, 2020).

Coss, Peter, *The Lady in Mediaeval England 1000–1500*, (Stroud: Sutton Publishing, 1998).

Cox, J. Charles, 'Duffield Castle; its history, site, and recently found remains; with some account of the seven Ferrers earls who held it', in *Journal of the Derbyshire Archaeological and Natural History Society*, Vol. 9, (1887), pp.118–178.

Crosswhite, Anastasia B., 'Women and Land: Aristocratic Ownership of Property in Early Modern England', *New York University Law Review*, October 2002, pp.1119–1156.

Crouch, David, 'Marshal, William (called the Marshal), fourth earl of Pembroke (c.1146–1219)', Oxford Dictionary of National Biography, 2004, (online version 2007).

Crouch, David, *William Marshal, Knighthood, War and Chivalry, 1147–1219*, (London: Longman, 2002).

Crouch, David, *Medieval Britain, C.1000–1500*, (Cambridge: Cambridge University Press, 2017).

Cummins, Neil, 'Lifespans of the European Elite, 800–1800' in *The Journal of Economic History*, 77/2, (June 2017), pp.406–439.

Curtis, Edmund, *A History of Medieval Ireland*, (London: Routledge, 2013).

Davis, Paul, R., *Three Chevrons Red, The Clares: A Marcher Dynasty in Wales, England and Ireland*, (Almeley: Logaston Press, 2013).

Debrett, James, *The Peerage of the United Kingdom and Ireland*, (London: J.G. & F. Rivington, 1817).

Duby, Georges and Howard, Richard, (trans.) *William Marshal: The Flower of Chivalry*, (New York: Pantheon, 1985).

Dugdale, William, *Monasticon Anglicanum*, vol. 5, (London: T.G. March, 1849).

Everett, Nicholas, *The Alphabet of Galen*, (Toronto: University of Toronto Press, 2012).

Filippini, Nadia M., *Pregnancy, Delivery, Childbirth: A Gender and Cultural History from Antiquity to the Test Tube in Europe* (London: Routledge, 2021).

Flanagan, M.T., 'Clare, Isabel de, *suo jure* countess of Pembroke (1171X6–1220), *Oxford Dictionary of National Biography*, September 2004, (online edition 2010).

Flanagan, M.T., 'Clare, Richard fitz Gilbert de [called Strongbow], second earl of Pembroke (c.1130–1176), *Oxford Dictionary of National Biography*, September 2004, (online edition 2010).

Flanagan, M.T., 'FitzGerald, Raymond fitz William [known as Raymond le Gros] (d.1189x92), *Oxford Dictionary of National Biography*, September 2004, (online edition 2004).

Foucault, Michel, *Society Must Be defended: Lectures at the Collège de France, 1975–76*, Bertini, Mauro and Fontana Alessandro, (eds), (New York: Picador, 1997).

Gilchrist, R, 'The contested garden: gender, space and metaphor in the English castle garden', in Gilchrist, R. (ed.), *Gender and Archaeology: contesting the past*, (London: Routledge, 1999), pp.109–145.

Gold, Claudia, *King of the North Wind: The Life of Henry II in Five Acts*, (London: William Collins, 2018).

Hanawalt, Barbara A., *Growing Up in Medieval London, The Experience of Childhood in History*, (Oxford: Oxford University Press, 1995).

Hand, G. J., *English Law in Ireland, 1290-1324*, (Cambridge: Cambridge University Press, 1967).

Hickey, Julia A., *Medieval Royal Mistresses, Mischievous Women who Slept with Kings and Princes*, (Barnsley: Pen and Sword, 2022).

Hogan, Arlene, 'Wales and Ireland: monastic links' in Burton, Janet and Stöber, Karen, (eds), *Monastic Wales: New Approaches*, (Cardiff: University of Wales, 2013), pp. 163-174.

Holden, Brock, *Lords of the Central Marches, English Aristocracy and Frontier Society, 1087-1265*, (Oxford, Oxford University Press, 2008).

Holt, J. C. 'Feudal society and the family in early medieval England,' IV, 'The heiress and the alien', Transactions of the Royal Historical Society, 5th series, 35, (1985), pp.1-28.

Holt, J. C., *Colonial England, 1066-1215*, (London: Bloomsbury Academic, 1997).

Johns, Susan M., *Noblewomen, Aristocracy and Power in the Twelfth-Century Anglo-Norman Realm*, (Manchester: Manchester University Press, 2003).

Jones, Dan, *Realm Divided: A Year in the Life of Plantagenet England*, (London: Head of Zeus, 2015).

Jones, Dan, *Magna Carta: The Birth of Liberty*, (London: Viking, 2015).

Kenny, Gillian, *Anglo-Irish and Gaelic Women in Ireland, C.1170-1540*, (Dublin: Four Courts, 2007).

Kenny, Gillian, 'The wife's tale: Isabel Marshal and Ireland' in Bradley John, O Drisceoil, Cóilín and Potterton, Michael, (eds), *William Marshal and Ireland*, (Dublin: Four Courts Press, 2017).

Kerr, Nigel, & Kerr, Mary, *A Guide to Norman Sites in Britain*, (1984).

Kostick, Conor, *Strongbow: The Norman Invasion of Ireland*, (Dublin: O Brien, 2013).

Leask, H.G., 'A centotaph of "Strongbow's" daughter at new Ross, Co. Wexford', *The Journal of the Royal Society of Antiquaries of Ireland*, Vol.78, No. 1 (July, 1948), pp.65-67.

Leland, Thomas, *The History of Ireland from the Invasion of Henry II*, Vol. 1, (Philadelphia and New York: Hugh Gaine, Robert Bell & John Dunlap, 1774).

Leyser, Henrietta, *Medieval Woman, A Social History of Women in England 450-1500*, (London: Orion, 1995).

Lewis, Matthew, *Henry III, The Son of Magna Carta*, (Stroud: Amberley Press, 2016).

Lomas, Richard, *The Normans in Ireland*, (Edinburgh: John Donald, 2022).

Lynch, Breda, *A Monastic Landscape: The Cistercians in Medieval Ireland*, (Xlibris UK, 2010).

Mckerr, Lynne, 'Towards an Archeology of Childhood: Children and Material Culture in Historic Ireland', in Dommasnes, Liv Helga and Wrigglesworth, (eds), *Children, Identity and the Past* (Cambridge: Cambridge Scholars Publishing, 2021) pp.36-51.

McNamara Jo Ann, 'Women and Power through the Family revisited', in Erler, Mary and Kowaleski, Maryanne, (eds.), *Women and Power in the Middle Ages*, (Athens: University of Georgia Press, 1988) pp.83-101.

Mantel, Hilary, 'The Day is foe the Living', The BBC Reith Lectures, Lecture I, 13 June, 2017, downloaded from www.bbc.co.uk/radio4.

Marsh, John Fitchett, *Annals of Chepstow Castle Or, Six Centuries of the Lords of Striguil from the Conquest to the Revolution*, (Exeter: W. Pollard, 1883).

Mitchell, Linda, *Joan de Valence: The Life and Influence of a Thirteenth-Century Noblewoman*, The New Middle Ages, (New York: Palgrave MacMillan, 2016).

Mitchell, Linda, 'The Most perfect Knight's Countess: Isabella de Clare, her Daughters, and Women's Exercise of Power and Influence, 1190-ca.1250' in Tanner, H.J. (ed.), *Medieval Elite Women and the Exercise of Power, 1100-1400, The New Middle Ages*, (London: Palgrave MacMillan, 2019) pp.45-65.

Morris, Marc, *The Bigod Earls of Norfolk in the Thirteenth Century*, (Woodbridge: Boydell Press, 2005).

Morris, Marc, *The Norman Conquest*, (London: Windmill Books, 2013).

Munby, Julian, 'From carriage to coach: what happened?' in Kann, Anrea, Bork, Robert (eds) *The Art, Science, and Technology of Medieval Travel*, (Farnham: Ashgate Publishing, 2008).

Page, William, (ed.), *A History of the County of Gloucester: Volume 2*, (London: Victoria County History, 1907).

Painter, Sidney, *William Marshal, Knight-errant, Baron, and Regent of England*, (Baltimore: John Hopkins University Press, 1995).

Power, Daniel, 'The French interests of the Marshal Earls of Striguil and Pembroke', *Anglo-Norman Studies*, xxv, (2003), pp.199-224.

Power, Daniel, 'Henry, Duke of the Normans (1149/50-1189)' in Harper-Bill, Christopher and Vincent Nicholas, (eds), *Henry II: New Interpretations*, (Woodbridge: Boydell Press, 2007) pp.85-109.

Power, Eileen, *Medieval Women*, ed. by Postan, M.M., (Cambridge: Cambridge University Press, 1975).

Rose, E.M., *The Murder of William of Norwich*, (Oxford: Oxford University Press, 2015).

Round, J. H., 'The Family of Clare', *The Archaeological Journal*, Vol. LVI, Second Series vol. VI, (1899), pp. 221-231.

Round, J.H., *The King's Serjeants and Officers of State*, (1911).

Salzmann, L.F. 'Documents relating to Pevensey Castle', *Sussex Archaeological Collections*, 49 (1906), pp.1-30 accessed from archaeologicaldataservice.ac.uk.

Turner, Ralph V., *The English Judiciary in the Age of Glanvill and Bracton, c.1176-1239* (Reprint ed.), (Cambridge: Cambridge University Press, 2008).

Turner, Rick, *Chepstow Castle, Chepstow Bulwarks Camp, Runston Church*, (Cardiff: CADW, 2002; reprinted 2018).

Van Houts, Elisabeth (ed.), *The Normans in Europe*, (Manchester: Manchester University Press, 2013).

Van Houts, Elisabeth, *Married Life in the Middle Ages, 900-1300*, (Oxford: Oxford University Press, 2019).

Veach, Colin, 'Conquest and Conquerors', in Smith, Brendan, (ed.), *The Cambridge History of Ireland, 600-1500*, vol 1, (Cambridge: Cambridge University Press, 2018), pp.157-184.

Venning, Timothy, *Kingmakers: How Power in England Was Won and Lost On The Welsh Borders*, (Stroud: Amberley Publishing, 2017).

Ward, Jennifer, 'The Estates of the Clare family 1066-1317', (Unpublished thesis, 1962).

Ward, Jennifer, 'The Lowry of Tonbridge; *Archaeologia Cantiana*, Vol. 96 (1980), pp119-132.

Ward, Jennifer, 'Royal Service and Reward, The Clare Family and the Crown 1066-1154' in Allen Brown, R (ed.), *Proceedings of the Battle Conference 1988*, (Woodbridge: Boydell Press, 1989) pp. 261-279.

Warner, Kathryn, *Sex & Sexuality in Medieval England*, (Barnsley: Pen and Sword, 2022).

Weir, Alison, *Eleanor of Aquitaine, By Wrath of God, Queen of England*, (London: Pimlico, 2000).

Weir, Alison, *Britain's Royal Families: The Complete Genealogy*, (London: Vintage Books, 2008).

Wilkinson, Louise, J., 'Joan, Wife of Llywelyn the Great', in Prestwich, Michael et al, (eds) *Thirteenth Century England X, Proceedings of the Durham Conference 2003*, (Boydell and Brewer, 2005) pp.81-94.

Wilkinson, Louise, J., *Women in Thirteenth Century Lincolnshire*, (London: Royal Historical Society, 2015).

Yoshikawa, Naoë Kukita, (ed.), *Medicine, Religion and Gender in Medieval Culture*, Vol. 2, (Woodbridge: DS Brewer, 2015).

Acknowledgements

I continue to be grateful to the staff at Ashbourne Library for all their help and perseverance finding obscure texts. None of this would be possible without the team at Pen and Sword and, of course, to my family and friends who have encouraged me throughout.

Index